DECISION
ORDER AND TIME IN
HUMAN AFFAIRS

DECISION
ORDER AND TIME
IN HUMAN AFFAIRS

BY

G. L. S. SHACKLE

*Brunner Professor of Economic Science in
the University of Liverpool*

CAMBRIDGE
AT THE UNIVERSITY PRESS
1961

PUBLISHED BY
THE SYNDICS OF THE CAMBRIDGE UNIVERSITY PRESS

Bentley House, 200 Euston Road, London, N.W. 1
American Branch: 32 East 57th Street, New York 22, N.Y.
West African Office: P.O. Box 33, Ibadan, Nigeria

©

CAMBRIDGE UNIVERSITY PRESS

1961

Printed in Great Britain at the University Press, Cambridge
(Brooke Crutchley, University Printer)

2/22/71 Bru. Dept 8.50

TO
J. W. N. WATKINS

CONTENTS

Part IV

EXPECTATION OF CHANGE OF OWN EXPECTATION

Part V

SOME ECONOMIC ILLUSTRATIONS

PREFACE

Let us make a supposition about the nature of things, namely, that the rival possible outcomes which a man will imagine for an available act of his own cannot be listed from a knowledge, however complete, of what is and what has been. Two things amongst others follow. Decision, by which a man finds and adopts that one amongst his available acts which promises or suggests the outcome that he most desires, is more than mere response to circumstances and contains an element which we may call inspiration, which brings essential novelty into the historical sequence of states of affairs. *Decision* thus becomes the locus of unending creation of history, and acquires the meaning which intuition and working attitude to life give it, in contrast to the character, implied for it by those who seek a sequential calculus of human conduct, of a passive link in chains of necessity. Secondly, in analysing decision, the use of a distributional uncertainty variable, that is, probability, becomes in principle inappropriate and must give way to a non-distributional uncertainty variable such as possibility, understood as discriminable in some manner into degrees; for example, by being identified with potential surprise.

Such is the kernel of this book's argument. It offers an escape from the conclusion that choice and creative freedom are illusory; illusory, because there is in general only one act by which a man of consistent tastes can rationally respond to given circumstances. We do not assert that our premises are true, only that the meaning they imply for 'decision' is interesting and corresponds to people's unselfconscious feelings and the assumptions by which they live in practice.

When a number of actions, distinguished from each other by the sets of outcomes respectively assigned to them, are *available* and choice amongst them is open to the decision-maker, the sets of outcomes, each considered as a whole, are mutually exclusive rivals of each other. Within each set, the members also are mutually exclusive rival hypotheses. Thus these outcomes cannot be matters of fact but are things imagined by the decision-maker. They exist in his imagination, not after but *before* his commitment to a particular act; their existence is within the moment of decision and forms part of that act. Thus all the business of decision, however long the meditation that has led up to it, comes to a crisis in a single moment, the *solitary present* or the *solitary moment of actuality*, and is therein consummated. This 'event-moment' is not an *instant* or point of time, for an event, that is, a transition from one to another instantaneous state of affairs, occurs within it, but is yet quite different from the spatial and extended time used by sophisticated minds as a vessel or frame for mathematical conceptions of motion or process or for historical narrative. My insistence upon its exclusive and solitary actuality may prove shocking to those sophisticated minds themselves. I can appeal only to the argument advanced in Part I of this book.

The scheme of thought, of which I have tried above to give some forewarning, has been criticized by a number of writers who have already encountered it in some of those partial versions which have at various times appeared. I hope these writers will read into the discussions of their quoted works, with which the argument of this book is at several places interrupted, the warmth of gratitude which I feel to them for having somewhat relieved my inevitable isolation. I shall not refer to these writers by name in this preface, since their names appear prominently in the following pages. There are, however, a number of writers to whom my gratitude is no less intense, but whom I have not, in the course of the very complex task which the consideration of a large mass of critical publications has set me, had occasion to quote from. It is to these especially that I wish here to make amends for the omission of their names from the text itself.

At rare moments a writer is suddenly afforded a sense of the completeness of life. These moments bring, from someone else's written word, the assurance that he has himself succeeded in communicating to other minds something which they find acceptable. The memory of two such experiences is for me perpetually vivid. In the *British Journal for the Philosophy of Science* Mr J. W. N. Watkins wrote of my *Expectation in Economics*. In the *Revue d'Economie Politique* Professor Henri Guitton discussed my *Time in Economics*. To each I owe an immeasurable encouragement.

The generosity of my friend of many years, Professor Eraldo Fossati, in devoting two numbers of his journal, *Metroeconomica*, to a symposium on those earlier presentations of my argument, is beyond any words of mine. To the contributors to that symposium I owe also a debt, which in respect of some of them will become apparent in the following pages. The contributors who are not there mentioned include Professor Kenneth Arrow, whose fame as a writer on stochastic economics (as well as other branches) needs no announcement to economists, and whose criticism* of the notion of neutral outcome was the reason for my writing chapter xv of this book. Professor Albert Hart is a pioneer of expectational economics, and his symposium article is a beautifully ingenious application of the gambler indifference map to monetary theory. Professor Carl Shoup is one of the foremost authorities of our time on public finance, and his application of some of my ideas to this field has given me the greatest pleasure. Dr Margaret Wray has carried these tools into yet another piece of country, that of the fashion trade where the soul of success is change for its own sake, and where, therefore, decisions which businessmen must take about what to produce, or what to buy for resale, face the most acute hazards even when they look no more than a year or six months ahead.

If the thesis of this book is in any degree acceptable, it follows that such a subject as economics must not be looked on as self-contained. Human nature and action as a whole is the proper object of study, and philosopher, psychologist, economist, and historian must work hand in hand. I have been fortunate indeed in numbering amongst my friends such psychologists as Professor Patrick Meredith, Mr David Duncan, and Professor Leslie Hearnshaw, and to have corresponded, to my very great pleasure, with Professor Jerome S. Bruner of Harvard, and Professor Stanley Stark of the University of Illinois, and very lately with Professor John Cohen of the University of Manchester, whose brilliant book *Chance, Skill and Luck* affords some experimental evidence in support of the notion of focus values.

Professor Raffaello Maggi has honoured me with a very

* 'Alternative Approaches to the Theory of Choice in Risk-taking Situations', *Econometrica*, vol. xix (October 1951).

extended discussion of my work in his great critical survey *Momenti dinamici dell'Economia* in which any economist would be proud to see his name.

The analysis of notions of profit, which forms chapter xxviii of this book, is based on one of four lectures which I was privileged to give in the universities of Uppsala and Stockholm in 1955, through the kindness of the late Professor Erik Lindahl and that of Professor Pålander and Professor Herman Wold, and especially through the generosity of Professor and Mrs Ingvar Svennilson who received me in their home on Drottningholm. The lecture in question was published in the *Ekonomisk Tidskrift* in December 1955, and the other lectures were included amongst the proceedings of the Pittsburgh conference on 'Expectations, Uncertainty and Business Decisions' which was organized in that year by the Social Science Research Council located in New York. To the Editor of that volume, Dr Mary Jean Bowman, I owe an immeasurable debt for her luminous and sympathetic appraisal of my ideas, in a brilliant Introduction.

The occasion for some part of the effort of organization and refinement, which underlies this final attempt on my part to communicate my scheme of thought, was an invitation to me in 1957 to give three lectures in the University of Amsterdam under the Foundation set up in honour of Professor F. de Vries. It is impossible to describe the kindness with which I was received on that occasion, by Professor Hennipman of the University of Amsterdam, Professor Lambers of the Rotterdam School of Economics and Professor Zimmerman of the Institute of Social Studies at The Hague. Professor Pen of the University of Groningen then and since has done me the greatest kindness by sympathetic criticism, and I had also the privilege of a brief discussion on probability with Professor J. A. Hartog, the Dutch mathematician.

The discussions I had at Lund, and at beautiful Ringsjögården, in September 1959, and all the kindness of Professor and Mrs Johan Åkerman at that time, have given me some inkling of how Part I of this book is likely to strike the reader. I have, however, left the ideas of that Part in the same shape as I then presented them.

My line of thought on uncertainty is in this book presented in two forms carefully distinguished from each other. In one I have avoided entirely the assumption that possibility, or potential surprise, can be treated as a cardinal variable like length or mass. The argument can be developed and presented in its entirety on this basis. The recognition that this is so was brought home to me as a consequence of reflecting on an article by Mr Maurice McManus in the *Review of Economic Studies* of February 1958, as well as some oral remarks of Mr E. S. Mills (then of the University College of North Staffordshire) and the basis proposed for part of my argument by Professor K. R. Popper, reported by Mr J. W. N. Watkins in his contribution to *Uncertainty and Business Decisions*, second edition.

The search for a content for the word *decision* must have occupied many minds. A few weeks ago Professor Owen Sauerlender of Pennsylvania State University told me of his own pre-occupation with this problem. He also was dissatisfied to treat a decision as something fully explainable by the confrontation of a man's tastes with his knowledge of his own circumstances. Is decision *mere* response? Unless human beings are mere computers, no. Then there must be in a decision some element beyond that of rational coping with an action-problem. Professor Sauerlender, not to his own complete happiness, had resolved to call this a *random* element. This (plainly) is the mathematical statistician's natural answer. I have ventured, as the reader will see, to call this originative element in decision, *inspiration*. The reader is entitled to ask how this word, in its turn, is to be filled with meaning. But I can go no further. Can we, Professor Sauerlender also asks, in principle write down what I will call a man's *conduct-function* in which his every action will appear as dependent on and wholly determined by his history and current circumstances? Again Professor Sauerlender is compelled, by the resolve he shares with me to treat men as non-machines, to answer No; we can, he says, write down 'partial' functions, in which action and conduct are shown (as I understand him) to be *constrained* but not *dictated* by a man's situation and the events which have led up to it; there will be a number of such functions, but we cannot combine them into one all-embracing, all-determining function.

Such, then, are the problems which have imposed themselves

upon the enterprise initiated some twenty-three years ago, to replace *probablity* with a new concept; an enterprise which would scarcely have gained even such attention as it has, without the decisive action of Professor Austin Robinson in securing for me publication of my *Expectation in Economics* in 1949.

I wish to record my deep gratitude to all those who have had any part in the production and publishing of this book, for the happiness I have in their friendship and for their incomparable work. I wish also to thank Mrs E. C. Harris for her endless patience and care in typing and indexing this book.

G. L. S. SHACKLE

1 October 1960

PART I

TIME

I

DECISION

Decision means literally a cut; and this I take to be the most essential aspect of its meaning in our spontaneous, intuitive, everyday and almost universal usage, betraying our attitude to our life and the human condition and our apprehension of the essential nature of that life as a process of creation. Decision, as all of us use the word, is a cut between past and future, an introduction of an essentially new strand into the emerging pattern of history. To elucidate and elaborate this statement and draw some of its consequences is what this book attempts.

There are some assumptions about the ultimate nature of things, about what the cosmos is, that are incompatible with the unspoken and instinctive but deep-seated and commanding assumption, which most western people or perhaps in the last resort all people make, that when a person decides he innovates; he destroys the possibility or meaning of attempts based on knowledge, no matter how perfect or complete, of what was the state of affairs before his decision, to predict what would be the state of affairs, or the sequence of such states, after his decision; and that he thus creates something new. The most obvious of such incompatible assumptions is that of a cosmos whose history is predestinate, a cosmos behaving, in every detail, in a manner settled and determinate from the start. If such is the cosmos, it is plain that we deceive ourselves in thinking that history is made, in any interesting sense, in human acts of decision. These acts, or our awareness of them, in a predestinate cosmos, can be no more than the clicking of the machine as it works, and if they are worth investigating (the very notion of worth is totally out of touch with that of the determinism of history) it is as something wholly different from that explosion of essential novelty which they seem to be to the person whose tense thought and feeling give them birth. Any meaning that could be given to the word decision in a determinist scheme of thought is no concern of this study, whose first pre-supposition is that, on the plane of conceivable human knowledge, human history is non-determinate.

History can be thought of, we would say, as a sequence of instantaneous states of affairs. When two of these states differ, otherwise than in that particular respect which we are using as a definition of the lapse of time or as a means of graduating the calendar axis, we have an event. Whether, therefore, we prefer to look upon history as a sequence of states or as a sequence of events is immaterial. By a hypothesis about the outcome of an available act we mean a description, in all those respects which the individual feels to be of concern to him, of a sequence of situations or events which he imagines to follow that act. Decision can take place only when several distinct and mutually exclusive acts appear to the individual to be available to him. If, for each available act, he sees one and only one outcome, and if also he assumes that an act necessarily has an outcome, and if further he can order all the outcomes (one for each act) according to his greater or less desire for each, then we say that his choice amongst the available acts will not involve decision, but will by contrast be a mechanical and automatic selection of that act whose outcome he most desires. Thus the second assumption which, in our view, would render uninteresting any analysis of decision is that the individual making a choice amongst available acts supposes himself to know precisely, completely and for certain what consequences for himself would flow from any given one of the available acts. We say that perfect foresight would render decision *empty*.

In a cosmos lacking order, that consistency of nature that we think of as cause and effect, a cosmos in which no act placed any constraint whatever upon the character of the sequel, choice amongst acts would be pointless. If, in place of the one–one correspondence between act and supposed outcome that we have used to define perfect foresight, we suppose a correspondence having that extreme degree of degeneracy in which every outcome would correspond to each act and every act to each outcome (the most complete state of many–many correspondence) no purpose would be served by deliberate selection amongst available acts and again decision would be quite uninteresting. In such a cosmos, foresight would also be at the opposite extreme from perfect, and would be non-

existent: uncertainty would be unbounded. Unbounded uncertainty is the third of the assumptions about the character of
the cosmos and of the human condition in it that we must reject
if decision is to be an interesting object of analysis.

The model of human affairs which we choose to investigate
is established by rejecting the three foregoing assumptions and
thus bringing into existence (in the sense of the word *existence*
that we use in requiring that an 'existence theorem', that is, the
logical possibility given a set of axioms, of some mathematical
idea be proved) non-illusory, non-empty, non-powerless decision. Decision, we have claimed, is choice, but not choice in
face of perfect foreknowledge, not choice in face of complete
ignorance. Decision, therefore, is choice in face of bounded
uncertainty. Thus, for the purpose of this investigation, we
define it.

Perhaps these premises of our subsequent argument need
some defence. We find it in the claim, which to some will only
confirm their suspicion that this inquiry lacks all scientific
objectivity, that human beings for all they can tell may be what
they seem to think themselves to be, sources of unexplainable
initiatives. So far as the writer of this book can judge, people
in their attitude to life and their manner of conducting it, and
in their spontaneous workaday conversation, do implicitly reject
all three of the contrary assumptions, and do implicitly take it
for granted that they can make non-illusory, non-empty and
non-powerless decisions. It may not be altogether foolish to
give their instinctive working assumption the benefit of the
doubt.

Let us review a number of words to which we are already
proposing to give rather special meanings. For 'state of affairs'
we shall often use the shorthand *situation*. So far as it can be
specified by numbers (standing for measurements, rankings and
so on) a situation can if we like be thought of as a vector or
ordered set of such numbers where the place of each number in
the order shows what subject-matter its measurement refers to.
A situation exists at an instant. If the column vector representing the situation at some named or identified instant (some
named date on the calendar axis) is multiplied on the left by
a diagonal matrix which transforms it into the situation existing
at a different identified instant, this matrix will stand for an

event in the same way as the column vector stands for a situation. Starting with any situation, we can represent the carrying of this situation into any subsequent situation, through any chosen number of intermediate situations, by writing the appropriate set of matrices on the left of the column vector representing the initial situation. This is what we meant by saying that history can be pictured equally as a sequence of situations or a sequence of events.

In denying to choice without (subjective) uncertainty the name of decision, or in calling such choice *empty* decision, we think of uncertainty as more than the existence in the decision-maker's mind of plural and rival (mutually exclusive) hypotheses amongst which he has insufficient epistemic grounds of choice. Decision, as we mean the word, is creative and is able to be so through the freedom which uncertainty gives for the creation of *unpredictable hypotheses*. Decision is not choice amongst the delimited and prescribed moves in a game with fixed rules and a known list of possible outcomes of any move or sequence of moves. There is no assurance that any one can in advance say what set of hypotheses a decision maker will entertain concerning any specified act available to him. Decision is thought and not merely determinate response.

Non-empty decision we define as choice which cannot be explained as in every respect the inevitable consequence of what went before; as choice which is not *structurally identical* with the cosmos that pre-existed this choice, no matter how comprehensive our knowledge of that cosmos, its nature and principles, may be. Whence, then, does choice arise? If 'choice' were merely part of the working out of a plan perfectly complete from some beginning, we should surely have to say that 'creation' had wholly occurred in that beginning: if nothing *new* can enter into the scheme of things, if history exists as a book whose pages are merely being turned by the hand of time; then nothing is thereby created, nothing is created by any event or aspect of the lapse of time, nothing is created by choice and choice is empty. Non-empty choice corresponds to continuing creation. We do not know what we mean by creation except the sudden, spontaneous emergence of essential novelty. But to refer to continuing creation at least makes explicit one aspect of the position which we are taking up in electing to assume that decision is non-empty. Can we then find a name for the source of that part of decision which is not simply the reflection or actualization of something already implicit in the structure of past history? We shall call it, simply, inspiration, and we shall sometimes refer to non-empty decisions as *inspired* decisions. One of our chief endeavours will be to show that there could be inspiration in this sense in the scheme of things without its implying that human conduct is arbitrary in face of given circumstances.

For if, in the moment of decision, the decision maker's knowledge and the state of his interpretation of it and his inferences from it are given, how can there be room for inspiration? Are we saying that he will respond *arbitrarily* to the presentation of a given system of apparent opportunities and available acts? More especially, if his tastes and relative desires for this outcome or that are given, and if each available act is linked in some intelligible fashion and degree with an outcome or a set of outcomes, how can there be any third possibility, besides conduct or choice determined according to desire, on the one hand, and on the other, irrational, senseless conduct which ignores desires and fails to seek advantage? Our answer to this objection is one of the central strands of the argument of this volume, and consists in our interpretation of *uncertainty*. We do not confine uncertainty to the mere existence in the decision maker's mind of plural hypotheses of the outcome of some available act, if such plural hypotheses are understood to compose a list known to be complete. For in the first place we claim that such knowledge is unattainable and cannot exist. But more relevantly we claim that the possible outcomes of any act do not, in general, constitute a limited and finite set such as would exist if we were concerned with a game with stated rules. It is in the creation of the range of imagined outcomes of an available immediate act that inspiration can be supposed to enter the process of history.

II

IMAGINATION, EXPECTATION, ANTICIPATION

In order to have a full identity, an act must be thought of not merely as a specified intellectual, moral or physical motion on the part of an individual, but as one of these performed in a particular context of circumstances and of the concomitant acts of others. It will always be impossible for the performer to know any such context completely at the time when he performs his act; but that context can nevertheless be pinned down as a particular thing, which will ultimately in principle become, *ex post facto*, knowable in some or perhaps all relevant respects, by naming its date; and so when the date is included amongst the specified particulars of the proposed act, we have in the act thus specified one potential means of filling what is a unique historical occasion, a unique and individual empty place which will inevitably be somehow filled and which the decision-maker has, perhaps, the power to fill in one or other of a number of mutually exclusive ways; that is, *by rival available acts*.

We assume that choice amongst a set of rival available acts will be made in view of consequences associated in some manner and degree by the decision-maker with the acts. We also assume that the only consequences relevant for this choice are experiences of the decision-maker. What kind of experiences can these be?

For three separate reasons, each sufficient in itself, they cannot be experiences coming from outside the decision-maker's mind from sources of stimulus observable in principle by others; they cannot, that is to say, be what we ordinarily speak of as 'real' experiences requiring the intervention of sense perceptions of the external world; they cannot be 'news'. For in the first place, 'real' experiences derived from externality, by means of sense perceptions, cannot be *exchanged* for others belonging to the same moment of history: they are beyond the reach of choice. Secondly, the individual's total real experience of any moment, the actuality of his present, is unique. There is no question of his comparing of one such content of his 'present moment' with another; this we shall elaborate and emphasize in chapter III, for, obvious as it may seem, elaborate analyses of human conduct have ignored it. Thirdly, the experiences which the decision-maker looks to in making his choice of action do not all belong to one and the same brief interval of the calendar axis but are spread along it over an interval perhaps of years. The calendar axis that we here speak of is, of course, a construct in the mind of the individual. Our whole discussion is conducted from a viewpoint as far as possible identified with his own outlook. A consequence of the non-externality of the experiences which can be subjected to comparison, to exchange one for another, and thus can serve as the basis of decision, follows at once.

The outcomes by comparison of which an act is chosen from amongst rival acts must be *imagined* outcomes. These outcomes, which compose the basis of choice, are imaginations not merely *en passant*, as a preliminary stage on the way to actuality, but, so far as choice is concerned, for ever. When the chosen act has its actual, emerging outcome there will be no more choice but only unique fact. Choice amongst outcomes takes place in the individual's imagination. All the qualities these outcomes can display, all the pressure or attraction they can exert on his mind, are by virtue of imagined qualities and powers.

It will be natural for the reader to ask, whether these imagined qualities are to be thought of by us, detached observers, as false or true? In what circumstances will they be true? Or when they are true, need we insist upon their being imagined qualities? The reader who has been with us in the foregoing argument will not ask these questions, for he will see that our argument compels us to class them as *meaningless*. At the moment when the decision-maker is *free to choose* between acts, and still able to create for them fresh imagined outcomes, the future, which will be partly created by this choice and a million similar contemporary ones made by other decision-makers, does not yet exist. In a moment when the future is being created, it makes no sense to ask whether this or that figment concerning that future is true or false.

It is hard to give a sufficiently arresting emphasis to the idea, and what is implied by it, that outcomes are figments and imaginations. This idea and its implications lie at the root of our argument. For it is the contention that the outcomes, by comparison of which decision is made, are figments of the individual mind (no matter whether in some later actuality they shall be observed to have come true: nothing could be more irrelevant) that allows us to claim that, for all that observation can ever teach to the contrary, there can be what we have called inspired decision: decision not born wholly of the past. A cosmos in which outcomes have calculable probabilities which men seek to discover and upon which they act is a cosmos where in effect certainty and not uncertainty prevails; where the outcomes of any available act can be listed and where the list can be known to be complete; and where therefore there is no room for decision which is both *non-arbitrary and non-predictable*. Men imagine outcomes which come into their minds we know not whence; these outcomes can be *new* in the most absolute and radical sense, untraceable to the individual's past or present, sprung from nowhere. If these can steer his choice of act, the decision to perform that act can be properly called creative, opening on each occasion, perhaps we might almost say, an extra dimension to that abstract conceptual space in which things happen.

Decision is paradoxical. The formal content of those hypotheses, concerning the outcome of each available act, upon which decision is based, is labelled with dates in the future. Yet that future, as we shall maintain more strictly in the next chapter, has its effective existence only in the present. It is a system of rival figments imagined by the decision-maker in his moment of decision, in his *present*. The pressures or attractions that bear upon his mind are those exercised by imaginations of his, concerned indeed with what he locates at distant parts of a calendar axis which he conceives and uses as a frame of thought, but imaginations only able to give him experience, or the apprehension of rival and comparable possible experiences, by occupying his mind in the present.

It will no doubt be evident to the reader of the foregoing paragraphs that in using the word imagination we have in mind in the most general sense the power to make mental constructs, whether these take visual, verbal or mathematical form or any form whatever which allows of structure, inter-connectiveness and 'meaning' of some kind. The imagination of the poet, the dramatist, the landscape painter, the military commander, the geometer, may work in apparently unrelated subject matter. All of them have in common, however, the ability to detach their thoughts from present external experience and replace the latter with internal experience.

There are three degrees, we shall suggest, in which imagination can be constrained. With total absence of constraint it is mere fiction, fantasy or daydream, claiming no essential relation with the world observed except, presumably, in being built up from 'elementary particles' which directly reproduce sensations. Scenes conjured up, however fantastic, must perhaps consist in the last analysis of colours and sounds, and even of elementary shapes and patterns, which perception has supplied to memory, as well as emotions of which experience has at least supplied some hint. But the construct made from these elements need conform to none but arbitrary rules imposed by the individual. With this 'free' imagination, however, we are not concerned. It is not directly relevant for decision since it does not concern itself with the question whether what is imagined can come true.

For the decision-paradox has more to say. Although the effective hypotheses about the outcome of this available act or that are thoughts arising in the decision-maker's present moment, they are not free imaginations, for he will not choose an act which relies for its appeal on an hypothetical outcome which he thinks that act cannot bring to pass. To play its part in decision, imagination must be constrained to be congruous with what the decision-maker knows of the nature of things in general and of human nature; and constrained also to be congruous with the time available for transformation of the actual situation at the decision-maker's present into his desired situation at its specific calendar location.

When we say that in order to bear upon decision, a hypothetical outcome of any act must seem a *possible* consequence of that act, we mean that it must be deemed possible by the decision-maker. Decision is an operation of an individual mind, and for such decision only those things count which belong to that mind, which are available to it and are sanctioned by it. For us, in attempting to analyse decision, 'possibility' means the absence of fatal obstacles within the decision-maker's knowledge; it means possibility, of some degree, registered and admitted by him. A situation or an event, or some series of such which compose an outcome, all of them hypothetical, may have a *general* impossibility, that is, may appear contrary to the law of nature, so that in no circumstances can this situation or event be supposed to occur; or it may appear impossible within the time constraint imposed upon it. The transition from the existing to the desired situation is recognised by the decision-maker as requiring some time. If the date of the desired situation, being looked upon as one of its essential characteristics, is too near, the situation must be counted by him unattainable. This second source of impossibility is merely a more special form of the first. It is natural law and the constitution of the cosmos as these are assumed to be; and human nature and institutions; which constrain the speed at which history can be supposed to pass from one situation into another. But the distinction of the more special type of impossibility is valuable for our later argument. For we shall show a connection between the degree of uncertainty and the distance of the decision-maker's 'time horizon' from his viewpoint, and draw from this connection some explanations of observed human conduct.

The whole of Part II of this book is concerned with the formal analysis of possibility and of some notions with which it must be contrasted. We can go far in the analysis of decision by means of a mere possible–impossible dichotomy. Uncertainty as we ordinarily understand this word, however, includes a more subtle meaning of 'doubt' than the mere plurality of hypotheses placed in the 'possible' as against the 'impossible' class. There seems in the observed or reported working of our minds to be a faculty of adjudging degrees of possibility, and we shall be concerned below with formalizing this notion. The precise and detailed ground upon which an hypothesis, an answer to some question, is classed by a particular person in a particular moment as possible or impossible, or on which it is assigned a 'degree of possibility' can scarcely be supposed to be discernible even to the person concerned. His whole personal history and every detail of his experience and education and even of his heredity may be relevant to the understanding of such a judgement, which is in the highest degree a 'personal' or 'subjective' thing. But more. It is partly in the formation of such judgements that we think of the essentially new as being able to enter.

It is here that there can be inspiration. This is the locus of creative decision.

Imagination constrained to congruity with what seems in some degree possible we shall call *expectation*.

To expect is to imagine situations and events which this or that available act would make to seem possible. Decision is choice amongst available acts, and this choice is aimed at securing a preferred combination of experiences. Such experience, we have shown, must be experience by imagination. There are two quite distinct intensities of experience by imagination. Before the act of decision, while available acts are being compared, the imaginative experience in its full degree which each act would afford can only be discerned. When decision has been made, when the decision-maker has committed himself to one sole act out of the rival formerly available acts, then the act of imagination becomes a real experience instead of the intellectual appraisal of an experience, and we shall call it in this final and full intensity, *anticipation*, a *taking beforehand* of the imagined situation or event.

III

THE SOLITARY MOMENT

The foregoing argument, if such it can be called, has taken for granted a certain frame of ideas about time which must now be made explicit. We have tried to show that decision is based upon a comparison of imaginations. Expectation is *thought* taking place in the present but having a content labelled with future dates. Expectation is an activity of the decision-maker, part of his consciousness, and therefore part of his present actuality. It belongs to the present as much as seeing and hearing do. Two things distinguish it from sense perception. It arises from within rather than outside the individual's mind; and it is explicitly concerned with situations or events which are not part of the individual's present actuality. We have to consider two entirely distinct ideas of time.

The momentary time in which thought occurs is in arresting contrast with the endless extension of time which thought can be about. In each moment we are sure that there will be another moment, because the moment exists for us only by virtue of events which change it into another moment. It is the very evolution of one moment into another which constitutes the passage of time. We are convinced that this will continue, and so we acquire the notion of an endless sequence of moments constituting, as it were, an axis or a one-dimensional space. Yet this space ought surely to be labelled as a mental construct, even an abstraction. It is a highly sophisticated inference from, or interpretation of, the nature of that actuality which we know by conscious experience and which is wholly contained within a solitary present moment.

The solitary present or the moment in being is the time of actuality in which things happen and consciousness exists. Extended time or the calendar axis is a mental construct. Futurity is merely an aspect of the content of thoughts which are actual in the solitary present. This is the essence of that view of time which our argument in this book assumes.

We do not mean that the view of time as an extension is

baseless or needless. Memory informs us that we have experienced a number of moments which were distinct amongst themselves and which are not themselves actual in the present. The very nature of that 'present' presages other moments not yet experienced, since the present makes itself felt, and has its only mode of existence, by changing into another moment. The present comprises perceived events, and we have defined an event as what carries one instantaneous situation into another. The choice of instants at which we shall elect to observe 'the situation', and thus the choice of particular, identified intervals between situations, is in general arbitrary. But the moment, by taking place, brings forth another moment which in turn will surely produce another and so on. We need a scheme of thought to formalize the distinction between moments, on the one hand, and on the other their apparent organization into *history* or an understandable drift and flow of action. The scheme which has imposed itself on all western minds is that of the (topological) line, the linear sequence endless in both directions, which it is easy to think of as a geometrical straight line or axis. (Straightness in the geometrical sense is of course totally irrelevant, we could with equal aptness think of an equiangular spiral or other doubly endless and non-self-intersecting pattern.) We shall refer to the *calendar axis*.

The lapse of time can then be thought of in two ways, as 'the moment' changing into another moment, or as the variable *viewpoint* moving along the calendar axis, and there is nothing mutually contradictory or incompatible in these views. But there is a vital caution to be observed in using the notion of the axis. Memory, and the need to explain to ourselves the existence of records and to interpret their precise form, give to the notion of the past a certain objective reality. There is a danger that we shall transfer this objective reality to the future. What right have we to speak of this possibility as 'a danger' and thus imply that the view in question is false? We do not say that it is false; merely that in adopting our premises and defining non-empty decision, we have implicitly rejected it. If there is non-empty decision in our sense, there is no objective future.

There is no objective future. This follows from our chosen axioms. By it we mean that there is no attainable future, out-

side our own minds, with which we can have any contact whatever. All that is, is in the present, which exists *alone*.

We are not here, let it be repeated again and again, attempting a statement about any deeper reality than is presented to our experience. For us, conscious humans, there is
nothing but the present. This is all we say, but we claim it,
within its limits, as an immediate fact about which no argument
is necessary or possible. The past exists in memory, but memory
is a mental act of the present. Records which describe the past
exist, but they exist in the present and are consulted in the
present. These rejections of the actuality of future and past are
what we wish to convey when we adopt the phrase *the solitary
moment* or *the solitary present*.

The idea which we wish to convey by this phrase is indeed
commonplace, once thought about. It is the extreme of the
obvious. Yet it has been neglected and even rejected in much
thought about human conduct and the nature of history. In
the social sciences in particular there is a tendency to speak of
means whereby we can 'find out' the future. The standpoint
we have adopted, if one more repetition can be forgiven by the
reader, is that the future is not there to be discovered, but must
be created.

Time as a scheme of thought contrasts in a way that must
astonish us, when we examine it, with time as the vehicle of
experience. To the mathematician all the points of an abstract
space are, *a priori*, equally valid and equally important. They
exist in his mind together, and, in the logical sense of the word,
simultaneously. This remains true if he considers by itself one
dimension of such a space and labels it 'time'. If this dimension
is the range of a variable, all values of that variable are equally
meaningful, equally necessary to the *general* validity of his
theorems or his equations involving that space. The different
points of his conceptual time co-exist. But the single momentary
thought in which he can embrace all those points manifestly
lies in a different time, a different world. In relation to his
thought-world, he himself is a detached observer viewing that
thought-world from a place of vantage and of superior wisdom.
The same sort of statement can be made about the historian.
For him the history of the past may appear as a sort of Bayeux
Tapestry brought to life. From any chosen date he can look

before and after, and there may seem to be a pattern to which his historiography can be a guide and an interpretation. He also is, in relation to the past, an outside observer and superior being. For both the exponent of classical physical dynamics writing his differential equation of the motion of a particle, and for the historian explaining the past, time is an extension all of whose points or parts belong to one and the same world of thought. The solution of the differential equation can be imagined as a curve, a segment of which can be drawn on a piece of paper, and the whole of that drawing and all its points can be seen in one momentary glance. Yet the different points correspond to different points of that 'time' in which the particle is supposed to be moving.

With this extended time seen from outside by an extra-temporal observer, we must contrast the time in which things happen to, and are perceived in their actuality by, an intra-temporal observer, a living person in his act of living. The time of actuality or consciousness in which perceptions, thoughts and emotions occur is a unique moment unaccompanied by any other moment, the sole possessor of all that is, the solitary present. Granted that expectation and memory are thoughts, it follows that nothing *is*, within the reach of human consciousness, except the present. There is but one moment, though it exists by changing. If the reader accepts, for some purpose of argument, this point of view, he will declare it so obvious as to be not worth putting into words. Yet it has consequences which social sciences have often overlooked.

Its chief victim is the distinction between rational and irrational conduct, when the latter is defined as a decision whose consequences, when they become actual, are exactly those in view of which the chosen act was selected, but which also, when they become actual, are regretted. Such a conception assumes that the experience in view of which the decision is made, and the experience which at a different moment becomes actual, are things belonging to 'one world', which are of a nature to be confronted with one another and to be compared, and to have meaning and validity together. Such comparison is possible only to the extra-temporal observer, who has no business whatever to pronounce on a question in which he has no competence. Any such argument speaks, in one and the same breath and span of thought, of two distinct moments as though what is actual in one could be compared in its actuality with what is actual in the other; it speaks as though these two actualities could be brought face to face on some sort of common ground. What we are saying in this chapter, fundamentally, is that no statement involving two actualities, that is, actuality at two distinct dates, can have any meaning; for it is a logical self-contradiction, a contradiction in terms. The present moment of actuality, the moment in being, is not only unique but alone, solitary, unaccompanied by any other moment, a world to itself all-embracing and by its existence denying the existence of any other moment; so far as the thoughts and feelings, perceptions, judgements, decisions and actions of the human individual are concerned. Comparison of the individual's *actual* experiences at two distinct moments is impossible and meaningless.

Suppose, then, that at a viewpoint labelled, on the calendar axis, t_0, a decision-maker adopts a scheme of action whose assumed outcome involves by anticipation both pleasures and pains, the pains having to be accepted as the price of the pleasures. The pleasures are associated in his mind with a calandar label t_1 and the pains with a calendar label t_3. Since he chose this action-scheme it is plain that at the viewpoint the anticipations of the pleasures outweighed those of the pains. But if, as outside observers, we take our stand at a calendar date t_2 partway between t_1 and t_3, what feelings shall we observe him actually experiencing at that date? When his viewpoint has reached this date t_2 there is no longer, we are assuming, anything pleasurable for him to look forward to amongst the consequences of the action-scheme but only its pains that are the price, still to be paid, of the pleasures which now are only a memory. May it not be that in this moment he will regret his choice of this action scheme? It is not certain that he will, for memory has pleasures of its own. But if, as outside observers, we see him regretting at t_2 the action course which, at t_0, had seemed preferable to all others, we may want to ask: Which of these two views, taken at different dates by the same man about the same act, is just? The position which we have tried to define in the preceding paragraphs can now be pinned down in relation to this question, for, we say, this question is *meaning-*

less. It may not on the surface appear meaningless to us: as outside observers, altogether detached from the time-world of the decision-maker, we can treat both dates t_0 and t_2 as co-existent and co-actual, so that, if the question were, what view *on our part* would be just? it would have a meaning. But the question does *not* concern *our* view. It concerns the view of the participant, the person for whom these various dates are not co-valid points on an extended axis but are *mutually exclusive* locations of a unique and solitary moment in being.

To the experience, the satisfaction and enjoyment which the moment in being affords the individual, memory may evidently, in some circumstances, contribute the feeling that an action-scheme conceived and adopted at an earlier date has since been adhered to, that it has yielded an outcome which is felt to correspond with what was then imagined, and that thus the present is in some sense a fulfilment of the past. This conception does not in the least conflict with our foregoing contentions about the singleness and solitariness of the actual present.

Plainly the comparisons relevant to decision are between *mutually exclusive* things. Between things which (for the individual decision-maker) are not mutually exclusive there is no need to choose. The actual experiences of the solitary present, taken as a whole, are unique. If they are taken as a whole, there is no alternative with which to compare them, nothing which is not too late to replace them. Parts and aspects comprised within this total actual momentary experience can no doubt be compared or contrasted with each other: but these parts or aspects are not mutually exclusive. Choice between actualities is, then, impossible. Between what can choice be made? Only between figments or imaginations. If the reader is weary of reading this statement, our excuse must be that, however obvious, it is essential and it has often been neglected, even implicitly denied and overridden. This neglect sometimes appears, in the literature of economics, as a reference to the 'undervaluation of future goods'. We need scarcely articulate the fallacy that we see in this expression. This phrase plainly assumes that the actual satisfactions obtained from the consumption of certain goods at one date can be meaningfully compared with the enjoyment by anticipation which was experienced at an earlier date by imagining the future consumption of these goods, and found to be 'equal', or 'less'. Alternatively we may say that it speaks as though a choice between two dates as the locus of otherwise specific satisfactions could be made by comparison of *actual* satisfactions. It is plain that so-called intertemporal comparisons are comparisons of imagined experiences, and that each such comparison is made as a single mental act in one and the same moment, so that it is baseless to argue that one of the two comparanda suffers under any 'irrational' disadvantage.

One kind of movement in time is evidently inseparable from the very nature of the solitary moment. Such a moment, looked on as belonging to the consciousness of the individual, consists of experiences, that is, of events, which in turn we have defined as transitions between one instantaneous situation and another. It is plain that our conception of 'moment' is sharply distinct from that of 'instant' and that we must conceive of the moment, however brief, as containing an infinity of instants, most of which we may disregard by taking an event to be a transition between two instants separated by a finite interval. It follows, however, that the moment by taking place also gives place to another moment, and this in turn to yet another and so on: there is 'lapse of time' or 'movement along the calendar axis'. It is also true that one of the events composing the moment can consist of thought which fleets along the calendar axis at a 'speed' that renders negligible, by comparison, the movement of the viewpoint itself entailed by the occurrence (the 'passage') of that thought. Thus there are two kinds of 'movement in time' to be considered. There is the kind which allows or consists in the actual occurrence of events, including thoughts. When such an event is a thought, the movement of this first kind consists in the *taking place* of the thought quite regardless of its content. But secondly there is the kind of movement which consists in a thought having for its content or substance a swiftly successive contemplation of distinct and perhaps widely separated dates in that figment or abstraction which in this book we have referred to as the calendar axis. Except that the notion of a calendar axis enters conveniently as a means of expressing both ideas, there is little similarity between the two kinds of 'movement', which, it is surely needless to say, must be kept wholly distinct in any dealings which involve both.

One such context, where we may meet both ideas in close company with each other, is the bundle of notions under the heading of 'change of expectation'.

Change of expectation, whatever form this change may take, can concern either what is to exist or occur at some fixed, named and identified calendar date, or it can concern what is to exist or occur at each date which will successively lie at a constant time-distance ahead of the moving viewpoint; the viewpoint moving, that is, of course, in the first of our two senses. The two meanings of change of expectation may be compared to the two kinds of change of scene which are visible from a moving vehicle. When the observer keeps his eye fixed on a point half a mile ahead of the vehicle, new tracts of country come continually into view as it moves; when he keeps his eye fixed on a stationary object which the vehicle continually approaches, fresh aspects and details of this object are continually revealed to him.

IV

INSULATED DYNAMIC SCHEMES

Decision in the meaning we have elected to give it is a cut between past and future, a moment of invention and not merely of calculation. In his vision of outcomes, looked upon as possible in some greater or less degree, for each rival available act, the decision-maker (we suppose) finds something more than could be explained by any observer, however well informed, by reference to the decision-maker's knowledge, to the previous conditioning of his mind by experience, and to his desires. Expectation can be something more than what is implicit in the sum of the past. If the reader rejects this view, let him admit that decision is, in our sense, 'empty', or else that judgement in face of uncertainty is arbitrary in a fundamental sense. We are assuming that men are reasonable, but also creative, in face of an orderliness of nature.

Decisions of the kind we here postulate are by their essential nature not predictable. No proof is needed, we have declared our assumption that some of the expectations by comparison of which these decisions arise are not fully explicable as consequences of what has gone before. Can we then have a system of calculation, a 'dynamics', which will enable us to make *prophecies* of the course of future history? We make here deliberately a distinction between conditional inferences from postulates adequately restricted, on the one hand, and unconditional prophetic statements based on an assumed sufficient knowledge of the past and present.

It is often held that any scheme of thought which purports to give *understanding* of how things happen, whether in nature or society, must therefore make possible *prediction* of what will happen. It must, at least, make possible such prediction (so it is believed) subject to precise assumptions about the existing state of affairs and what has led up to it. Those who wish to predict, however, often feel themselves to possess such firm and sufficient information about the present and the past that no distinction need be made between what they assume, in these respects, as the basis of prediction and what is demonstrably true. Thus their conditional predictions take on the quality of prophecies. For our part we recognize that predictions emphatically stated to be conditional, with the less easily discerned conditions given special prominence, are allowable; we differ only in being compelled, by the meaning we have adopted for *decision*, to include amongst the conditions the provision that, given the set of decisions which the members of the society are about to act on, no further decisions must be taken before the most distant date to which the prediction refers. Whether such a limitation renders any predictive scheme (any 'dynamics') worthless we shall discuss below.

However, we cannot agree that a scheme of thought must be worthless unless it makes possible prediction having almost the status of prophecy. Prophecy implies omniscience. The very living of conscious life is a thing unthinkable and logically excluded if we suppose the living beings to have knowledge of an objective future. For consciousness is experience, experience is the registering of stimulus, of what was hitherto outside consciousness, and how can there be stimulus, how can there be freshness of impression from what was already known, accepted and familiar? A scheme of thought can perform a valuable service in rendering experience *acceptable*, in an intellectual sense. Insight is not rendered *a priori* nugatory or invalid by our having to accept 'a mystery at the heart of things'.

We have defended our view that a descriptive, as distinct from a predictive, analytical scheme can have value. We turn to consider how far we can concede, to those who believe that only predictive power is worth while, the practicability of a limited predictive tool.

We have already used the term *action-scheme* as a mere equivalent of 'course of action' or 'act'. A person who supposed himself to know precisely, completely and for certain what each other person would do in response to any given action of his own, and also knew what nature would do by way of weather, harvests and so on, would no doubt lay down for himself an unconditional series of acts which would, at his viewpoint, give him a more preferred experience by anticipation than any other intended series of acts. A person having this perfect foresight would not be a decision-maker in our sense.

To allow for his uncertainty about the responses of others to his own acts (we may use the word 'response' in the most general sense to include acts which would be the same no matter what was done by our own individual) and about the behaviour of nature, a decision-maker would have to prescribe for himself alternatives of action for dates beyond the immediate future, this or that alternative to be adopted in case of this or that reaction of the total human and natural environment to his own acts. Such a scheme, where the later adoption of this or that alternative will not, *in certain circumstances*, require a new *decision*, but merely the recognition that, as things have turned out, the original decision implied alternative *A* rather than *B*, we call an action-scheme. The essential character of the circumstances, that is, the relation between events and previous expectations, which will be such as not to require a new decision, we cannot specify until we have set out our account of the nature of decision. Meanwhile we can use the concept of action-scheme in the sense of a prescription by the decision-maker of his own future acts which makes allowance for his uncertainty.

With this preamble, we can say that as detached, extra-temporal observers we are at liberty to construct a dynamics, for a whole society, on the assumption that after the initial moment every member of the society adheres to the action-scheme which he laid down for himself in that initial moment. So long as this adherence is going to last, so far our dynamics may be deemed free from the objection that decisions are by their nature unpredictable. There is still a difficulty. Our proviso cannot really be given any content, for we cannot say how long it will be before a decision is taken. Yet perhaps we have in our formula an excuse for constructing conditional inferential schemes; what we shall call an *insulated dynamics*.

An insulated dynamics satisfies logic rather than practical need. In defining expectation as imagination constrained to congruity with the possible, we employed the notion of the greatest speed at which a viewpoint situation could change into some specified desired situation; such desired situation, if linked with too early a date, would evidently be an impossible outcome, in the decision-maker's judgement. If, when the decision-maker has imagined an essentially new path of events, it still remains true that the social machine with its habitual, institutional, technical and epistemic equipment can only follow that path, or allow the decision-maker to follow it, at a definitely limited speed; if the pace of divergence, from the path which calculation from the recorded past would point to, is bounded; then it follows that the degree to which such calculated forecasts can, within a given space of time, be wrong is also bounded. We must be cautious, however, in relying on the *initial* speed at which a system of established policies and plans can be induced to swing away from its apparent aim. Ideas breed ideas in their own kind. Thus if it be true that decision is only non-empty when it is choice amongst outcomes newly imagined and containing an essential germ of inspired novelty, it seems to follow that a great part of the ultimate effect of a non-empty decision will lie in its setting a new background for the thought and decision of others. But such a propagation itself takes time. Suggestions take effect, new efforts of thought are made, on those discrete occasions when problems arise or become pressing. There are intervals between these occasions. Thus although a new idea (new in our special sense of radical non-explainability in terms of antecedents) may initiate an accelerating tide of change, we as outside observers may still claim that the past illuminates a little of the future. Such a defence of the attempt to calculate from past to future relies on a sort of momentum in affairs, and we shall refer to it as an *inertial dynamics*.

By a dynamics we mean a scheme of calculation or inference by which, when the situation at each of a certain set of dates is specified, sufficiently according to some stated test, the situation at one or more later dates can be determined. In the foregoing sentence we have not used the words past and future. They were not needed. A strict dynamics is independent of the notion of past and future, except in the fact that calculation may have to proceed from earlier to later. Having worked out the sequence of situations for a particular stretch of time, the extra-temporal observer can arbitrarily select any point within that stretch and say: Let us call this 'the present'. Within its own particular strait-jacket, our concept of an insulated dynamics is a strict dynamics in the foregoing sense. The inertial dynamics that we then outlined is not a strict dynamics. It neglects the effect of decisions instead of assuming their absence. Its validity fades gradually instead of being abruptly cut off, as that of an insulated dynamics is by a new decision. Nonetheless, these two kinds of dynamics have features in common which sharply contrast with the essential character of our own analytic scheme. The latter's purpose is to illuminate the structure of decision and not to show how decision-making could be annihilated and rendered needless, nugatory and ineffective by prediction of what the decision would be.

Our own scheme has evidently its dynamic aspect. Given the set of outcomes, one set for each available act, imagined by the decision-maker (and it is the product of this imagination which we claim to be unpredictable) our scheme shows how he will elect one of those available acts and, in order to obtain by anticipation, within his solitary actual present, the fruits of that decision, will commit himself to the elected act. Thus our scheme shows (in so far as its premises and argument can be accepted by the reader) how a tension will be set up in the decision-maker's mind (and thus in the society of which he forms a part) whose release requires certain action. Ours is, perhaps we may say, an extremely short-term dynamics. It shows, up to a point, how those decisions arise which in a particular moment *rig* the human society which we are concerned with to produce a specific set of immediately-next actions. Up to a point: that point is the barrier beyond which, by our own elected definition of *decision*, there can be no insight and no explanation; the point at which those who accept the idea of creative decision must resign from their analytical task and signal that relinquishment by some such word as inspiration. Decision which can be *wholly* explained is not, in our sense, decision at all, but mechanical and determinate reaction to circumstances.

Remote in purpose, meaning and pre-suppositions as our scheme of thought about decision is from those schemes of 'calculation of history' which economists call dynamics, there may still be some gain in setting out explicitly the various aspects of this contrast. Most fundamental, most powerful in determining all the other differences, is the question: *Whose* scheme of thought? The interior dynamics of the decision-maker's moment in being can, at most, be apprehended only by him. It is entirely and inviolably private. Moreover it is 'subjective' in a very special sense, for our whole effort in this Part I has been directed to show how the history-creating process can find room within the individual decision-maker's reasoning and appraising search for a best experience. Whatever lies behind his inspiration, it is, if our concept of decision is valid, something forever unexplainable, and thus we may say that the decision is the child of his own originative power. Something that springs up in the individual mind from an unaccountable source? What a starting-point, some will say, for an analysis claiming to be scientific.

If the observer's own thoughts, feelings and decisions are forbidden him as matter for observation, he becomes detached from the system he is observing, he is our 'outside observer', free to construct schemes for the 'calculation of history'. The maker of history and the calculator of history cannot be one and the same person, for the man who can make history cannot know in advance what history he will later make ('make' in the sense of genuine creation). But if the system being studied is something outside the student of it, there can be many such students all watching and explaining one and the same object, or at least, all able to understand and test each other's explanations. Thus an exterior dynamics, a scheme for calculating the future from a knowledge of the past, is public and objective.

One character which our scheme of thought must have in common with any exterior dynamics, if both are to offer an 'explanation' in the same ultimate meaning of the word, is that both must describe *structures*, or the complex interrelations of elements. Such descriptions of structure, whether or not involving elements labelled with different calendar or clock points, are the fundamental mark of science of any kind from genetics to cosmology and from historiography to mathematics. The elements whose interrelations and possibilities of interrelation are studied or proved by a science can be anything at all; the mark of science is description of structure whether of an atom, the ladder of biological ascent, a period of history or the sudden fusion of thoughts in a decision. In these terms the contrast between the interior dynamics of the individual's moment, and the exterior dynamics of an extensive calendar interval, can be stated simply as a difference in the elements involved. The interior dynamics involves elements private to a single mind and belonging, in their actuality, to a single moment. The exterior dynamics involves public and objective observables whose 'actuality' is not that of being thought or felt by a participator but that of being noted by a detached student to whom all dates are equally valid. Our student, moreover, is not only extra-temporal, but also extra-personal, and is interested in the actions of a society instead of the action of a single decision-maker.

Chiefest of all the aspects of contrast between the two kinds of analysis is that the exterior dynamics, of whatever type in detail, has as its main purpose the prediction of events or situations from a knowledge of events or situations. The interior dynamics, if we can find for it no more felicitous name, has as its goal insight into the structure of a mental event.

We have now completed the task of this Part I, namely, to define non-illusory, non-empty, non-otiose decision as choice in face of creative uncertainty bounded by natural order. We have sought to answer the questions, how can choice be other than determinate calculation without being arbitrary and capricious? How can the orderliness of nature be reconciled to the originative imagination of men? Amongst what do men choose, when the notion of plural rival actualities is a contradiction? We elected as our basis of argument the pre-supposition that there is such a thing as effective history-making decision, and we preferred anwers of a sort to the questions that sprang from this assumption. These answers have left us with a further central problem: How are we to conceive of uncertainty, how is it to be defined; described in concrete instances; analysed and even quantified; so that its part in decision can be understood? This will be the subject-matter of Parts II and III.

V

THREE CRITICS

The foregoing chapters contain, we believe, a minimum set of postulates concerning the place of decision in the bringing of history to birth from moment to moment; and concerning the nature of the human experience of time; and concerning the meaning to be given to the word decision itself; to make possible an analysis of how decision occurs when we accept the evidence of our own attitude to life, the attitude 'I am responsible'.

From these postulates we deliberately seek in the first place only one consequence, the freedom to suppose that decision is originative or creative in the deepest sense. But from these postulates there also flow, of course, other consequences, variously discerned and interpreted by various critics. Three of these critics, sympathetic to the general enterprise itself of studying decision as creative and non-empty, have found some of these other consequences disconcerting or at odds with their own frames of thought. In this chapter by liberal quotation of what they have written I hope to present their views and to attempt some reply.

Professor Johan Åkerman of the University of Lund has, out of a very great generosity, on three occasions intensively examined the questions which I have tried to formulate and the inferences which have seemed to me to flow from my proposed system of axioms. In *Kyklos** his article-review of my *Time in Economics*; in *Metroeconomica*† his contribution to a symposium; and in correspondence his notes‡ on a lecture which I was privileged to give at Lund, embodying the substance of the four preceding chapters of this book, have that quality of critical insight which enables another writer to see more plainly and more fully what he himself has asserted and what its implications are. Professor Åkerman says:

* 'Professor Shackle on Economic Methodology', *Kyklos*, vol. xi (1958), pp. 341–61.
† 'Shackle's System and Theories of Business Cycles', *Metroeconomica*, vol. xi (1959), pp. 3–11.
‡ 'Comment on Professor Shackle's Lecture', reproduced below.

But the absolute subjectivity and uniqueness of decisions and the impossibility of testing a choice as to its correctness—which forms the kernel of Shackle's system—severs the connection between the individual's action and its outcome in the economy as a whole, i.e. in macro-economics.... If we accept this as a psychological model of the single decision-maker, we are, however, confronted with the big problem of connecting the decision thus engendered with decisions of other single decision-makers and then throwing a bridge between all these decisions and their collective outcome. Finally, we cannot shirk the main problem of connecting this total outcome with the actual structure of the economy as a whole—how it will be transformed, what cumulative process may arise as a result of the new decisions. To put it squarely one may say that Shackle has justly criticized the logic of the psychological assumptions of econometric as well as of general economic models, which cannot consider real decisions because they are automatically eliminated by the functional, deterministic form of reasoning, but that by doing this he has deprived himself of every tangible link between decisions and the whole economic structure—its attributes, its mechanism, and its changes. Confronted with the antinomy between a psychologically plausible type of free, real decisions and a functional, mechanistic and unrealistic theory of relations between changes in the value of variables ('decisions') and their results in the macro-economic system, Shackle has opted for a theory that places 'individual human consciousness' and 'non-empty' real decisions in the centre; but he does not see that by doing so he has shut the door to macro-economic theory and perhaps even to micro-economics. His psychological theory of decisions is autonomous and hence non-economic, because it has no necessary and sufficient references to economic relations and processes. I do not say that such connection between real decisions and economic change is possible; on the contrary, the antinomy between free-willed action and determinate process makes such a junction paradoxical. My main objection to Shackle's ideas in *Time in Economics* is the fact that he does not seem to have grasped this paradox as a fundamental question.

Professor Åkerman has here, I think, stated with arresting clarity the dilemma that confronts the would-be 'scientist of human affairs'. If, on the one hand, the word 'human' means nothing in particular; if men are cogs in nature's machine and nothing more; if history is fate; then *decision* also is a meaningless and otiose word, a 'fifth wheel' in the theories of what is happening to us as time unrolls our destiny. Such theories, in this case, have merely (however complex the task may be) to discover and state the set of equations by which the future may be calculated from the past. But if, instead, decision is improvisation, then it is in decision that we must seek an understanding of how things happen; but to be able to gain such an insight is not the same thing as being able to tell *what* things will happen. Shall we then opt for a theory about decision, or shall we opt for one about 'necessity', the rigid, precise sequential implication of states or events? The two are incompatible.

It is true that I have tried to present this dilemma with its own uncompromising force. But if we opt for non-empty decision this does not, in my belief, cut us off from supposing that the decision-maker uses knowledge, logic and a tense and anxious judgement in composing his imaginative picture of what might lie beyond each gate that each rival choice of act might open. What might lie beyond is what he creates. The outcomes that he thinks of for any one act are not, so our suggestion runs, determined by his previous history nor, therefore, even in principle determinable from it; but they are bounded by his judgement of what is possible, and in making such judgements he calls upon his knowledge of physical laws and of the existing situation of affairs and of what other people, by their acts, appear to have decided. It is thus, I would say, that decisions of different men may interact and influence one another. But to say this is, of course, to make no concession whatever regarding the basic choice: if we assume meaningful, effective decision we must abandon the strictly interlocking sequence of earlier and later general situations.

It is plain that a man's decision and the act that follows can play a part amongst the things that another man takes account of in forming his own decision. One decision can influence and contribute to another. But when all these influences of act and situation are added up, perhaps we are still short of being able to know what the new decision will be. If so, we have real decision, if not, we have a determinate system. There are important contexts, such as the economic one, where it seems that a large part of conduct is given little effort of true decision, being instead a passive response to circumstance. If this is true of most people, and if the true decisions have little early effect on the passively responding majority, we can study markets in the established way. It is of the very nature of economics, I would say, to have to be content with an imprecision of concept ('income', 'general price level' and so on) and a type of reasoning which consequently calls for sympathetic supplementation and interpretation on the part of the hearer, and for caution and reserve in use; needs which were exceedingly well understood by Alfred Marshall and John Maynard Keynes. Economics, like life itself, is practised subject to acceptance of uncertainty.

Professor Åkerman has stated my positions with the utmost fairness and sympathy. In only one main respect I feel that he has missed something of what I have tried to say. In his contribution to the *Metroeconomica* symposium* Professor Åkerman says

The kernel of Shackle's system, the theory about the isolated individual's unique decisions, eliminates all connections between the individual's mind and his own experiences as well as the experiences and actions of other individuals.

My means of expression have been at fault if I have given the impression of saying this. The decision-maker forms *expectations*, by which word I mean conceptions of outcomes looked on as *possible*. What seems to him possible, from the viewpoint of a particular, unique moment, depends not only on the supposed laws of nature but on the particular detailed state of affairs, a state of affairs which is the consequence of previous decisions and actions of others. Each decision of any individual does something to shape the background of beliefs and assumptions, and of data for judging possibility, against which the later decisions of others and himself will be taken.

The passages quoted hitherto are from Professor Åkerman's criticisms of my *Time in Economics*. At his kind invitation the substance of chapters I through IV of this present volume were delivered as a lecture in the University of Lund on 28 September 1959, and Professor Åkerman on that occasion wrote the *Comment* which, with his permission, I reproduce in full below:

Many of Professor Shackle's theses are challenging: they challenge the premises of many conventions and traditions in economic

* Johan Åkerman, 'Shackle's System and Theories of Business Cycles', *Metroeconomica*, vol. XI (1959), p. 4.

analysis. And I am perfectly at one with the contention that methodological and epistemological discussion of so-called ever-valid economic laws is necessary—now more than at any earlier date. Professor Shackle treats a non-determinate world, in which the isolated subject in a moment-in-being can decide freely. The problem on inter-actions between individuals and the question of the relation between individual decisions (plans) and the total (macro-) result are not yet sufficiently elucidated.

I will now shortly comment on seven points.

1. 'When two consecutive states differ—there is an event' says Professor Shackle. When two consecutive states of the macro-structure are identical—there is equilibrium, according to common definition. Equilibrium hence constitutes an 'empty situation': it has no content—and should not be used as a starting-point when constructing dynamic theoeris. Lord Keynes' contention about equilibrium with under-employed factors of production as well as Schumpeter's 'neighbourhood of equilibrium' does not apply to any real facts. 'Equilibrium' is a fiction of classical and neo-classical economics, not a description of a real situation.

2. 'Inspired decision implies a *new* choice in face of bounded uncertainty.' This inspired decision affects a future structure, but the expectation which explores this future structure merely represents the screen on which the decision is projected. Is it not necessary to explain the relation between expectations and decisions (plans) in some such way?

3. I have used 'activity periods' as concepts denoting the time horizon of different groups. With Professor Shackle's very graphic parable I could say that activity periods are shortened, when for instance monetary stringency looms on the horizon; then they meet with a wall and are successively reduced—the longest ones first; finally all are reduced to nil in the acme of a crisis.

4. 'The future is not to be discovered but to be created'—a challenging statement; all sorts of econometric forecasts are prepared daily. Of course one can say that speculation predicts the movement of prices and prediction—of W. M. Persons' ABC-system and J. Tinbergen's 'explanations' of time-series—but one must grant that such prediction *either* is focused on transactions changing income-distribution i.e. speculative profits, not profits from creative new investments or from current production, *or* just the observer's (economist's) ordering of the material in a 'causal' pattern.

5. 'No statement involving two actualities has any meaning.' Hence it is wrong to distinguish between rational and irrational conduct, because such a dichotomy presupposes two dates; one acts

in T_0—and in T_n it should become evident if the action was rational or irrational. But this presupposes 'ceteris paribus'; it is really impossible to prove or disprove. When Myrdal in 1930 criticized the concept of general welfare as the result of rational conduct he maintained this to be circular reasoning—rational conduct making for welfare and welfare defined as the result of rational conduct. He glimpsed something of this time-relation and of the fictitious 'ceteris paribus' but he did not reach its general implication according to Professor Shackle's approach.

6. According to Milton Friedman, theory is to be identified with prediction. Professor Shackle accepts predictions on the explicit condition that all decisions are concluded with the 'initial' decision. This statement does as a matter of fact efficiently criticize Erik Lundberg's model sequences (ch. ix in his treatise of 1937 on economic expansion) because Lundberg places all the determining data in T_0 and then moreover declares that all plans are made each time the sequence crosses a demarcation-line between two periods. Hence the sequence is necessarily and sufficiently determined by the data given in T_0 and unquestionably *over-determined* by adding the declaration about new decisions at the passage from one period to another due to differences between ex ante and ex post values. In this case also Professor Shackle's approach gives a more general, philosophical proof than that obtained by a purely economic analysis.

7. Finally a question: 'Does Professor Shackle reckon with a change of the subject's mental structure and also with a change of the observed (economic) macro-structure?' Or are such changes irrelevant as decisions constitute the whole content of economics and new, inspired decisions are made by isolated individuals in a moment-in-being of infinitesimal length?

*   *   *

With a rare sympathy and understanding Professor B. S. Keirstead has suggested to me the dangers of any attempt to fix *time* into a scheme of thought. His first criticism, at first sight so radical, seems on examination to bring strong testimony in my favour. In his contribution to the *Metroeconomica* symposium Professor Keirstead says:*

One doubts if really great historians stand 'outside' the time they are describing. As one reads Herodotus or Livy, even Julius Caesar, and, of the moderns, Vico, Lecky, Gibbon, Motley or Halèvy, one

* B. S. Keirstead, 'Professor Shackle on Time in Economics', *Metroeconomica*, vol. xi (1959), pp. 44-50.

must realise how far they have imaginatively entered into the period of history they have set out to display.... The possible relevance arises from this: that if historians can enter imaginatively into their 'period', what happens to the proposed distinction between 'lived, moment-in-being time', and 'outside, observed time'? In fact— and this leads us to our second philosophic objection—can this distinction be maintained in the case of the historian or any subject who enters imaginatively into the past or the future?

I do not question that the real historian can live his way through the episodes he studies, can make the crises of decision, which his characters suffered, crises for himself in imagination, can ask himself with vivid realism 'What would I do if this were my situation?' To admit this is merely to say that the historian understands what time is for those who live in it. The historian who can feel, like the dramatist, the passions, perplexities and doubts of his actors; still more, the one who can imagine for them the field of possibility from which they were free to gather a sheaf by their selection of one act rather than any of its rivals: this is the great historian. If this power to raise, as it were, imagination to a higher power, and, though still living in a solitary 'present', to elect for that 'present' a different date from the natural one, to shift his personality, thoughts, judgements, fears and hopes to a moment different from the 'present' of other living people, and place himself instead alongside the actors in his own historiography, is the chief gift of the historian, then this truth reinforces rather than refutes our contentions. For to cause oneself to be thus completely rapt into the past would require an intense self-discipline: all that lies between this elected present and the natural present would have in the literal sense to be 'ignored', to be not known; else the whole point and truth of the exercise would be lost. This unknown region would indeed be free for the historian to explore in imagination looking forward from his elected present, provided he could really forget his knowledge of the record. In helping to storm the Bastille he must know nothing of the Terror, in crowning the first Kaiser he must have no inkling of the world wars as the history books describe them. I cannot assert that there are none to whom such a feat is possible. But their existence would in no way blur the distinction between the lived moment, tense and fleeting, on the one hand, and that 'interior distance',* time as a space, the imagined or hypothesised calendar axis, on the other.

The second philosophic objection [Professor Keirstead continues] has to do with the matter of identity.... With every sympathy towards Professor Shackle's views, the present author cannot find any systematic attempt to explain the identity of the something which experiences 'inside time'. There is implied a 'flow of consciousness' philosophy which reminds one of fashionable literature of the 1930's.

I have never suggested, but quite the contrary, that the experiencing, imagining, decision-making subject has not *memory*, nor denied that in every moment he draws upon a mental stock bequeathed by previous moments back to the beginning of his life or even of his race. Out of this stock we can, perhaps, suppose him to make something not to be found in the stock itself, something 'new' in a profound sense; and if not, how are we to say his decision is creative? But how, if not by memory, can I reach back to my former self? What there is of me, is now. To *be* is to be now. Let me say again, the task this book attempts is a modest one, concerned with men's condition of existence as they can see it to be, and not with transcendentals. I do not think anything in the conception of the 'solitary present' denies a man the right to look upon that personality, who performed the past acts he remembers as his own, as *belonging* privately and securely to that self who exists in the solitary present. For that other personality exists doubly in the present. The present self is in every way his child, 'inheriting' much of his character and physical traits and inheriting also the rich stock of memories, knowledge, skill and ideas that earlier selves have gathered. I can catch a glimpse of the difficulty that Professor Keirstead feels; but seeking to hold it in a steady gaze, I find it evaporate.

Professor Keirstead quotes Locke by way of warning to me not to understate the role of experience and of the decision-maker's careful endeavour to interpret the record of the past:

If to break loose from the conduct of reason, and to want that restraint of examination and judgement which keeps us from doing or choosing the worse, be liberty, true liberty, madmen and fools are the only freemen.

* I borrow this remarkable phrase from the title of the book called in English *The Interior Distance*, by Georges Poulet, translated by Elliott Coleman (Johns Hopkins Press and Oxford University Press, 1959).

It is useful to note the criticism here implied, although Professor Keirstead does not press it against me; for in presenting my scheme of thought afresh in the present book (which Professor Keirstead has not seen) I have specially sought to make prominent that element of it by which it attempts one of its central purposes, namely, to show how decision can be undetermined without being arbitrary. My decision-maker is by no means free from 'that restraint and examination of judgement which keeps him from doing or choosing the worse': his freedom lies in creating, in some sense, the imagined outcomes of the acts amongst which he chooses; and no one, unless a super-human detached observer, can say that these imagined outcomes are not legitimate: there is nothing objective to compare them with. A paper of mine called 'The complex nature of time as a concept in economics' was read at a meeting of the Econometric Society at Uppsala in 1954. The paper itself was printed in full in *Economia Internazionale* of November 1954* and the discussion which took place is recorded in *Econometrica* of April 1955.† A rather inexplicit statement of the matter now in question appears in the paper itself, an explicit one in the discussion. The idea (which is I think part of the kernel of my whole scheme of thought) is again stated in *Time in Economics*,‡ p. 27:

Looking back on the convergent paths we have followed to this position, you will see that I want to make the term 'free will' point in a somewhat different direction from that of its meaning in ordinary discourse, where if we examined our attitude with exactness we should perhaps be led to define the free-willed individual as one who acts or is capable of acting *arbitrarily* in face of a *given* situation. I am proposing instead to say that it is his situation, his structure of expectations, that he is in some sense free to create, or to derive from some unexplained and essentially unpredictable inspiration, but that his conduct in face of any *given* expectational vista, any given set of assessments of the possible consequences of specified rival action schemes open to him, will be non-arbitrary; if you like, that it will be rational.

*   *   *

---

* *Economia Internazionale*, vol. VII (1954), pp. 743–57.

† *Econometrica*, vol. XXIII (1955), pp. 207–8.

‡ *Time in Economics*. Three lectures given in the University of Amsterdam in May 1957, under the Professor F. de Vries Foundation. Published for the Foundation by the North Holland Publishing Company, 1957.

In a most luminous and arresting article, and a most generous one, Professor L. M. Lachmann has touched in a highly individual way on some of the questions which have engaged Professor Åkerman and Professor Keirstead. Like Professor Keirstead he urges that there must exist some receptacle of gained and accumulated experience, a vehicle which shall preserve and convey what, of knowledge, judgement and interpretation, is achieved in one moment, from thence to another and another moment, so that we may conceive a basis of decision being built up gradually in the decision-maker's mind until the moment comes for acting on it. Both writers seem to ask whether my scheme can accept such an idea, or at any rate whether it is meant to. But most certainly I do think exactly this, certainly I have always thought of each moment as the child of its predecessor in the decision-maker's mind, inheriting characters though also undergoing mutations. In speaking thus of a *basis* of decision I mean, of course, a means by which the individual can judge possibility, a means of testing the outcomes he imagines for any available act to see whether they deserve the status of expectations. 'Whatever may be discontinuous in us, the human mind is continuous', Professor Lachmann says. But he proceeds, 'The acts of mind of which our conscious life consists, follow each other ceaselessly. Bergson and Husserl have shown that the content of our consciousness is best regarded as a continuous stream of thought and experience.' When we compare this with Professor Keirstead's words: 'The *tabula rasa* which Locke postulates as the origin of experience is also the "self" whose identity must be explained... the present author cannot find [in Shackle] any systematic attempt to explain the identity of the something which experiences "inside time", the "moments-in-being"', we find a clue, I think, which can resolve all important differences of view between the three of us. All are agreed that the content of each moment is partly, or perhaps overwhelmingly, an inheritance from previous moments. Whether we prefer to think of the essential continuity as 'an identifiable object which passes through time'* or as the conservation from moment to moment of an *impress* or pattern of thought, a *reproduction* in each moment of part of the content of earlier moments, seems to me to belong to that realm

---

* *Metroeconomica*, vol. XI, p. 66.

of transcendental questions which I wish to avoid. It may be that Professor Keirstead prefers the former of these conceptions while Professor Lachmann would accept the latter.

However this may be, Professor Lachmann emphasizes that something which is both objective and vitally relevant to the making of a decision is indeed preserved from one moment to another. This thing is the *formal* aspects of knowledge of the past. If we can find a suitable interpretation of the word 'formal' which I have here on my own initiative introduced into the discussion, then I should feel bound to agree with Professor Lachmann in this. It is plain that the answers which history gave to certain questions will be identically stated by many men no matter when we consult them. The dates of the deaths of kings, the wording of parliamentary enactments, the figures of elections, the details of balance sheets; each such item offers an inter-temporal and inter-personal fix-point which will be preserved, or identically reproduced, from moment to moment. Yet all such facts are the mere surface of things. The meaning which is found in them, the emotional colour that they wear, what they stand for in imagined history are private to the individual mind. When I add this, am I justifying Professor Lachmann in saying:

But if we were to take Professor Shackle's thesis literally, there could be no testing the success of plans, no plan revision, no comparison between *ex ante* and *ex post*. In fact planned action would make no sense whatever

It will appear in subsequent chapters that the individual's power to decide, as I conceive it, depends essentially on his preparedness to judge whether or in what degree some outcomes are possible; such judgements themselves rely, of course, on knowledge, however imperfect, of the physical properties of nature, of human character and history, and of the current state of affairs; and such knowledge can, of course, be available only as a consequence of the storing of experience by memory. It is in neglecting my references to memory that my critics have, I think, somewhat misjudged my view:

There is a third category of mental acts related to time, those of memory. These in one way resemble our interpretations of sensory perceptions, in that we suppose the events or situations which are their content to have a character of truth.... Expectation and memory are part of the essence of the moment in being, they are in it and of it.

The content of a thought can include, as part of itself, a label referring it to any date; but when that thought takes place it does so, of course, in the individual thinker's present. In these two ideas there is surely no contradiction. Thus I do not think the axioms on which I am seeking to found an analysis of decision entail that 'planned action would make no sense'. But since all three of the critics discussed in this chapter have mis-understood me in a somewhat similar way, it is evident that my earlier expositions have been at fault.

Professor Lachmann raises in a somewhat different form a question which is also one of Professor Åkerman's main objec-tions to my viewpoint. This is the question of communication and interaction of the individual decision-maker with others. Here again it seems that in bending my efforts intensely on certain special ideas I have allowed it to be thought that I can accept nothing which I have not explicitly referred to. But in my view the decision-maker decides and acts. His actions are observed, and the effects of those actions are felt, by others, who add these items of news to their dossier of knowledge, to their outfit of tools for adjudging degrees of possibility to imagined outcomes of acts available to themselves. Amongst the acts which will be noted by others are evidently the acts of buying in markets and thus affecting prices, whether those markets be ordinary or forward markets. Thus, so far as markets of either of these kinds can enable the plans of different indivi-duals to be harmonized, there is nothing in my own views which conflicts with the establishment of Hayekian equilibrium, that is, the perfect dovetailing and mutual compatibility of plans, by means of markets. But again I must accept responsibility for a failure of exposition.

Professor Lachmann is one of the very few who have outlined a general system of economic thinking in which time is not merely a tiresome addendum or something allowed rather grudgingly to play a 'role', but is, as with Marshall, the heart of the matter. Growth of knowledge is the entelechy and inseparable upshot of the lapse of time: thus, perhaps, we may express the essence of his vision, which in his contribution to the *Metroeconomica* symposium is condensed to a few brilliant passages:

[Shackle's] general thesis about the creative power of the mind and our inability to predict its acts would still hold, because men would still be interpreting experiences, acquiring knowledge, planning and revising plans. We are able to imagine a world in which tastes do not change but unable to imagine one in which knowledge does not spread from some minds to others. Even continuity of ends does not entail an invariant means-ends pattern; men would still be eager to make better use of the means at their disposal. *Time* and *Knowledge* belong together. The creative acts of the mind need not be reflected in changing preferences, but they cannot but be reflected in acts grasping experience and constituting objects of knowledge and plans of action. All such acts bear the stamp of the individuality of the actor.

The impossibility of prediction in economics follows from the facts that economic change is linked to change in knowledge, and future knowledge cannot be gained before its time.

As soon as we permit time to elapse we must permit knowledge to change, and knowledge cannot be regarded as a function of anything else. It is not the subjective nature of expectations, any more than that of individual preferences, which makes them such unsuitable elements of dynamic theories, it is the fact that time cannot pass without modifying knowledge which appears to destroy the possibility of treating expectations as data of a dynamic equilibrium system.

'Future knowledge cannot be gained before its time'; 'knowledge cannot be regarded as a function of anything else'. In these last two sentences Professor Lachmann grants me all that I require.

VI

TIME AND DECISION IN SUM

The subject's position in space can be elected, but his position in time cannot be elected. This should warn us that, in human experience and perception as distinct from human intellectual construction, time is of a different nature from a space whether we mean by that word the space of the senses or the mathematician's purest abstraction. For the subject, the living individual, there is but one moment—the present. Within this same solitary moment-in-being must lie all the *actual* consequences in view of which any decision is taken in that moment. For no two or more moments can be 'in being', can be actual, together; the present alone is uniquely actual in total solitary exclusiveness. What kind of actual consequences can occupy the same moment as the decision which aims at them? Such consequences, to be *relevant* for decision, must be experiences of the decision-maker; to be realized in the moment of decision they must be experiences *by imagination*.

We assume that decision aims at the most *preferred* experiences, using the freedom of imagination constrained only by judgement of what is possible; for imagined experiences will not be interesting unless they are deemed possible. An available action can, however, have many rival imaginable outcomes. Must imagination dwell on all of them? It can confine itself without arbitrariness or lack of logic to the best and the worst amongst the 'sufficiently possible' imagined outcomes.

As the locus of consciousness, or as consciousness itself, the moment exists only in the perceptions, feelings, thoughts and decisions which take place in it. These things are events, transformations carrying one instantaneous state of affairs into another, and it follows that the moment cannot exist without changing into and giving place to another and different moment. Like a phase of a wave the moment is individual but continuous with the preceding and the following phases. Transformation of one moment into another is inherent in the idea of the moment. The *detached* observer can adopt the figment of a

'calendar axis' along which he supposes the viewpoint of the
engaged observer, the time-experiencing individual, to move.
Movement of another kind along the calendar axis is possible
for the engaged observer: this is the shift of the date with which
his imagination is concerned.

In a predestinate world, decision would be *illusory*; in a
world of perfect foreknowledge, *empty*; in a world without
natural order, *powerless*. Our intuitive attitude to life implies
non-illusory, non-empty, non-powerless decision. This attitude
is revealed by our ordinary speech, in which the word *decision*
suggests the power to initiate a new train of impulses in the
wave-pattern of history. Since decision in this sense excludes
both perfect foresight and anarchy in nature, it must be defined
as choice in face of bounded uncertainty. If decisions are
creative, each injecting into history something essentially novel,
something which is not purely the inevitable outgrowth of the
past, decisions are unpredictable and so, therefore, is history.

If the individual's *ends are given*; if the dossier of knowledge
which at any moment he possesses, however imperfect, prescribes the course 'most likely' to attain his ends; is not his
action determinate? Can there be non-empty decision which
is not merely arbitrary and non-rational? We say that the
individual's ends are not given in this sense. The set of rival
hypothetical outcomes of each available action is not prescribed
like those of a game with completely stated rules. The outcomes
imagined by the decision-maker for each act may not be
determined by his past but may contain something not to be
found in any account of his experience; an element of
'inspiration'.

PART II

UNCERTAINTY

VII

UNCERTAINTY AS PROBABILITY

To dismiss as unquestionably wrong some suggested answer to some question is an act of mind which we shall take to be one and the same thing for every one, needing no definition. It accords to that answer a status distinct from the status of any not-dismissed answer to the same question. Can we further discern distinctions between the status of this and that not-dismissed answer? Can these answers or *hypotheses* be ordered, that is, arranged in a sequence implying that the person's feeling about one hypothesis is more remote from absolute dismissal of it than his feeling is about another hypothesis? Yet again, we shall treat as in no need of argument the idea that such comparison is sometimes made. To express such comparisons, we assign to each hypothesis a value of some variable. What should be the nature and character of this *uncertainty-variable*, in order that it may best serve this purpose?

The essential choice we have to make is between what I will call a *distributional* and a *non-distributional* uncertainty variable. In the preceding paragraph we took as our point of departure the idea of certainty that some hypothesis is wrong. We did so because this idea has a plain direct meaning common, as we shall subsequently argue, to both distributional and non-distributional kinds of uncertainty-variable, while the idea of certainty that a hypothesis is right has a *simple* meaning only when we use a distributional uncertainty variable, since with a non-distributional uncertainty variable the idea of 'certainty of rightness' must be constructed. However, in order to discuss the concept of distributional uncertainty variables we shall assume that certainty of the rightness of a hypothesis is, like that of certainty of wrongness, a mental act or state familiar to everyone and needing no definition.

When a man is certain that a particular answer to some question is right, he means that that answer by itself exactly fills the vacant place constituted by the question, leaving no room for any other suggested answers. He may then represent to himself this completeness by the integer one. If now that answer can be split up into additive components which, when all taken together, come to the same thing as that answer, and if he wishes to represent to himself the share of any one component in the completeness achieved by the entire set of components, he will have to assign it some proper fraction determined on a principle such that when all the fractions, one for each component, are listed, they sum to unity. Let us restrict p to be a number such that $0 \leqslant p \leqslant 1$. Then when values of p are assigned, on some principle which satisfies the additive test we have described, to a set of suggested answers to some question, p is serving as a distributional uncertainty variable.

The suggested answers or hypotheses can be those elicited by any question. What will my situation in such and such respects be at such and such a date? How will that situation differ if I now adopt course A from what it would be if I now adopted course B? If I have a stated set of physical objects, such as a coin or dice-box, and execute with them a stated kind of performance, what will their resulting configuration be, when I next do this, or when I do it on the tenth occasion from now? When I do it a thousand times, how many of these times will yield such and such a result? What is the length of this page in inches? The question can be one to which by its nature the suggested answers are discrete, or it can be one to which the suggested answers form in logic a continuous range of a variable. But when in practice we test a hypothesis which is a value from a logically continuous range, we call it 'right' on condition that it falls within some specified interval. Thus in effect the suggested answers to even a 'continuous' question are treated as discrete. Because we are interested in psychic reality, and because we thus avoid problems of transfinite arithmetic, we shall unless we say otherwise treat all suggested answers to all questions as discrete.

If a book is written in a living language of the British Isles, what is its language? English, Welsh and Gaelic are answers which might be suggested. A man who is unable to find any additional suggestion might say to himself that these three hypotheses are components which, taken together, make up an answer which is certainly right: the language of the book is one or other of the three languages, English, Welsh and Gaelic.

Then he could apply a distributional uncertainty variable to the three hypotheses. What necessary conditions for using a distributional uncertainty variable are fulfilled by this example?

Two things about this list are noticeable. First, it is regarded by the individual as certainly complete. Secondly, every item in it is specific (particularized); it does not contain any such item as 'some other language'. The combination of these two ideas can be expressed by saying that, for the person whose list it is, the list is *complete without a residual hypothesis*. The term *residual hypothesis* is a mere label on a closed door behind which there may lie anything whatever in the way of outcomes unspecifiable as to their nature or their numbers. The inclusion of a residual hypothesis in his list of suggested answers is his acknowledgement that he has no basis for considering his existing list of particularized hypotheses to be comprehensive. If he does hold that list to be complete without a residual hypothesis, one kind of obstacle to the use of a distributional uncertainty variable is absent, the obstacle, to wit, that if hypotheses of unknown character not yet included in the list are liable to appear and claim a share, and if, because nothing is known of these hypotheses, not even the total of their shares can be determined, then plainly the total of the shares of the already-listed specific hypotheses, and therefore the respective shares of these individual hypotheses, cannot be determined either. Let us call this kind of obstacle the arithmetical obstacle to the use of a distributional uncertainty variable, and let us repeat that the arithmetical obstacle is absent when the list of specific, particularized hypotheses is held by the individual to be complete. Now we can formulate our answer to our question posed at the end of the preceding paragraph, and summarize its grounds, as follows: The essential condition for the use of a distributional uncertainty variable is that the list of suggested answers should be complete without a residual hypothesis. For on what conceivable principle and with what meaning could the individual make a distribution when, besides his list of particularized hypotheses, he acknowledges that an unknown number of other hypotheses of whose content and character he knows nothing are also liable to claim shares?

I can sense a possible objection from the reader. Admittedly, he may say, when the list in order to attain formal completeness must be rounded off with a residual hypothesis, there can be no distribution *a priori*, that is to say, no distribution which depends on an examination of each hypothesis as to what it says; but can there not sometimes be an empirical distribution? When the question asks what proportion of one thousand instances of some kind of performance with a given 'system' will yield such and such a result, what proportion will yield such and such another result, and so on, does it matter that the list of different specific results is incomplete? For even if some results were, so to speak, rolled up together in a cloak which concealed their number and their characters (as if some of the faces of a die should have no visible dots inscribed on them), would it not nevertheless be possible to observe the relative frequency of each of the unconcealed results? The confusion which lies at the heart of such an objection will be fully analysed in later paragraphs, but its nature can be seen at once. It arises from the simple failure to distinguish the question: what will be the result of this or that *particular instance* (for example, the next, or the tenth from now) of the performance, from the question: in what proportions will *one thousand instances* of the performance, taken as one whole, be made up of this result and this other result and this other result...? In our example, above, of one thousand performances, we are not really concerned with any residual hypothesis; a residual hypothesis only appears in this example quite incidentally, as part of the list of suggested answers to a *quite different question*.

Let us now consider a consequence which would flow from an insistence on using a distributional uncertainty variable even where the list of suggested answers contained a residual hypothesis. In preparing his mind to make a decision, a man must surely be supposed to use all resource in order to extend and clarify the list of suggested answers he can offer to each such question as: how will the outcome differ if I do *B* instead of *A*, or if I do *C* instead of *A*...? Thus if at any stage of this process he were to assign values of a distributional uncertainty variable to the particularized answers in any list containing a residual hypothesis, he would do so in awareness of the liability of the list to be at any moment extended by fresh claimants for shares. The mere existence of a residual hypothesis as part of his thought is a constant threat of disruption of any provisional distribution he might make. Now is there good reason for exposing the value of the uncertainty-variable, assigned to a particular hypothesis, to the liability to be changed because of a change in the number of other particularized hypotheses which have been listed? If the value assignable to a particular hypothesis is to be judged by considering the special factors and circumstances which seem to bear on its rightness or wrongness, then has the *number* of other hypotheses, rivals to this one, a claim to be considered one of these special circumstances? If I am asking myself whether it will rain today, am I best occupied in studying the air pressure, the wind direction and the cloud formations, or in counting up the number of other possible weather states, such as snow, fog, fine weather, which could, in general, occur instead? To allow the size of the crowd of hypotheses, which present themselves in answer to some question, to influence the value of the uncertainty-variable assigned to any particular hypothesis, would be like weakening one's praise for the chief actors in a play on the ground that a large number of supers were also allowed to cross the stage. It would be an abdication from the task of discriminating and an abandonment of all attempt to have insight into the texture of affairs. It is inherent in the use of a distributional uncertainty variable, that if extra hypotheses are each to be accorded non-zero values of the variable, some of the hypotheses in the initial list must be deprived of part of their shares of it.

A distributional uncertainty variable is peculiarly liable to misinterpretation. It assumes that the suggested answers in some finite list are all that need be taken into account for some particular question. It assigns to each such answer some proper fraction, and the whole set of these fractions sums to unity. The method of determining these fractions can sometimes be such as to legitimize the following proposition: If the question is asked on enough occasions, the variability of the circumstances of these occasions being bounded, each hypothesis will be right in a proportion of those occasions equal to the value of the uncertainty-variable assigned to that hypothesis. When such a statement can be made it is knowledge, and *pro tanto* is quite divorced from uncertainty. But what is it knowledge about? Evidently, it is knowledge about the entire set of occasions on which the question was asked, and *not* about any one particular occasion of asking it. We have, in fact, two quite different sorts of question. One is exemplified by: will it rain at Liverpool on 21 September 1961?, the other by: in what proportion of the next 500 Septembers will it rain at Liverpool on the 21st? With some assumptions about the general stability of that portion of nature (the sun, the earth's atmosphere and so on) which generates the weather, the second question can be answered on the basis of records of the past. The first question, *on those same assumptions*, which amount to a supposition that the weather at Liverpool will continue to show the same sort of irregular day-to-day fluctuations in the future as it has in the past, cannot be answered if we have only those data which are sufficient to answer the second. There is a temptation to think that the answer to the second question is also an answer to the first. Plainly, it is not. The answer to the second question claims to be *knowledge*, and in so far as its assumptions and data are well-founded, it *is* knowledge. This same numerical proper fraction, which answers the second question with knowledge, may *also* be able to serve as an uncertainty-variable indicating *a particular status* for some other answer, such as 'Yes, it will rain' or 'No, it will not rain', to the first question; but in serving thus it is filling an entirely different role from the one it fills when it *forms the substance* of the answer to the second question.

We are supposing that for the first of the two questions an unmistakably complete list can be made of all the hypotheses, each sufficiently specified for its *ex post facto* rightness or wrongness to be apparent in due course, that need be taken into account. This list consists, in our example, of the two hypotheses: it will rain, it will not rain. Now light can be thrown on the difference between the two kinds of question by saying that in answer to the first question, the two hypotheses are *rivals*, the truth of one denying and excluding the truth of the other, whereas for the second question the two hypotheses are members of a team, each of them providing, in a quite harmonious way, part of the substance of the answer to that question. For plainly, the statement that it will rain on one-third of all the occasions does not in any way conflict with the statement that it will be fine on two-thirds of all the occasions. The statement, however, that it will rain in Liverpool on 21 September 1961 does conflict absolutely with the statement that it will not rain in Liverpool on that date. In short, when an uncertainty-variable, whether distributional or non-distributional, expresses an *uncertainty-status* it cannot at the same time itself constitute the substance of *knowledge free from uncertainty*; with a non-distributional variable there is no distribution, no knowledge of the kind in question and hence no danger of mistaking the role of the variable.

We made a formal reference above to the need for choosing appropriately the method of distributing the values of a distributional uncertainty variable over the hypothetical answers to some question, if these values, in addition to their role of indicating the uncertainty status accorded by some particular individual to these hypotheses as answers to a single question relating to the particular circumstances of a specific occasion, are also to provide a substantial answer to a generalized form of the question relating to a 'large number' of 'similar' occasions. In fact, there are two types of such appropriate methods, and when either is adopted we may abandon the rather empty generalism of the term 'distributional uncertainty variable' and speak henceforth of *probability*.

The two types of method may be indicated as follows. On the one hand, the question to which we have a list of proposed answers may refer to the behaviour of a system whose structure we can inspect, and from which we can deduce the relative frequency with which this answer or that will, on certain assumptions about that structure, occur when the question, in a form applicable to *any* occasion, is repeatedly asked on one occasion after another. The resulting relative frequencies we may call *a priori* probabilities. On the other hand, we may repeatedly observe the behaviour of the system in practice and record the frequency with which it gives this or that answer to the generalized question. The relative frequencies thus obtained by repeated trial we may call *statistical* probabilities. The distinction is thus stated by N. Georgescu-Roegen:*

According to the Laplacian or Classical School, probability is measured by the relative frequency of favourable cases among all possible cases, *provided these are equally possible* [italics in original]. According to the Frequency School, probability is measured by the

---

* *Expectations, Uncertainty and Business Behaviour* (Social Science Research Council, New York, 1958), ch. 1, p. 13.

frequency limit of favourable cases in an infinite sequence of observations, *provided the limit exists and the sequence satisfies the condition of randomness* [italics in original].

After summarizing the logical objections brought by the Frequency School against the Classical view and those which have been levied in turn against the Frequentists, Dr Georgescu-Roegen refers to a definition of the probability co-efficient resting on the notion of the phase-space of a mechanism. An example of such a mechanism is the coin tossed by hand, whose phase-space consists of all possible, distinct trajectories of the coin. The main difficulty remains, which troubles the Classical definition: 'how to tell whether all phases are equally probable.' It will be noticed that in the passages quoted Dr Georgescu-Roegen has used indifferently and as though they were equivalent the expressions 'equally possible' and 'equally probable'. For our own analytical purposes we shall divorce completely from each other the ideas of 'probable' and 'possible', and shall give at least to the latter an intuitive meaning which is, I think, alien to Dr Georgescu-Roegen's discussion of the Classical and the Frequentist views. It seems appropriate and sufficient here to point out that, with us, 'possible' will mean intuitively or subjectively possible, possible in the judgement of a particular individual at a particular moment.

We shall not here discuss Dr Georgescu-Roegen's luminous account of the mathematical and semantic difficulties of defining probability. These difficulties, so far as they concern the general 'ratio' view of probability, have been explained with a beautiful and masterly simplicity by Professor R. B. Braithwaite* who offers a new model to deal with the dilemma that 'the bag from which balls are drawn must be both finite and infinite'. His 'many-handed Briareus' model enables the mind to picture with ease and exactness a self-consistent meaning for ratio probability. This does not, of course, in any way render it better able to serve as an uncertainty-variable, a purpose with which, I think it may be fair to say, Professor Braithwaite is not concerned. When probability is used as an uncertainty-variable by someone who is marshalling his thoughts for a decision in the business of real life, or by the scholar in analysing and

* *Scientific Explanation*, by R. B. Braithwaite (Cambridge University Press, 1953), pp. 118 f.

describing such a process, those deep-seated semantic problems are masked by others equally essential and less excusably ignored. Some of these, arising from the distributional aspect of probability, have already been mentioned and will be further examined below. But two others stand apart and call for special emphasis.

In the business of real life, it is plain that no examination of the 'system' or the 'mechanism' will yield an *a priori* determination of probabilities. This is a separate matter from the assertion we have made in earlier chapters that the whole conception of mechanism is incompatible with that of non-empty decision. Let us for the moment waive that contention. To insist on the contrast between the ineffably complex, conflicting, confusing and unseizable reality of life on the one hand, and the simple, definite and technically expressible features of a mechanism such as a spun coin, a dice-box or a shuffled pack of cards, on the other, is superfluous. If probabilities are to be found for the contingent outcomes of an act in the field of general human concerns, this cannot be done otherwise than statistically. Even statistically, it will only be possible under a condition analogous to that which prevails in coin-spinning or dice-throwing, to wit, some stability of the system, permitting variations of circumstance only within fixed limits. This is fulfilled in certain aspects of life. The life-tables of insurance companies do require revision as years go by, but they make the business of life insurance highly calculable. One man's physical constitution and environment are like enough to those of many others to enable the question: how many men out of a thousand in such-and-such a walk of life, and in such and such a climate, will live n years? to be answered well enough for the practical purpose of insurance. But in a great multitude and diversity of matters the individual has no record of a sufficient number of sufficiently similar acts, of his own or other people's, to be able to construct a valid frequency table of the outcomes of acts of this kind. Regarding these acts, probabilities are not *available* to him. This is the less fundamental of two obstacles to the actuarial abolition of uncertainty, its replacement by knowledge.

It can be argued that pooling of dissimilar acts is meaningful and sensible. The failure of one set of ventures may be offset by the success of another, even if all these ventures are of quite diverse kinds. Thus I gamble on finding a particular book interesting, and on being pleased by the food in a particular unfamiliar restaurant, and on getting good results from a particular nurseryman's grass seed, and on liking the company at a particular party. To regard all these gambles as contributing to the curate's egg of life as a whole, no greater concession is needed than is habitually granted to the economist who argues that a loss of comfort through decreased consumption of one good can be compensated by the gain of comfort through increased consumption of another. But we could look at all this differently. None of the outcomes of these ventures would, at worst, be heart-rending (or so we think, blinding ourselves perhaps to the remoter 'accidental' consequences that can flow from any act). Such acts promise minor pleasures or threaten minor disappointments. I may be a little unhappy because of one of these results, but will forget it in contemplating another which has 'come off'. I think this argument is valid and is one of the saving clauses in the terms laid down for the lives of men. However, there is a kind of experiment to which all such considerations are purely irrelevant and where there can in the nature of things be no possible neutralizing, no pooling and no probability.

When an individual elects to marry or not to marry, to become a surgeon instead of an engineer; when a statesman decides to challenge rather than appease an aggressive enemy; when a general stakes everything on a particular battle-plan; when a ruler brings his whole people into official adherence to a spreading religion; in all such instances the entire subsequent career of an individual or a nation is swung into one rather than another of two wholly different channels. After such a decision there can be no going back to the state of affairs which prevailed while the choice was still open; the basis and background and the means and imaginable consequences of all subsequent actions are irretrievably different, because one 'experiment' was chosen, from what they would have been had some other experiment been chosen. It is, accordingly, logically impossible for a person who has to make a decision in such an instance to contemplate *repeating* his experiment: such experiments are *self-destructive*.

By a self-destructive experiment I therefore mean one which, in being performed, irreversibly destroys some circumstances which are essential to it. Among such essential circumstances, when the outcome of the experiment will consist in the attitudes, reactions and conduct of human beings, are evidently the 'ideas', the knowledge, beliefs and remembered experiences of these human beings, and these must inevitably be changed by any public act, of any influential or power-holding person, which goes beyond the merest routine or trivial manipulation. There is a strong contrast here between 'experiments' in the narrower technical sense of controlled physical and chemical events produced in order to observe some limited aspect of some particular stage or effect of these events, on the one hand, and on the other the idea of an impulse given to human history, whose consequences, even those relevant for the decision-maker, cannot be easily bounded by any horizon in time or any defined range of human concerns. When the experiment is of this latter kind; when it is an action-scheme presenting itself to a man in his capacity as enterpriser, as politician, as military commander, as apostle of a faith, or merely as an individual shaping his own life, there will be a multitude of circumstances which are just as much an integral and inseparable part of the experiment itself as are the reagents in a chemical experiment, but which, unlike those chemical reagents, will be irreplaceable when once they have played their part in this once-for-all, strictly and inherently unique experiment. When an experiment which involves a human person adds to that person's total stock of experience, that experiment cannot, in the nature of things, ever be repeated, for he cannot be made to unlearn his new knowledge and unlive his experience. Not only personality, however, but institutions are changed by experiments involving them. The political configuration of the world, once it has been changed by a battle, a treaty, a voyage of exploration, an election or a speech, cannot be put back to what it was as if that battle or discovery had never happened. The one-way traffic of human history allows no repetition of the kinds of experiment which change men's ideas. They are self-destructive experiments.

Less fundamental, less theoretically interesting but perhaps of no less practical importance are two other sources of virtual uniqueness and unrepeatableness in an experiment. One of these is the large scale of the resources which the experiment may require in relation to the total resources at command of the decision-maker. A firm whose continued existence hangs on the commercial success of a new block of equipment or an expensive technical innovation cannot, when its decision-maker is weighing the question whether to invest in the equipment or not, treat this 'experiment' as one item of a series of such experiments, for it is only on condition of success in this particular and therefore special instance that there will be any further items in the series. The 'seriability' of the experiment will only be realised provided such seriability is unnecessary.

Non-seriability from this source can be looked on, if we prefer, as giving rise to a special kind of self-destructive experiment. They could be called semi-self-destructive, since such an experiment *can* destroy some circumstances essential to its performance but does not necessarily do so. However, these experiments whose large scale, relative to the decision-maker's available resources for making them, marks them off as non-seriable for one reason, are also non-seriable for another, to wit, that any further performances of even approximately similar experiments, of kinds which, so far as their technical character goes, might be 'pooled' with the first experiment, are likely to be spread over such long stretches of time, and performed if at all at such long intervals from each other, that they will be *isolated* from each other, more especially when they are business ventures. The reasons for treating business experiments remote in time as isolated experiments are two-fold. First, a series of experiments cannot be safely treated as seriable when the remoteness in time of the various items makes it very uncertain whether they will ever really be performed. The outcome of such distant experiments is *doubly* uncertain: it is uncertain whether there will ever be an experiment, and it is further doubtful whether, even if the experiment is made, it will yield 'success' rather than 'failure'. Secondly, when the experiments are business ventures there comes in the phenomenon of discounting at compound interest. The well-known formula for the equivalent in spot cash of a sum of A money units due to be received at the end of N years from today is

$$P = \frac{A}{(1+r)^N},$$

where r is the proportion by which any principal P would increase in one year if lent at today's market interest-rate applying to loans of N years' term. It can be seen that if r lies in the ordinary range from, say, 2–7 %, and if at the same time N is a matter of decades, then P will be so small compared with A that a failure of a business venture on a given scale today could by no means be offset by a success of a business venture of similar scale in, say, thirty years' time, unless the degree of success was far greater than the degree of failure. The seriability or pooling of widely time-spread experiments is thus for two reasons excluded.

For convenience in subsequently referring to some of the arguments of this chapter, I want now to define the term *non-divisible non-seriable experiment*. When the question is: If I throw these dice 36,000 times, how often will they show a double six? experience or thought may entitle us to answer: about one thousand times. The experiment is *divisible* into a large enough number of items, each consisting in a performance undertaken in some stable set of circumstances, to allow actuarial principles to give us an answer with the status of knowledge. When the question is: I am about to throw these dice once, what will they show? no such division is possible, the experiment and its answer are a unitary whole and actuarial principles are not able to give that answer. We shall call such an experiment *non-divisible*. Sometimes, however, an experiment which can only be performed once by a single individual person (such as finding out whether he will live to be sixty) can be pooled with similar experiments made by others so as to compose an experiment which, if all these people can be treated as a single entity, becomes divisible. The people *can* be treated as a single entity provided they agree to share out the result of the divisible experiment amongst themselves on some principle which to each of them seems equitable. Thus although no one can tell whether any particular person will live to be sixty, an insurance company can write him an endowment policy whose terms are based on knowledge. Then we can say that his experiment is *seriable*. An experiment which is non-divisible and whose outcome cannot be pooled with the outcomes of other experiments we shall call a *non-divisible non-seriable experiment*.

Let us try to sum up our argument about the use of probability as the uncertainty variable. When probability is objective and claims to found itself on observation, it consists in relative frequencies. So far as the observations are properly made and interpreted, the relative frequencies are knowledge. Knowledge and uncertainty are mutually exclusive, and when we are discussing uncertainty we cannot qualify or specify its degrees by a variable whose values are knowledge of the kind which answers the question about which we are uncertain. This is fundamental. Objective, actuarial probability has no relevance for the analysis of decision in face of uncertainty, because when objective probabilities can be applied there is no uncertainty. Actuarial probabilities can be applied to a *divisible* experiment, and a non-divisible experiment can also shelter under the actuarial umbrella provided its outcome can be pooled with the outcome of many similar experiments to *compose* a divisible experiment. Thus when the question is: What will be the outcome of this divisible, or this seriable, experiment? the decision-maker is in no need of an uncertainty variable, he need not formulate a list of rival hypotheses, for he can get an answer which, within a reasonable interpretation, is exact knowledge. When the question is: What will be the outcome of this non-divisible non-seriable experiment? the decision-maker can make no use of objective, actuarial probability. He is reduced to using *subjective* probability, which has no claims to be knowledge, which cannot offer any objective support to such constructions as the mathematical expectation, cannot validly or meaningfully be used to arrive at a *weighted average* outcome, save when this phrase has a purely formal meaning and indicates no more than that an arithmetical procedure of multiplications and additions of the resulting products has been performed. For now we are brought face to face with the core of the matter: When the experiment is a non-divisible one, the hypotheses regarding its outcome are cut-throat *rivals*, denying and excluding each other. What, then, is the sense of *averaging* them?

One more question supervenes upon the discussion. How important in life are the two kinds of experiment, the divisible or seriable kind whence uncertainty is absent, banished by probability, and the non-divisible non-seriable kind for which probability has only the relevance of *an uncertainty variable*, albeit, and not without disadvantages, a distributional one? We have disclaimed any appeal to the idea that, in strictness, the situation encountered by the individual at each different moment of life is for him unique and never to be repeated, and that therefore every action-scheme open to him in any one moment is different in its circumstances and in its range of imaginable outcomes from every action-scheme open to him in any other moment. We cannot appeal to this idea, because we have refused to enter into the ultimate mathematical subtleties of the definition of probability, expressly contenting ourselves with a 'working idea' of relative frequencies such as that on which the whole actuarial structure of insurance rests. Our notion of probability being somewhat coarse, we must accept that some action-schemes or experiments which in strictness differ from each other can for practical purposes be lumped together. But, by contrast, there are other situations where the choice is amongst experiments every one of which is essentially and logically incapable by its very nature of being pooled with others or split up into a number of component trials. These we have called self-destructive experiments. Each is such that the very act of performing it permanently destroys some conditions which are an essential part of it.

Probability, we conclude from all this argument, cannot claim that the part it plays in the fabric of actuarial *knowledge* makes it in the smallest degree better fitted for the role of an *uncertainty-variable*. But neither can the role of uncertainty-variable be dismissed as unimportant. In abolishing the experimental character of many acts, and virtually depriving them in effect of any uncertainty as to their relevant outcomes, statistical probability yet leaves a vast field of action untouched. Isolated and, above all, self-destructive experiments, numerous enough and of crucial and dominating importance when they arise, are inherently untouchable by it.

VIII

PROFESSOR NIEHANS ON PROBABILITY

Professor Jürg Niehans has kindly allowed me to reproduce
below sections I and II of his contribution to the symposium in
Metroeconomica, to whose Editor I am also most grateful for the
necessary permission. I did not see Professor Niehans's article
until a year after I had written the foregoing chapter VII,
neither, of course, had Professor Niehans seen my chapter. The
reader will see that the central thesis of my chapter and that of
the following passages by Professor Niehans are essentially the
same. Professor Niehans, however, has given a specially
arresting and concise expression to the essential truth:

...every decision is by logical necessity unique and whenever
similar experiments are consolidated into groups they cease to
demand individual decisions. The usefulness of probability *as a
measure of uncertainty* [italics in original] thus depends entirely on its
usefulness for unique decisions.

Professor Niehans proceeds to speak of 'two different types of
probabilities'. It will be seen in what follows that he has in
mind the two different *roles* of probability which I thus referred
to above: 'In short, when an uncertainty variable, whether distributional or non-distributional, expresses an *uncertainty-status*
it cannot at the same time itself constitute the substance of
knowledge free from uncertainty.' Professor Niehans begins:*

What men will do largely depends on what consequences they
expect of their actions. Generally, these expectations are uncertain.
The most we can say is that a future event will conform to one of a
number of hypotheses, but we do not pretend to know to which one.
Each alternative course of action is thus linked to a bundle of
possible outcomes and its rank in the order of preference will
usually change according to which of the various possibilities
becomes true. As a consequence it is impossible to select the most
desirable alternative simply by finding the most desirable outcome,
and additional assumptions are needed for the determination of

* Jürg Niehans, 'Reflections on Shackle, Probability, and our Uncertainty about
Uncertainty', *Metroeconomica*, vol. XI (April–August 1959), pp. 74–88.

choice. These assumptions are the core of any theory of decision under uncertainty.

The problem may be more precisely stated in terms of the familiar

	s_1	s_2	...	s_n
a_1	r_{11}	r_{12}	...	r_{1n}
a_2	r_{21}	r_{22}	...	r_{2n}
a_m	r_{m1}	r_{m2}	...	r_{mn}

Uncertainty is expressed by specifying two or more future *states of affairs* (states of nature)s_h. What is to be explained are decisions in the face of this uncertainty. A decision consists of a choice of one among several *alternatives* a_i. Each alternative is characterized by the gains (or losses) $r_{i1}, r_{i2}, ... r_{in}$, which may result from it, called *outcomes*. These outcomes may be defined either by a description of actual consequences, say the loss of a battle, victory at the polls, death of a patient, quantities of some commodities, profits, etc., or by the utilities of these consequences measured by some utility index. In the first case we may speak of 'real outcomes', in the second case of 'utility-outcomes'. If in each column the best outcome happens to be found in the same row, choice between alternatives presents no problem. This, however, is a special case. In general, it will be impossible to select a row so that the outcome is maximised for each column. What decision principles shall then be substituted for simple maximisation? The search for a solution of this problem has produced quite a number of ingenious hypotheses. The most venerable of them is Bernoulli's principle of mathematical expectation. According to this principle a number p_h is attached to each state s_h expressing its probability. These numbers are non-negative and add to unity for all states. In each column the outcomes are then weighted with the probability of the respective state and the weighted outcomes are added horizontally for each alternative. Choice is supposed to fall on that alternative for which this 'mathematical expectation' is highest. Against this valuation principle, Shackle has raised several objections. The main purpose of this paper is (1) to evaluate the validity of these objections and (2) to see if there are other difficulties which Shackle did not mention.

Before entering on this discussion it must be made clear, however, *what kinds of probabilities* are at issue. This question shall be the subject of the following section

II

It seems to be generally agreed that there are either certain kinds or certain applications of probability against which no serious objections can be raised from any point of view. The question is how this area of happy agreement may be marked off from the area of doubt, discussion and disagreement. Shackle tries to draw the line by distinguishing between unique decisions on the one hand and recurring decisions on the other. The use of probabilities is then said to be legitimate for recurring decisions but not for unique ones. This procedure seems to reflect a widespread impression that probability is quite useful for decisions which are repeated a large number of times, while on the other hand its application to unique decisions is usually felt to be open to serious doubts. Whenever this view is adopted, the discussion of probability is in danger of degenerating into a sterile discussion about how often similar decisions may be expected to repeat themselves. It cannot be said that Shackle has been entirely successful in avoiding this blind alley. It seems better, therefore, to adopt a terminology which draws the line not between different types of decisions but between different types of probabilities.

With regard to decisions, it is clear at the outset that their unique or recurring character must be considered from the *ex ante* perspective of the deciding mind. It does not matter how often they may prove *ex post* to have repeated themselves or how often an outside observer may expect them to be repeated. Now, consider a series of 'similar' experiments $e_1, e_2, ..., e_q$. If the decision about e_2 may be influenced by the observed outcome of e_1, the decision situation anticipated for e_2 is obviously not the same as for e_1. Thus the decision about e_1 is unique. It may be, however, that the experiments are independent in the sense that the outcome of e_1 has no influence on $e_2, ..., e_q$. If in this case the decision on e_1 is taken without regard to $e_2, ..., e_q$ it is again subjectively unique, because the actual recurrence of e_1 is not reflected in the decision matrix. If, on the other hand, the full sequence $e_1, e_2, ..., e_q$ is taken into account at the moment of e_1, choice is in fact not concerned with e_1 alone, but with the group of e_1, $e_2, ..., e_q$ as a whole. What is then decided upon, is not an alternative for the experiment e_1, but a policy or strategy covering all expected experiments. This decision, however, is by necessity unique. On the individual experiment no decision is then made at all. This may be summarized by saying that every decision is by logical necessity unique and whenever similar experiments are consolidated into groups they cease to demand individual decisions. The usefulness of probability as *a measure of uncertainty* thus depends entirely on its usefulness for unique decisions.

On the other hand, however, there are two different types of probabilities. This is readily seen on the background of the decision matrix. A probability distribution of the first kind assigns a probability number to each state of affairs; these numbers add to unity over all states. Of this type are the probabilities in the above decision matrix. By contrast, a probability distribution of the second kind serves to characterize one individual state of affairs; probabilities then add to unity for each state separately. Probabilities of the first kind are supposed to describe the uncertainty of the various possible states; they may thus be called 'uncertainty-probabilities'. Probability of the second kind, however, has nothing to do with uncertainty. It rather results from the fact that a given state of affairs may sometimes be described by specifying the frequency with which certain values occur within a group of similar experiments. So a lottery, taken as a whole, may be described by the frequency distribution of prizes. In this case, the term 'frequency probability' seems to be appropriate.

In the light of these considerations, the traditional view may be restated by saying that frequency-probabilities are of unquestionable usefulness, but have nothing to do with decisions under uncertainty, whereas uncertainty-probabilities are indeed relevant to the theory of decisions but at the same time present rather difficult problems. I do not want to suggest that by this restatement anything materially new is added to Shackle's formulation; indeed I tried to express Shackle's view. I feel, however, that his own concepts are not well suited for this purpose and lead to irrelevant discussions.

Towards the end of his article Professor Niehans goes far towards admitting that we have no criterion for selecting either a *rational* or a *practically successful* decision principle:

In most cases, however, the set of axioms underlying the Bernoulli principle is meant to be a definition of 'rational' rather than a description of actual behaviour. At a glance this interpretation might seem to give such a system a better chance, for it might then be useful, even if it were unable to explain or predict actual decisions. On the other hand, however, the problem of evaluation is then desperate indeed: how on earth can science judge the validity of a definition of rational behaviour? No satisfactory answer to this question seems to exist. Contrary to axioms on actual behaviour or axioms, say, in geometry, axioms on rational behaviour under uncertainty have no chance to justify their existence by the fruitful applications which they permit, for it is logically impossible to find out if a certain application is 'fruitful' or not. One might perhaps argue that axioms on rational behaviour are fruitful if decisions which are based on them result in satisfactory outcomes. But the outcome of a decision is as much the result of the ensuing state of nature as of the decision principle. It is impossible, therefore, to find out from *ex post* outcomes of unique decisions if the decision principle was good in view of the very uncertainty of outcomes *ex ante*. How should we ever find out whether the satisfactory outcome was due to our clever decision theory and not just to our good luck?

The reader of the foregoing chapters of this book will know why I myself fail to find meaning in the question whether a decision principle is 'rational'. The human world, in contrast with all the rest of terrestrial nature, is driven by hope. It is access to good hope which men seek in their decisions.

IX

UNCERTAINTY AS POSSIBILITY

A man cannot, in general, tell what *will* happen, but his conception of the nature of things, the nature of men and of their institutions and affairs and of the non-human world, enables him to form a judgement as to whether any suggested thing *can* happen. In telling himself that such and such a thing 'can' happen, he means that its occurrence would not *surprise* him; for we are surprised by the occurrence of what we had supposed to be against nature. When, in the course of this argument, I refer to a man as saying that such and such a thing 'can happen', or 'is possible', I shall be supposing him to make a statement about his own mind and thoughts, not, except indirectly, about the objective and external world. A judgement is made by some person in some particular moment, when, therefore, he has in mind a particular conception of the then existing state of affairs of all sorts. The attainment of a given other situation, from the existing starting-point, may seem 'against nature' in a general and basic sense, so that no matter how much time was available the attainment would be judged impossible; or it may be judged impossible in the time separating the moment when the judgement is formed from the date envisaged for the attainment. For our analysis this distinction does not lie in the foreground. If a man feels that, should his knowledge and understanding remain as they are, the occurrence of a given thing would not surprise him in the slightest degree, we may say that, for him, that thing is *perfectly possible*. We are taking *certainty of the wrongness* of a proposition to be a state of mind familiar to everyone and needing no definition. Thus when the proposition is 'This given thing will happen' (the specification of the happening may of course include any degree of comprehensiveness of detail of its temporal unfolding and sequence of events) we shall assume that absolute rejection of such a proposition is a state of mind that all of us accept as known. This state or act of mind, expressed in other words, is a judgement that the thing in question is *impossible*. The occurrence of something hitherto judged impossible would cause a man a degree of surprise which is the greatest he is capable of feeling. If this be so, we have, corresponding to *perfect possibility*, a zero degree of surprise; corresponding to *impossibility*, an *absolute maximum* degree of surprise. Can there be *degrees of possibility*? A theory due to Professor Jerzy Neyman divides events into the possible and the impossible. We have already gone beyond this in speaking of 'perfect' possibility. We shall go further still. There are degrees of surprise. If surprise corresponds to possibility, then we can say that there are degrees of possibility. The greatest surprise is caused by the occurrence of the impossible. If a lesser degree of surprise occurs, it must surely be because the occurence was judged not quite impossible. So we may proceed. A very slight surprise indicates something which the individual had little difficulty in imagining to come true. Surprise provides us with a means of knowing how strongly we doubted the possibility of a given happening or a given outcome of some act of our own.

Surprise felt at the actual occurrence of something to which we had conceded less than perfect possibility can evidently not serve as an uncertainty variable, since the latter must qualify *imagined* happenings and outcomes. It is the degree of surprise to which we expose ourselves, when we examine an imagined happening as to its possibility, in general or in the prevailing circumstances, and assess the obstacles, tensions and difficulties which arise in our minds when we try to imagine it occurring, that provides the indicator of degree of possibility. This is the surprise we *should* feel, if the given thing *did* happen; it is *potential* surprise. In these first two paragraphs of this chapter we have expressed in summary form the basis of our proposal for a non-distributional uncertainty variable. The rest of this chapter elaborates and completes the statement of this idea; the next chapter quotes extensively from critical discussions of the idea and considers these criticisms.

To serve our purpose, potential surprise must be able to establish two primary claims. We have already asserted that *actual* surprise, a feeling occasioned by an actual rather than an imagined happening, has differing and distinct intensities in various circumstances: there are degrees of surprise. When, instead, the happening is imagined, and the individual asks himself what his feelings would be in case this happening became actual without there having been in the meantime any change in his own knowledge or inferences, it seems reasonable to claim likewise that he will distinguish between the degrees of potential surprise which he ascribes to this or that supposed event. We shall assume that he does so. A question which may here arise in the reader's mind must at once be answered. Are we supposing the individual's judgement in this matter to be always correct? Can he always tell just what degree of surprise he *would* feel, *if* some event, which he now merely creates in imagination, were to emerge into actuality? If the reader has been able to accept the argument of chapter III, he will be prepared for our answer: such a question is meaningless. The moment of actuality wherein he *assesses the potential surprise* is a different moment from the one in which the *actual surprise could be experienced*. There can be no comparison of the two actualities; the act of judgement is an actual mental act, the feeling of experienced surprise is another actuality, but they belong to two different points of the calendar axis and therefore *do not co-exist*. Only potential surprise called up in the mind, and assessed, in the moment when decision is made, is relevant for that decision, and alone can have any bearing or influence on it. In the moment of decision, the surprise aroused in a subsequent moment by the objective happening itself is remoter than the galaxies. We defer for a little the task of considering what more must be required besides the mere existence of distinct degrees of potential surprise; such questions as: What sort of relation must subsist between these degrees? Can we, and do we need to, suppose that *differences* between these degrees, as well as the degrees themselves, can be compared? must wait. We wish first to consider the second of the primary claims, to wit, that potential surprise is non-distributional.

When I feel that some given happening would not surprise me in the least, there is nothing in this state of mind which conflicts in any manner or degree with a similar feeling which I can entertain about some quite different, rival suggestion about what may happen. I can simultaneously feel, about each of two or many mutually exclusive hypotheses, that it is perfectly *possible*. Show me a hat-box, assuring me that it contains some kind of hat. I know no reason why the hat should not be a bowler; but equally I know of nothing which suggests that it cannot be a straw, or again that it may not be a soft felt. Zero potential surprise can be assigned to each of an unlimited number of rival, mutually exclusive, hypotheses all at once; any number of suggested answers to a question, any number of distinct happenings arising out of a given set of visible present circumstances, any number of different outcomes of some action-scheme on which the decision-maker contemplates embarking, can all be regarded by him as perfectly possible. The same is true of any other degree of potential surprise: there is no limit in logic to the number and diversity of suggested answers to a question, which can all simultaneously be accorded any given degree of potential surprise from zero to the absolute maximum, the degree which means total rejection and exclusion of an answer. Potential surprise is completely non-distributional.

On the lines of the two foregoing paragraphs we claim, then, that potential surprise can represent by its variations the various degrees, between and including perfect possibility and perfect impossibility, of the status accorded by some individual decision-maker to suggested answers to any question, including, especially, such questions as: What will be the outcome for me if I embark on such-and-such an action-scheme, if I make such-and-such an experiment? Secondly, we claim that potential surprise is non-distributional and indeed this scarcely needs demonstration. Now we pass to a more detailed survey of this concept.

When, in the next chapter, we turn to the criticisms of potential surprise, we shall find it suggested that a mapping can be made of potential surprise and probability upon each other. Many such mappings can undoubtedly be constructed on various arbitrary principles, but it behoves us to ask whether any one of these has a claim to arise naturally from the meanings of the two variables and so to illuminate those meanings. More pointedly we may especially inquire the following. Whereas potential surprise claims as one of its anchorage points in psychic reality the idea of *perfect possibility*, which it represents unequivocally by a zero degree of potential surprise, what *probability* represents perfect possibility? Is every contingency whose probability is less than unity to be regarded as less than perfectly possible? But if so, we are identifying perfect *possibility* with perfect *certainty*, and this, we cannot too strongly insist, is in our view a fundamental error. But if not unity, then what probability corresponds to perfect possibility? Where, on the downward path from unity, do we stop? Has it not to be admitted that *any* probability greater than zero can correspond to perfect possibility? Or should we not rather say, that there is *no* natural and self-justifying basis for a mapping of probability on possibility, and therefore, on potential surprise?

In his review of the Liverpool symposium* Professor Robert Dorfman has the following comment:

Carter also questions Shackle's attitude toward the relationship between those two slippery concepts, 'degree of surprise' and 'degree of belief'. The problem is that while both of these concepts are intuitively appealing substitutes for mathematical probability, they are almost undefinable; reasoning based on the one contradicts reasoning based on the other, and no accepted basis for reconciling the two exists. The vagueness of the relationship between the two is illustrated by the fact that a man using a telephone has a low degree of belief in getting a wrong number but also a low degree of surprise if he does.

We would say that an individual's degree of belief in a hypothesis can be easily and exactly expressed by means of the potential surprise he assigns to the least (potentially) surprising rival hypothesis. Since, in any exhaustive set of rival suggested answers to some question, one at least must carry zero potential surprise, it follows that either the hypothesis we are concerned with has some rival carrying zero potential surprise, in which case, no matter what degree it carries itself, the degree of belief in it is zero, or else while itself carrying zero potential surprise it has no rival carrying zero potential surprise. In this latter case the individual's degree of belief in it is measured by the least degree of potential surprise accorded to any one of its rivals. We are, however, here giving to 'degree of belief' an interpretation which will not be accepted by those who think that one may have some positive belief in each of two rival (mutually contradictory) hypotheses at the same time. Professor Dorfman's example of the telephone number can evidently

---

* Review by Robert Dorfman in *Review of Economics and Statistics*, vol. xxxvii, no. 3 (August 1955) of *Uncertainty and Business Decisions*, edited by C. F. Carter, G. P. Meredith and G. L. S. Shackle (Liverpool University Press, 1st ed. 1954).

be perfectly easily accommodated in our construction: I can attach zero potential surprise to getting a wrong number, but also zero potential surprise to getting the right one. Thus both my degree of belief in getting a wrong number, and my surprise if I do, will be zero. It is when we interpret 'degree of belief' in some sense resembling subjective distributional probability that we can find no basis for, or meaning in, a formal reconciliation of the two concepts of belief and surprise.

There is nothing in this contention, let it at once be added, that conflicts in any way with the entirely different idea that a man's assignment of potential surprise to a given hypothesis may be based on, or influenced by, objectively given frequency-ratios. Plainly for every individual faced with the knowledge that out of every n trials of a particular kind, a specified outcome A has proved right about m times, there will be some numerical value of m/n below which the outcome A will seem, as we may alternatively say, somewhat surprising or less than perfectly possible. The critical level of m/n will vary with the individual and the circumstances. But it would be absurd to deny, for example, that a man would be surprised if, in fact, he threw ten successive double-sixes with two dice within the first hundred trials. In this book we have little to say about the exact psychic process of forming those judgements which we are supposing to be expressed by means of an uncertainty variable. It is the expression and application of these judgements that we are concerned with. But nowhere, in this or earlier treatments, have we said that statistical frequencies are not amongst the materials out of which such judgements arise.

We shall have occasion to refer again to this point below, especially in chapter XI where it has a central bearing on the criticisms and suggestions of Mr Gerald Gould and Mr M. B. Nicholson.

Probability cannot represent degrees of possibility nor discriminate between perfect and other-than-perfect subjective possibility; by contrast, potential surprise can precisely represent perfect certainty and in doing so can show something about the structure of this state of mind. For when a man is perfectly certain that a given hypothesis is right, this implies his perfect certainty that all hypotheses rival to this one are wrong. Thus we represent his state of mind by supposing him to attach zero potential surprise to the hypothesis of whose rightness he is certain, and the absolute maximum potential surprise to each of its rivals. This idea can be generalized. When we consider together as one whole all the hypotheses which are rivals to a given hypothesis H, they constitute the *contradictory* of H. If, then, we wish to express the individual's *degree of belief* in a hypothesis, we shall think of this degree of belief as consisting in a degree of potential surprise associated with the hypothesis, and in another degree associated with its contradictory. If this is a very little more complicated than the simple assertion that a (subjective) probability directly represents a degree of belief, it is also much more illuminating; for it tells us something about the degrees of *possibility* which underly the degree of belief, and give the latter a structure. For example, if I think it is 'very likely' to rain today, I can say that the idea of its raining carries zero potential surprise, and the idea of its not raining carries some greater than zero degree. This latter hypothesis, the contradictory, however, will itself comprise such items as 'sun', 'overcast sky', 'fog', 'snow', and it is to one of these in particular that I shall perhaps attach a lower degree of potential surprise than to any of the others. This one will then project upon the contradictory as a whole its own degree of potential surprise. The contradictory may, for example, carry a very low degree of potential surprise while the hypothesis itself carries a zero degree; or the hypothesis itself may carry some greater-than-zero degree while the contradictory carries a zero degree. Degrees of belief in the hypothesis thus become not merely degrees but, in a sense, qualitative explanations.

There is evidently no logical obstacle whatever to prevent the individual from assigning zero potential surprise both to a hypothesis and to its contradictory. To do so will surely often respond to a strongly felt need, and express precisely the mood of a moment. Such-and-such a thing, a man says to himself, could perfectly easily happen; and it could perfectly easily not happen. Thus the happening E and its absence, not-E, are each assigned zero potential surprise. But not-E can nearly always be split up into many or even infinitely many component particular happenings. If E is rain, not-E will have come true if there proves to be sun, or fog, or snow, or hail. How can probability deal with this need to accord equal status to E and to not-E? To give a probability of $\frac{1}{2}$ to rain will leave the remaining $\frac{1}{2}$ to be shared amongst sun, fog, snow and hail, and if, as may well be the case, he feels that each of them deserves an equal status with rain, he will be totally frustrated. By contrast potential surprise, because it is non-distributional, can be assigned in zero degree to an unlimited number of particularized components of not-E and so to not-E itself.

There is one constraint upon the relation between the degrees of potential surprise accorded respectively to a hypothesis and its contradictory: one or other of these degrees must be zero. For the hypothesis and its contradictory constitute between them an *exhaustive set of rival hypotheses*: everything that can happen, every meaningful answer to the question, is included by the individual under one or other of these heads, whether or not he feels able to particularize all such possible happenings or answers. And provided that the question is a meaningful one, the individual is logically bound to suppose that there is some right answer to it. To assign greater than zero degrees of potential surprise to both the hypothesis and its contradictory would therefore betray an unresolved mental confusion.

Before we turn to summarize our comparison of potential surprise with probability, let us describe our concept in less formal terms than those of the foregoing discussion of its logical properties. We must once again insist that when the uncertainty in a person's mind arises from the plurality of the answers which suggest themselves to him for some one question, these answers are rivals mutually excluding each other. To believe in one of these answers is therefore to disbelieve in the others. By contrast it is *not* true that to disbelieve in one answer is to believe in the others. Thus it seems more natural, when we require the notion of uncertainty-variable in order to label various answers with this status or that in relation to 'certainty of rightness' or 'certainty of wrongness' to use a variable expressing *disbelief*. Zero potential surprise expresses *zero disbelief*. When a suggested answer, a happening, an outcome, seems in no way incongruous or incompatible with the essential nature of things and their existing particular state, as far as the decision-maker knows them, then this hypothesis or happening or outcome seems perfectly possible, his disbelief in it is zero, and he accords it a zero degree of potential surprise. We must, therefore, distinguish sharply between the notions, on the one hand, of a man's degree of actual belief in some hypothesis, and on the other hand, of the degree of 'believability' which he accords it. To believe positively that some hypothesis is right is *pro tanto* to dismiss all rival hypotheses as wrong. But to regard a hypothesis as credible or plausible is not necessarily to pass any judgement on the credibility or plausibility of other hypotheses: the insufficiency of any man's knowledge, of principles and of facts and perhaps of essentially unknowable things, leaves room for him to accept as believable very many diverse and mutually contradictory hypotheses about any one matter. Is it believable that it will be raining at noon tomorrow in Liverpool? Of course it is. Is it believable that it will be fine at noon tomorrow in Liverpool? Of course it is. Do I believe that it will rain at noon tomorrow in Liverpool? I neither believe it nor reject it. Thus we may say that potential surprise indicates plausibility or possibility, understood as a judgement made by the particular individual, and further, that a hypothesis attracts such a judgement by virtue of its own special features and their relation with the general features of the world at large and with those of the existing situation in particular, and not by virtue of its having few rivals in his mind.

To invert a problem is a well-known resource of the mathematician. We too, in adopting as our uncertainty-variable a measure of *disbelief*, are in a way inverting our problem, and we are thereby guaranteeing our solution against any attempt to turn it back into a distributional variable. Formally, it would be open to us to define a measure of possibility directly. A zero value of this measure would stand for impossibility, an absolute maximum value for perfect possibility. But it would then be tempting for those who favour a distributional solution to add together (contrary to reason and the nature of the problem) the respective degrees of possibility assigned to the members of an exhaustive set of rival hypotheses, and to treat the resulting total as unity. This total could then, at no greater cost in perversity, be looked upon as 'distributed' over the various rival hypotheses. By contrast, when we represent perfect possibility by a zero value of a measure of disbelief, no such summation can in general be meaningfully carried out, since, for example, the sum of a set of zero values is zero. Any number of rival hypotheses can be accorded *zero* potential surprise, at least one in every exhaustive set *must* be accorded zero potential surprise; and this is tantamount to saying that at least one hypothesis, if we used a direct instead of an inverted measure of possibility, must be accorded the absolute maximum of possibility. Thus with a direct measure of possibility, a distribution, however bogus, could always be performed. But with an inverted measure, distribution in one highly important case, that of perfect possibility of every hypothesis in an exhaustive list, can hardly be accorded any clear meaning. What is conveyed by saying that every member has a share of nothing?

We end this chapter by setting out in a series of numbered points a comparison between the distributional uncertainty-variable, probability, and our own non-distributional variable, potential surprise.

(i) Probability cannot discriminate or express degrees of *possibility*. Potential surprise is, precisely, the expression, in terms of feeling, of degrees of possibility.

(ii) An arbitrary probability-fraction could in any concrete instance be selected as representing 'perfect possibility'; or the probability of the most probable contingency, whatever probability had been assigned to that contingency, could be taken to represent 'perfect possibility'. But this procedure would in general represent 'perfect possibility' by a different probability in each instance. The probability of the mode is in general different in different distributions. Perfect possibility is, on the other hand, unequivocally represented by zero potential surprise in all instances.

(iii) The numerical probability accorded to a hypothesis which has many rivals of equal or not too disparate status has inevitably to be a fraction much less than one-half, a 'small' fraction, notwithstanding that this hypothesis may in itself be in every way consonant with the decision-maker's conception of the nature of the world and its immediate state. Thus a hypothesis can be rated 'improbable' not because anything in its own nature disqualifies it but because it is crowded out from attention.

(iv) A hypothesis can be rendered more 'improbable' merely by an increase and improvement, or any change whether well or ill founded, of the individual's knowledge, inferences and insight which particularizes additional hypotheses but leaves quite unaffected the relation of this hypothesis to that knowledge and his interpretation of it. Potential surprise is invariant against such changes.

(v) When what we have called a divisible experiment is in fact performed, the outcome will be a frequency-distribution of the various results which can arise from the individual trials composing the divisible experiment. If the frequency-distribution thus obtained was looked on by the experimenter, before he began the experiment, as certain to be closely approximated, then that judgement cannot be impugned in the light of the factual result. When the experiment is a non-divisible one, a probability-distribution which, before the experiment was made, assigned to the hypothetical outcome that in the event proves true any probability other than unity must be adjudged to have been at fault. However, to assign a probability of unity to one hypothesis and a probability of zero to every other means that the individual is *certain* that the one hypothesis will prove true. It follows that any *distribution* which represents a mental state of uncertainty inevitably entails an *ex post facto* verdict of 'faulty judgement'. By contrast, the use of a non-distributional variable enables the net of non-surprising hypotheses to be spread as wide as the individual thinks needful, and no matter how wide it is, the judgement will turn out correct if the net proves to have caught the one hypothesis which proved true. We must notice that with a divisible experiment, the frequency-distribution can *itself* be a hypothesis. With a non-divisible experiment, the probability-distribution is not *itself* a hypothesis but assigns values of a distributional uncertainty variable to the hypotheses included in its scope. The two roles, which we have sought to keep separate here by calling one a frequency-distribution and the other a probability-distribution, must be kept rigidly distinct. A critic has objected that in supposing probability-judgements to be refutable we are misunderstanding the nature of such judgements. We assume that this critic is speaking of the use of probability as what we have called a distributional uncertainty variable assigned to rival hypotheses about the outcome of a non-divisible experiment, and that each such hypothesis is stated so that in the event it must prove either right or wrong. If, when such a hypothesis proves right, the probability of, let us say, one-half assigned to it in advance is not to be regarded as having been refuted, then it appears that probability is a non-operational concept. But I doubt whether my critic would accept this conclusion.

(vi) There is a psychic necessity, surely experienced by everyone, to be able to accord equal status to a hypothesis E and to its contradictory not-E. If, as will usually be the case, not-E can itself be split up into, say, G and not-G, to each of which the individual may need to assign equal status at the same time as he assigns equal status to E and not-E, then we have him requiring to assign equal status, on the one hand to E and not-E, and on the other to E, G and not-G. In one assignment, E receives a probability of one-half, in the other it receives a probability of one-third. This contradiction appears, with probability, to be inescapable. With potential surprise there is no difficulty in assigning a zero degree to E, to G and to not-G and thus also simultaneously assigning a zero degree to E and to not-E.

We proceed in the next chapter to an axiom system and in the following one to a review of criticisms and discussions of the concept of potential surprise.

X

POTENTIAL SURPRISE AXIOMATIZED

It became fashionable in the 1950's to set out deductive arguments about human conduct in the strict form of numbered axioms and theorems. This method, a return to the classicism not only of the seventeenth century but of the ancients, has a beauty and incisiveness, and offers safeguards against loose reasoning, which amply justify it. What here follows is a variorum of the attempt to axiomatize potential surprise, which was made in the first edition of *Expectation in Economics* of 1949 and revised in the second edition, the latter incorporating one change, made in deference to a critic, about which I am now doubtful. Both versions of the axiom 7 in question are reproduced below.*

Although I have sought to make my set of propositions fulfil the requirements of an independent, self-contained, abstract system... we are not really unconcerned with the relation of our system to the observable or subjectively experienced world. We wish to make it serve to analyse and interpret that world, and as a consequence the terms we use, though undefined so far as the self-contained system itself is concerned, must be linked up with our notions of reality. The embryonic 'system' which follows is therefore introduced by a passage (falling outside the list of numbered propositions) in which are grouped a number of explanatory statements and definitions. The numbered propositions themselves comprise nine postulates and eight theorems.

By a hypothesis is meant any suggested answer to any question, and by the contradictory of this hypothesis is meant the hypothesis that the suggested answer will turn out to be wrong. By *rival hypotheses* is meant two or more mutually exclusive hypotheses concerning the same question. By an *exhaustive set of rival hypotheses* is meant any set of heads under which the individual feels certain that the true answer to some particular question, the true outcome of some particular experiment, when it shall become known, will prove to be

* Apart from the reformulation of axiom 7, the passage here quoted appears identically in both editions except for the renumbering of propositions consequent on shifting one of them from its position as no. 5 (an axiom) to become no. 10 (a theorem), as it is here shown.

classifiable. Any set of rival hypotheses can evidently be made exhaustive by the addition to it of a *residual hypothesis*, defined as covering every particular hypothesis, whether the individual has formulated it precisely or not at all, having any character which would exclude it from classification under the hypotheses in the initial set. Of the seventeen propositions which follow, numbers 1–9, inclusive, are the *postulates* or *initial propositions*:

(1) An individual's degree of belief in a hypothesis can be thought of as consisting in a degree of potential surprise associated with the hypothesis, and in another degree associated with its contradictory.

(2) Degrees of potential surprise can be zero or greater than zero. No meaning is assigned to a degree of potential surprise less than zero.

Degrees of potential surprise are bounded by that degree $\bar{y}$, called the *absolute maximum* of potential surprise, which signifies the absolute rejection of the hypothesis to which it is assigned, absolute disbelief in the truth of the suggested answer to a question or the possibility of the suggested outcome of an 'experiment'.

(3) *Equality* between the respective degrees of belief felt by an individual in two hypotheses will then require, for its expression in terms of potential surprise, *two* statements, viz. that some given degree of potential surprise is attached to both hypotheses, and that some given degree is attached to the contradictories of both.

(4) The degree of potential surprise associated with any hypothesis will be the least degree amongst all those appropriate to different mutually exclusive sets of hypotheses (each set considered as a whole) whose truth appears to the individual to imply the truth of this hypothesis.

(5) All the members of an exhaustive set of rival hypotheses can carry zero potential surprise.

(6) When H is any hypothesis, the degree of potential surprise attached to the contradictory of H is equal to the *smallest* degree attached to any rival of H.

(7) [version in first edition]. The degree of potential surprise assigned to the joint (simultaneous) truth of two hypotheses is equal to the *greater* of the respective degrees assigned to the separate hypotheses.

(7) [version in second edition]. Let y_A^B be the degree of potential surprise assigned to a hypothesis B when y^A is the degree assigned to a hypothesis A, and let y_0^B be the degree assigned to B when $y^A = 0$. Then y_A^B is not greater than the greater of y^A, y_0^B.

(8) Any hypothesis and its contradictory together constitute an exhaustive set of rival hypotheses.

(9) At least one member of an exhaustive set of rival hypotheses must carry zero potential surprise.*

The remaining propositions, numbers 10–17, are *theorems*:

(10) From (8) and (9) it follows that the degree of potential surprise that a person associates with the contradictory of a hypothesis cannot be greater than zero unless the degree he associates with the hypothesis is zero; and vice versa.

(11) From (5) and (8) it follows that a hypothesis and its contradictory can each carry zero potential surprise (notwithstanding that the contradictory may itself be capable of being resolved into two or more mutually rival hypotheses).

(12) Let H be any hypothesis. Then from (6) it follows that the degree of potential surprise attached to the contradictory of H cannot be greater than zero unless *every hypothesis rival to H* carries some degree of potential surprise greater than zero.

(13) From (10) and (12), the contradictories of two rival hypotheses (i.e. two mutually exclusive hypotheses both concerning the same question) cannot both carry degrees of potential surprise greater than zero. For if H_A and H_B are two rival hypotheses, and the contradictory of H_A carries some degree greater than zero of potential surprise, this implies by (12) that H_B carries some degree greater than zero of potential surprise; but (10) implies that the contradictory of H_B cannot then carry any degree of potential surprise greater than zero.

(14) From (3) and (13) it follows that if *equal degrees of belief* are felt in two rival hypotheses, the contradictories of both must carry zero potential surprise. The highest degree of *equal belief* which can be reposed in two rival hypotheses consists in assigning to both of them, and to the contradictories of both of them, zero potential surprise.

(15) Let $H_1^1, H_2^1, ..., H_n^1$ be an exhaustive set of rival hypotheses concerning a first question, and let them carry respective degrees of potential surprise $y_1^1, y_2^1, ..., y_n^1$. Let Υ be the degree of potential surprise assigned to a hypotheses H^2 suggested in answer to a second question. And let y_i^2 be the degree that will be assigned to H^2 if H_i^1 shall prove true. There are then two cases. First, if the y_i^2 are all equal we assert that $\Upsilon = y_i^2$. For by (9) at least one of the y_i^1, say y_k^1, is zero, and by (7) Υ will then be not greater than y_k^2. Since the set H_i^1 is exhaustive, at least the degree y_i^2 must be assigned to H^2. Thus $\Upsilon = y_i^2$.

(16) Secondly, if the y_i^2 are *not* all equal, we assert that Υ will be equal to the *least* degree which can be found amongst the complete

---

* But it is possible for all the rival hypotheses which are in any degree particularized or specified to carry potential surprise greater than zero, only the residual hypothesis carrying zero potential surprise.

set consisting of the *greater member of each pair* y_i^1, y_i^2. For by (7), Y cannot be greater than the greater member of some pair amongst this set. But by (4) it will be the least amongst these greater members.

(17) Let symbols have the meanings given them in (16). Then the individual will attach a degree *greater than zero* of potential surprise to the hypothesis that, when the answer to the first question shall have become known, he will *reduce* the degree y of potential surprise he attaches to any hypothesis H^2 concerning the second question. For to assert the contrary would be to assert that there is some hypothesis H_k^1 to which the individual initially assigns potential surprise y_k^1 equal to *zero*, and that the degree of potential surprise which this answer to the first question implies for the particular answer H^2 to the second question is *less* than the degree y of potential surprise *initially* assigned, in *ignorance* of the answer to the first question, to H^2. But this would involve a contradiction. For out of the pair y_k^1, y_k^2 we have $y_k^1 = 0$, and therefore by (2) y_k^2 is not less than y_k^1. But if y_k^2 can stand for the greater of the pair y_k^1, y_k^2, then it appears in the set amongst which, by (16), the *least* member is y, viz. the degree of potential surprise initially assigned to H^2. y_k^2 cannot, therefore, be less than y.

Concerning the first version of axiom 7, Professor H. S. Houthakker, then of the Department of Applied Economics in the University of Cambridge, wrote to me:

My objections against the crucial axiom 7 are of a more fundamental nature. It obviously does not apply to two mutually exclusive hypotheses, which I suggest should be stated explicitly. This is a mere quibble, but what about two hypotheses which are 'dependent' in some sense? For example, I associate zero potential surprise with the hypothesis that the left eye of Mr X, whom I do not know, is blue. Similarly I should feel no surprise if the right eye of the unknown Mr X proved to be brown. The hypothesis, however, that Mr X has one blue and one brown eye would meet with considerable potential surprise, though on your axiom that surprise should be zero.

It is plain that the wording of axiom 7 in its first version makes it unacceptable in face, not only of two hypotheses which are mutually exclusive but even of two which are mutually *hostile*, like the hypotheses that Mr X has one blue and one brown eye. The wording of the second version satisfied Mr Houthakker and still allowed axiom 7 to play its part in the proof of the theorems numbered, above, (15) and (16). I now think, however, that axiom 7 could be given the following form, slightly stronger and in one respect more explicit than the second version:

(7) Given the degree of potential surprise y^A assigned to a hypothesis A, and the degree y_0^B which would be assigned to a hypothesis B if y^A were zero, the degree in fact assigned to B will be the greater of y^A, y_0^B.

The purpose of inserting the word 'given' in this formulation is to guard against the following sequel.

(7A) Given also the degree y^B which would be assigned to B if no regard were paid to what degree is assigned to A, and given the degree y_0^A which would be assigned to A if y^B were zero, the degree in fact assigned to A will be the greater of y^B, y_0^A; hence by (7), the degree of potential surprise assigned to the *joint truth* of A and B will be the *lesser* of: max $[y^A, y_0^B]$ and max $[y^B, y_0^A]$.

The fallacy involved in this sequel is manifest. We cannot at one and the same time make the degree of potential surprise *in fact* assigned to B liable to be governed by that assigned to A, and also take it to be assigned 'regardless of what is assigned to A'. It would not be worth while to spell out this obvious fallacy, except that it helps to explain what it was that at first went wrong with axiom 7. The first version of that axiom entirely ignores the essence of its intended problem, that is to say, that the decision-maker is considering two hypotheses which will be put to the test *successively*, first A and *afterwards B*, and that he comes to a judgement first about A and then, given that judgement, about B. Axiom 7 was in origin my attempt to find a place in the axiom system for the ideas of our present chapter XXIV. This is one of the most striking aspects of the radical semantic difference between potential surprise and probability. Whereas the probability of the joint occurrence of two events is a unitary idea with one and only one numerical value, and we do not have to ask which event occurs first,* the degree of potential surprise accorded to the idea that A will occur and *afterwards B* need by no means be the same (and will in general be different) as that accorded to the idea that B will occur and then A.

Mr M. B. Nicholson has skilfully used the axiomatic scheme reproduced above to bring to a sharp focus a question which

---

* See below, chapter XXIV, pp. 200, 201.

has troubled me for many years. Potential surprise we have defined as the decision-maker's means of stating to himself his judgement of the *possibility* of an outcome, or of the coming true of an hypothesis. Is an outcome, then, rendered 'less possible' than before by an increase in the number of rival outcomes, all recognized as in some degree possible, the occurrence of any one of which would constitute the non-occurrence of our own outcome? We have suggested that the possibility of an outcome is less than perfect only when the individual forming a judgement concerning it has in mind some positive obstacle or difficulty to his imagining its coming true. Does the numerousness of rival ideas constitute such an obstacle? No physicist or engineer can point, in advance, to anything in the constitution or underlying principle, or in the particular design and construction, of the Electronic Random Number Indicating Equipment,* which renders the winning of a prize less than 'perfectly possible' by any Premium Bond. Yet the holder of just one such bond would no doubt be surprised if he won. How, then, are we to determine the point at which 'improbability' in the sense of the smallness of the ratio of favourable cases to all cases, begins to constitute less than perfect possibility? This point will evidently vary from case to case and from person to person: but what circumstances underly its particular location?

In a book not yet† published, Mr Nicholson writes:

Professor Shackle places it as one of the postulates of his system (Postulate 9): 'At least one member of an exhaustive set of rival hypotheses must carry zero potential surprise.' This postulate is qualified in a footnote which I quote: 'But it is possible for all the rival hypotheses which are in any degree particularized or specified to carry potential surprise greater than zero, only the residual hypothesis carrying zero potential surprise.' Now to take the previous example of 100 people applying for a job, all apparently equally qualified. [Let A_r denote the selection of the rth individual and $\bar{A}_r$ his rejection] $\bar{A}_1$ would be believed more than A_1. To translate this into Professor Shackle's language, he would say that A_1 carried a positive degree of potential surprise. To fit this into Postulate 9 he would say that $\bar{A}_1$ carried zero potential surprise. A_2 similarly carries a positive degree of potential surprise and from this any individual outcome bears a positive degree of potential surprise and

* 'Ernie'.   † December 1960.

his postulate is not fulfilled unless we are not permitted to specify more than a certain number of outcomes. On what basis we can say how many outcomes we can specify before having to declare the remaining as a residual outcome $A_r \cup A_{r+1} \cup A_{r+2}$ etc. is not stated.

In chapter IV of my *Uncertainty in Economics and Other Reflections* the question was discussed whether there can be circumstances where Postulate 9 is not valid. It was there argued that escape from Postulate 9 can only be afforded by the *complexity* of the rival hypotheses and of the subject-matter to which they refer. When we are concerned with values of a single variable, each constituting one hypothesis, Postulate 9 seems to us to impose itself invincibly. If this escape from the dilemma which Mr Nicholson poses is rejected (as we should reject it), there remain only two possibilities. Either the list of 'specified' or 'particularized' hypotheses is limited, according to some principle, in its numbers, so that when the total number of hypotheses is large enough to give rise to Mr Nicholson's dilemma, there automatically comes into being a residual hypothesis to carry zero potential surprise; or else the mere numerousness of the hypotheses rival to a given hypothesis is in itself a ground for attaching non-zero potential surprise to the given hypothesis. We cannot doubt that this last solution is the right one, but there remains the problem of locating the transition from perfect possibility to imperfect possibility as the number of rivals grows; or rather, of showing what circumstances and what character of the decision-maker will influence its location.

XI

CRITICS OF POTENTIAL
SURPRISE

In this chapter we shall reproduce from books, articles and reviews and from letters to the author extensive passages discussing the concept of potential surprise. The reader will thus be enabled to interpret for himself the words of the critics. Besides this we shall state our own interpretations, in order, first, that our answering arguments may be self-contained and their internal logic readily tested and, secondly, that the reader may be able to compare our interpretations with his own.

We begin with the view advanced by Professor C. F. Carter that in assuming *equal possibility* for several hypothetical outcomes we do not dispose of the question whether some of these outcomes may not be in some sense 'more likely' or 'more (subjectively) probable' than others:

The use of the new concept [viz. potential surprise] has the great advantage of freeing us absolutely from any false associations carried by the word 'probability'. But unhappily it can achieve this only at the cost of importing the associations of the word 'surprise', and these introduce a fundamental inconsistency....The trouble...lies with the width of the class of things which are unsurprising. Suppose I set up in business as a vendor of confectionary. Having no previous experience of the business, I have no basis for predicting my profits, it would not surprise me if they lay between £300 and £400 a year, and equally it would not surprise me if they lay between £1000 and £1100 a year. The converses of these propositions (that profits should be somewhere else than between £300 and £400, and so on) are also unsurprising. Then Professor Shackle wants me to say that I have an equal belief in the two outcomes. But I have nothing of the kind; in the common usage of words, I think it more *likely* that I should make the smaller profit, even though neither outcome would surprise me at all. There must be many business ventures for which *none* of the outcomes permitted by the terms of the venture would be surprising, in Shackle's sense of being incongruous or extravagant or demanding a stretch of the imagination. All the outcomes are either unsurprising or impossible; but all the unsurprising outcomes need not be thought equally likely.*

More recently Professor Carter has formulated his criticism thus:

This relates to [Shackle's] continued unwillingness to recognise any distinction between outcomes which are 'perfectly possible', or carry zero potential surprise. These outcomes are (on p. 47 of *Time in Economics*) both 'equally' possible and 'perfectly' possible. But surely these concepts are not the same; and I think that their difference explains some of the facts brought forward in disproof of Professor Shackle's theory. It is perfectly possible that the Conservative party will win the next election, and perfectly possible that the Labour party will win; both of these outcomes occasion zero potential surprise (whereas a victory for the Liberal party would occasion the maximum of surprise). But a Conservative victory and a Labour victory are not *equally* possible; if I am offered a choice between £1 for a Labour victory and 25*s.* for a Conservative victory, then on present anticipations my focus gain is not 25*s.* but £1. I suggest that for the sake of making more deadly his thrust at the statistical concept of probability, Professor Shackle has thrown away some of the reality of subjective probability.†

Professor Carter maintains that within a class of hypothetical outcomes every one of which the decision-maker regards as 'perfectly possible', and to every one of which, accordingly, he assigns zero potential surprise, some can appear to him 'more likely' than others. I cannot agree, but I cannot be sure whether the difference between his view and mine is one of substance or whether it merely arises from his giving a different meaning from mine to the expression 'perfectly possible'. I would say that if a man regards one outcome as more likely than another, this can only be because he perceives some positive hindrances to the second outcome; because he finds that in imagining that outcome to prove true he experiences, as it were, 'a hollow feeling'; because to do so requires 'a stretch of the imagination'; because there is a snag or an unrealism or an incongruity; a something belonging to those kinds whose

* 'The Present State of the Theory of Decisions under Uncertainty', being chapter xv of *Uncertainty and Business Decisions*, 2nd ed., edited by Carter, Meredith and Shackle (Liverpool University Press, 1957), pp. 142–52.

† See Professor Carter's review of *Time in Economics* (by G. L. S. Shackle, North Holland Publishing Company, 1958) in the *Economic Journal*, vol. LXVIII, no. 271 (September 1958).

presence is the very basis and essence of the idea of *imperfect* possibility. If this be accepted, it follows that when A is judged less likely than B, A is judged to be not perfectly possible, and calls for some greater than zero degree of potential surprise. In his review of *Time in Economics* Professor Carter wishes to use the expression 'perfectly possible' in such a sense that two things can both be 'perfectly possible' while yet one is 'more possible' than the other. Above I have preferred to use the expression 'more likely' in seeking to express Professor Carter's view; but from his use of words in that review it seems evident that what he really does is to make a distinction between the *absence of obstacles* to the truth of a hypothesis, and the *presence of something positive* which drives the individual to accept it. It is this distinction which I am unable to follow. The superior skill of one chess-player over another, which drives the spectator to conclude that the former will win, is the very same thing which makes him regard the latter's victory as less than perfectly possible, as potentially somewhat surprising. If, in Professor Carter's example, the Conservative party is judged by him less likely to win a particular election than the Labour party, this is because he considers the Labour party to have some means of preventing a Conservative victory, which thus becomes less than perfectly possible.

An interpretation which some, I think, will be inclined to put on Professor Carter's statement in his review of *Time in Economics* is that he is in effect proposing a two-dimensional concept of uncertainty, where one dimension would be potential surprise and the other 'likeliness' or subjective probability in some sense. This interpretation would give a more clear-cut meaning to his use of the expression 'perfectly possible', which otherwise must be understood as a merely qualitative feature, something which can be possessed in common by hypotheses very variously related to the ideas of 'certainly wrong' or 'certainly right'. I shall not here pursue this notion of two-dimensional uncertainty. J. M. Keynes hinted at something of this sort in his *Treatise on Probability** and Professor G. P. Meredith† has foreshadowed a 'Pattern of Evidence of Rational

---

* *A Treatise on Probability*, by J. M. Keynes (Macmillan, 1921).

† 'Methodological Considerations in the Study of Human Anticipation' by G. P. Meredith, being chapter IV of *Uncertainty and Business Decisions*, pp. 47–49.

Likelihood' which would require us to look upon uncertainty as many-dimensioned. Such proposals seem to me to involve too great a complexity for a practically useful analysis.

A view related to Professor Carter's, though reached independently and based on explicit psychological grounds, has been put forward by Mr J. Puthucheary as follows:*

It is questionable whether the mutually independent character of hypotheses regarding the same object, by the same man, at the 'same time' is valid. One would normally assume that as the hypotheses are by the same man, relating to the same object and formulated in a limited space of time, they will be inter-related, or related to a central hypothesis, which we will term the *primary hypothesis*.† The related nature of hypotheses on a subject in a limited period of time, can be deduced if we agree that hypotheses have a pattern and are the result of some ordering of the various factors that go into their formulation: that hypotheses are not the results of unrestricted forays into the unknown but the result of the correlating of information and anticipations and even informed guesses.... Given a mass of 'data' there would in the first instance be a grading process by which degrees of credibility of each member datum, and its significance to the problem at hand, is assessed. The degree of credibility attached to one set is related to the degree attached to others which it supports or contradicts.... Selection, ordering and integrating are essential parts of any thinking process, whether these parts are consciously separate or unconscious and telescoped.

The *primary hypothesis*, the central theme of the thinking on an investment project, is formulated from all the data considered significant and most credible. Secondary hypotheses will be formulated by the inclusion of factors rejected in the formulation of the primary hypothesis and by the inclusion of sets referring to factors already included, which were rejected in preference to other sets when formulating the primary hypothesis. Consequently, the primary hypothesis will have the greatest importance to the decision-maker and will have the greatest credibility to him. All the secondary hypotheses are deviations from the primary hypothesis and as such will have less importance and credibility. The primary hypothesis having the greatest credibility will have zero potential surprise and the secondary hypotheses will all have a higher degree of potential surprise, as they postulate outcomes, different from that postulated

* 'Investment Incentive and Income Tax', by J. Puthucheary. *Public Finance*, vol. xiv, 1959, pp. 218–35.

† Not to be confused with my *primary focus outcomes*, an entirely different concept [G.L.S.S.].

by the primary hypothesis, and as they were formulated by the inclusion of data rejected in the first instance.

In general terms the more a secondary hypothesis deviates from the primary hypothesis the greater will be the potential surprise associated with it.

We shall draw further on Mr Puthucheary's article in a sub-sequent chapter, since in it he examines generally how the concept of potential surprise should enter into the analysis of decision. Meanwhile it is clear that he is drawn like Professor Carter, though by a different route, towards the idea that one sole hypothetical outcome of some contemplated act, or at most a very compact group of closely similar outcomes, will claim for itself the exclusive status of zero potential surprise, all rival outcomes being assigned some positive degree. This view con-trasts with our suggestion, made below* in discussing the shape of the function linking potential surprise with desirability, or with some characteristic underlying desirability, that a full consciousness of the inadequacy of his data would almost always compel the decision-maker to recognize widely diverse outcomes as all equally possible, and, *pace* Professor Carter, therefore all equally 'likely'. While Professor Carter dis-tinguishes between equal *possibility* and equal *likeliness*, Mr Puthucheary, as we shall see below, distinguishes between 'expectations' and 'possibilities'. He says in effect that a decision will only be made when, out of all the 'possibilities' of each available action, one alone has been selected for that action as the 'expectation', that is, as the *assumed* result. There is, I think, a strong sympathy between the two lines of argu-ment. These two critics ascribe to the decision-maker, in my view, an urge to give to his actions an appearance of well-founded rationality which the circumstances of human life do not afford and which is therefore artificial. Even if artificial, it may still, of course, be what is in reality sought after; the figmenta-tion of rationality may be a real feature of decision making.

It will be most natural, I think, to consider next a group of closely inter-related contributions to the potential surprise debate which centre on the questions whether potential surprise can be mapped to subjective probabilities in such a way that it is a matter of indifference which of the two kinds of un-

* Chapter XVII.

certainty variable we use; and whether we give a realistic account of behaviour in the world by adopting an uncertainty variable such that we cannot meaningfully add together its values respectively assigned to several rival hypotheses, A, B, C, ...so as to obtain the value assignable to the hypothesis that *some one or other* of A, B, C,...is right. These questions, otherwise expressed, amount to the following: Is potential surprise a merely formal alternative to a distributional uncertainty variable, which can be legitimately obtained from it by manipulation? and: Does the realistic analysis of decisions in face of uncertainty require a distributional uncertainty variable? Special attention has been given to this group of questions by Professor Wilhelm Krelle in a review appearing in October 1957,* by Mr Gerald Gould in a correspondence with the author, published in December 1957,† and by Mr M. B. Nicholson in an article commenting on that correspondence, published in December 1958.‡

Professor Krelle writes as follows:

But is [potential surprise] really anything other than 'subjective probability'? Since in a set of exhaustive hypotheses at least *one* possible outcome must be ascribed potential surprise zero, there is a one-to-one mapping of the set of potential surprises y_i, $i = 1$, 2, ..., n to a set of magnitudes ω_i, $i = 1, 2, ..., n$ with $\sum_{i=1}^{n} \omega_i = 1$ e.g. by

$$\omega_i = \frac{\bar{y} - y_i}{\sum_{i=1}^{n} (\bar{y} - y_i)} \tag{1}$$

and

$$y_i = -\frac{\omega_i}{\omega_{j\,max.}} \bar{y}(1 - n\omega_{j\,max.}) + \bar{y}(1 - n\omega_i) \tag{2}$$

respectively, with $\bar{y}$ chosen arbitrarily. Let us call these variables ω_i 'subjective probabilities'. If the 'potential surprises' y_i are given, (1) gives us the 'subjective probabilities' ω_i which preserve the ratios of 'plausibility' $(\bar{y} - y_i)$ as given by the y_i. If the 'subjective

* Review by Professor Wilhelm Krelle of *Uncertainty in Economics and Other Reflections*, by G. L. S. Shackle, *Econometrica*, vol. XXV (October 1957).

† G. Gould and G. L. S. Shackle, 'Odds, Possibility and Plausibility in Shackle's Theory of Decision: A Discussion', *Economic Journal*, vol. LXVII, no. 268 (December 1957).

‡ M. B. Nicholson, 'A Note on Mr Gould's Discussion of potential surprise', *Economic Journal*, vol. LXVIII, no. 272 (December 1958).

probabilities' ω_i are given, we select the maximum, call it (resp., them) $\omega_{j\,max.}$, and get by (2) the co-ordinated y_i. Whether one prefers 'subjective probabilities' or 'potential surprise' as variable seems to be basically a matter of indifference.

While I believe that in the general direction of our thought there is a close sympathy between Professor Krelle and myself, I do not think that his suggested variable ω_i would be suitably described as a subjective probability. What I question is the meaningfulness of the summation $\sum\limits_{i=1}^{n} (\bar{y} - y_i)$. The very word *possibility* in the subjective sense I wish to give it is essentially an acknowledgement of a state of mind quite the opposite of that of a man who constructs a probability distribution. When a man speaks of probability he pushes ignorance as far as he can into concealment and an inconspicuous role; when he speaks of possibility he recognises his knowledge as merely setting bounds to a wide spectrum of mutually exclusive ideas. To sum the degrees of possibility assigned to various rival hypotheses is to fall back on the idea that it is the *number of its rivals* which gives a hypothesis its status, rather than its own particular character. An outstandingly well-qualified candidate for some post is not less likely to be appointed merely because a score, rather than half a dozen, second-rate applicants also present themselves. If we do not know what qualities are required, we cannot say which of a number of candidates *is* well qualified; but whichever man has, in fact, the requisite attributes, he has not them in less degree because of the presence of other men who do not possess them at all. To do what Professor Krelle suggests would give to a *perfectly possible* hypothesis a share, which might be a very small one, of the total $\sum\limits_{i=1}^{n} (\bar{y} - y_i)$. It is precisely this idea, that a *small share of a total*, and a share which *varies with the size of that total*, can suitably indicate the status of *perfect possibility*, that I cannot agree with. If an outcome or happening is looked on as perfectly possible, it is looked on as such regardless of what else is also looked on as perfectly, or in any other degree, possible.

It is with the second part of Mr Gerald Gould's contribution to the *Economic Journal* of December 1957, that we are here concerned: the first part cannot be considered until the focus-values construction has been presented in chapters XVIII and XIX. Mr Gould writes:

Let us look into potential surprise more closely. In the realm of vague non-numerical uncertainty the potential surprises form a partially-ordered set. Suppose for example, there are four hypotheses, *A*, *B*, *C*, *D*. The potential surprises may be partially ordered according to the following diagram (Fig. XI 1):

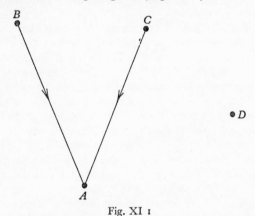

Fig. XI 1

Here *A* is more possible than *B* and also more possible than *C*, but no other pairs can be compared as to their degree of possibility. Now it is not difficult to find a realization of this model for which the hypothesis *E* defined as '*B* or *C* or *D*' can be fitted in the diagram shown below (Fig. XI 2):

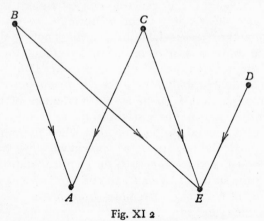

Fig. XI 2

In this case, A and E remain incomparable, even though E is more plausible than D, which itself is incomparable with A. In such situations, and I imagine that entrepreneur problems are typical of them, composite hypotheses (such as E) may carry no further weight than their individual components.

Mr M. B. Nicholson has commented as follows (*Economic Journal*, December 1958) on this part of Mr Gould's contribution:

Let us use the notation AsB to mean 'The hypothesis A is more possible than the hypothesis B', and AtB to mean 'The hypothesis A is as possible as the hypothesis B'—Mr Gould's model does no more than assert that the composite hypothesis 'B or C' may be no more possible than either of the individual hypotheses alone in situations where the probabilities of events happening are vague and unknown. It is tempting at this point to return to the firmer ground of probability theory and assert that this is only the case when the possibility of either B by itself or C by itself is so small as to be negligible. However, by firmly remembering our psychological rather than mathematical intent we might be induced to admit that sometimes 'B or C' tB when the possibility of C alone is not negligible. The question becomes, 'How great has the possibility of C to be before "B or C" sB replaces "B or C" tB?' Professor Shackle would hold that only in extreme cases would this happen.

It is in the phrase 'by firmly remembering our psychological rather than mathematical intent' that Mr Nicholson most clearly shows himself understanding of my position, a position to which Mr Gould makes generous concessions. It is, if without wearying the reader I can venture upon yet another re-expression, the *freedom* which the concept of potential surprise gives us, to make this or that assumption about the interior process of the decision-maker's thoughts rather than be rigidly bound to combine probabilities in the additive manner dictated by their nature, that I claim as the advantage of potential surprise in this regard. There seems to me to be no ground for assuming as a general proposition that when hypothesis B is assigned a particular 'status' in the sense in which we have been using this word, and hypothesis C an identical status, it must follow that the status of 'B or C' should be 'twice as good' as that of B or of C, 'twice as remote' from being looked on as certainly wrong, and so on.

Mr Nicholson continues:

The question which is relevant in the discussion of models of decision-taking is whether a model is applicable or not in the sense of its behaviour postulates being correct accounts of behaviour in the world. Hence the question to be asked of the Shackle model and the Gould interpretation of it is, 'Is the assumption of the non-additivity of a measure of uncertainty a correct assumption about people's thought processes in the face of uncertainty?' The model holds as a logical system irrespective of its applicability but its interest is small if the range of problems where it is applicable is small. The postulate may be unacceptable in one situation but not in another. Mr Gould gives an instance where the Shackle postulate does not seem to hold, but, as he himself makes quite clear, this does not necessarily mean that it does not hold in other and interesting situations. However, the non-additivity of the measure of uncertainty is a very strong assumption in all situations and contradicts what one is inclined to think intuitively about reactions to uncertain situations. Possibly it is applicable at times, but hesitation in accepting it without strong evidence is justified.

It is a matter of great interest that Mr Gould and Mr Nicholson should take so detached and even sympathetic a view, as their contributions indicate, of a concept whose chief purpose and *raison d'être* is to break the bonds of the traditional mathematical method of handling problems of uncertainty.

That method is traditional, however, not only amongst mathematicians. Its elaborate development and esoteric forms exist, of course, only for them. But the language of 'chances' or 'odds' is current with people of every kind, and it has to be admitted that they do sometimes use this language when they would express more accurately their mental posture in face of an uncertainty-situation by saying 'I should not be surprised if...' or 'It would surprise me very much if...'. Upon this question of the forms of words we use in ordinary speech, two differing conclusions are expressed by Professor J. Pen and by Dr C. L. Hamblin. Professor Pen writes thus:*

As regards the other decisive point—the one relating to Shackle's criticism of the conventional theory—I have a more positive opinion. This is an important question because the uncertainty phenomenon

* See Professor Pen's review of *Uncertainty in Economics and other Reflections*, *De Economist*, year 1955, no. 11, p. 794, in Dutch, from which I have had the above quotation translated.

is encountered everywhere and it is taken into consideration continually in daily life. Let us say...that there is a good prospect—say 80% probability—that Peter will pass his examination; we think then that we shall not be surprised if he passed. Now I have nothing against the last but I think there is no need, despite Shackle's criticism, to consider the first superfluous and in fact impossible. This way of thinking, with all its consequences, is firmly anchored in the human mind. Therefore there must be some mistake in Shackle's standpoint according to which [that way of thinking] is illogical and senseless. Nevertheless the logic of his criticism, reproduced above in outline, is impressive. It is in fact absurd to distribute a limited quantity, namely 100%, over an unlimited series of alternatives.

The way out of this dilemma is, according to my present and naturally preliminary judgement, quite simple. The cases cited by Shackle are all characterized by the same feature, i.e. the uncertainties considered form an endless series. Seeing that in a closed hatbox a bowler hat or a sou'wester, but also an ape or a lump of coal may be contained, it is indeed illogical and unpractical to attach probability percentages to these possibilities. Here only 'potential surprise' applies. The ape would give rise to greater surprise than the Sunday hat. Nobody would want to work with percentages in this case, even implicit ones. The position is quite different, however, when we have to do with clearly limited alternatives, namely two. It is no accident that Shackle's examples do not include this category, just as it is no accident that Rijken van Olst in his criticism cites the instance of Aunt's chance of recovering from her illness. Aunt will get well or she will not get well. There will be a war or there will be no war. These are cases characterized by Shackle as 'unique', to the extent that they may even be called 'crucial'. There are just two alternatives, and here the probability concept is not explicitly present. There reference may be made to the inaccuracy of Shackle's standpoint in the sense that the 'uniqueness' and *a fortiori* the 'crucialness' (the extent to which the further developments are influenced by a unique event) is made the basis of inapplicability of the conventional view. The real basis is the endless character of the series of alternatives. The hatbox may involve a unique situation but it is certainly not crucial. In really crucial situations, the alternatives are often two-fold and then I see no objection to application of the probability percentage, seeing that this is a subjective psychological factor, not to be confused with an actuarial value....

The difficult point is that Shackle builds his 'potential surprise' on the ruins of the customary way of thinking. Shackle's theory can do without this foundation.

Professor Pen, then, concedes to the language of chances and probability its own useful function in our ordinary speech, even as a means of stating a person's attitude to an uncertainty-situation, provided this language is confined to cases where the set of hypotheses or contingencies is a definite and limited one. The reader must be the judge of this view as against the one we have put forward. The whole tenor of Professor Pen's review of my book is so generous, that it would be doubly out of place to insist further at this point on my contrary opinion. Yet my view has found incisive support from a professional logician. In the opening paragraphs of a paper on 'The modal "probably"', Dr C. L. Hamblin* says:

Metrical probability-theory is well-established, scientifically important and, in essentials, beyond logical reproof. But when for example we say 'It's probably going to rain', or 'I shall probably be in the library this afternoon', are we, even vaguely, using the metrical probability concept? Is what we say about statements like these even *consistent* with their interpretation as metrical probability-statements, such as that the degree of probability of rain or of my being in the library is greater than some figure x, with all that this involves in the way of rules for arithmetic operations in the numbers representing degrees of probability? I want to suggest that, contrary to what is usually supposed, there is a case for answering these questions in the negative....I turn next to a concept analogous to one proposed by Shackle, and applied by him to certain problems in economics: it may be termed 'plausibility'. In terms of an... allocation of numerical indices to statements a modal logic of 'plausibility' is developed. The numerical indices are here, however, *non-metrical* in character: that is, no arithmetic properties are involved. It can in fact be demonstrated formally that 'p is plausible' can be interpreted simply in the form 'p does not occasion surprise'— a kind of reduction which is not possible in the case of the logic of 'probable'.

After developing a 'modal' logic of probability from metrical probability-theory, Dr Hamblin proceeds:

Without further discussion at this stage I shall proceed to outline the alternative system.

Shackle has discussed in detail the reasons for preferring, in most

* C. L. Hamblin, 'The Modal "Probably"', *Mind*, vol. LXVIII, no. 270 (April 1959), pp. 234-40.

real-life situations involving a choice between rival hypotheses, a measure of worth of the hypotheses concerned which differs in several respects from the probability-measure usually adopted by theoreticians. I shall not here repeat these reasons: it is enough to say that we want a measure which (i) can be allocated to a given hypothesis irrespective of the number and measures of contrary hypotheses, and (ii) is not limited by the usual probability addition rule....

In place of the addition rule for probabilities we have the following: the plausibility of any disjunction is equal to the *largest* of the plausibilities of the components....

Dr Hamblin then embodies this position in an axiom-system concerning which he says in a footnote: 'Shackle does not give a complete discussion of logical properties, and I have had to fill in some of them myself.' This is too modest a statement of what he has done in presenting his own axiom-system valuably extending the formal consequences of my conceptual apparatus. His use of symbolic logic gives his treatment an especial economy and beauty, but the main source of the happiness which his article occasioned me was its acceptance of the need for such a redirection of thought as this present book and my earlier ones propose.

Of even greater interest is Dr Hamblin's paper, presented to a seminar of the Australian National University in 1958, on 'Surprises, Innovation and Probabilities', in which the restricted applicability of von Neumann and Morgenstern's Theory of Games, arising from its essential dependence on probability, is shown to rest ultimately on the inherent nature of a *game with known rules*. Here Dr Hamblin shows himself in close agreement with the position taken up in my 'Time and Thought',* that in life itself decision is non-empty because the outcomes envisaged by the decision-maker for each act available

---

* Delivered as a lecture in the University of Toronto on 23 January 1958 and published in the *British Journal for the Philosophy of Science*, vol. XI, no. 36 (February 1959): 'The true basis of the disaster wrought upon economic theory by the *games of chance* universe of ideas is the notion of the existence and the attainability of a list, complete and known to be complete, of all the possible outcomes of an action. In games of chance this possibility, of listing completely all the contingencies, is assured by the very nature of these games, their inherent and essential dependence upon a set of explicit rules. It is the completeness of this list which makes it logically possible to distribute relative frequencies over the contingencies' (p. 291).

to him are not listable from a knowledge of anything corresponding to the stated rules of a game. Dr Hamblin says:

The mathematical theory devised by von Neumann shows that in the simpler context of a true poker-game it is possible to specify quite exactly the *frequencies* one should allocate to the various alternative moves in order to optimise one's long-term gain against opponents who play a similar 'perfect' game....

But there is one important difference between a 'game' in von Neumann's sense and a real-life situation. In a game there is at each stage a fixed and definite number of possible 'legal moves'.... The analysis of the game depends on this fact: each player can take stock of his own and his opponents' armoury of possible moves, bids, bluffs and surprises, and prepare a rational strategy based on his appraisal. Hence though it may not be possible for him to *predict* what his opponents will do, it is always possible for him to *enumerate the possibilities*—and to allocate *probabilities* to them.

But when we consider the economic-political sphere—and particularly when we specifically consider 'innovation'—it is clear that there are many circumstances in which we cannot with assurance even *enumerate* the possible future contingencies. We might say that the economic-political sphere is more like a special sort of poker-game in which at each stage each player can without prior warning invent a new sort of move for himself—in effect, invent new rules for the game.

One of the things that contributed to the appeal of the theory of games in its original form was its suggestion that rational strategy is possible even when there are unknowns in a situation. If we don't have certain knowledge on which to base our actions (it is suggested), why then, we can always fall back on probabilities; and these will do nearly as well. This is a dangerously misleading account.

The circumstances in which we *can* fall back on probabilities—or at least on the orthodox classical concept of probability—are in fact severely limited. We must *first* have a clearly delimited field of possibilities or contingencies, logically exhaustive and mutually exclusive—what von Mises called a 'collective' and modern statisticians call an 'ensemble'.

After some discussion of the concept of 'residual contingency'* Dr Hamblin proceeds:

...let me emphasise the fundamental nature of this problem. I have considered in particular the application of the theory of games; but

---

* See *Expectation in Economics* (1949), pp. 130, 131.

what has been said applies equally to *any* application of reasoning based on the orthodox concept of probability—and hence we exclude not only 'theory of games' reasoning but also any kind of actuarial statistics, and any of the probabilistic accounts of induction and confirmation, from Keynes to Popper.

Dr Hamblin accordingly proposes a resort to 'plausibility' of which he says:

The concept of 'plausibility' as I have described it, is close in character to the concept of 'surprise value' as suggested by Shackle. ...Shackle proposes in his problem of investment policy a *double* standard for evaluation of strategies; namely in terms of *both* the largest 'plausible gain' *and* the largest 'plausible loss'. This is clearly an improvement on the theory of games, since the question of how to balance risk against possible gain can be considered separately.

The contrast between the 'closed system', the game with *completely* stated rules, the fully posed problem requiring only to be solved and possessing an answer which, in some sense, waits to be found and exists before the attempt to find it and independently of that attempt, is again the theme of a passage, as I interpret it, of a paper on 'Temporal and Atemporal Foresight', in which from the viewpoint of a psychologist Professor Stanley Stark has contrasted my view of the nature of decision with that of Professor Herbert A. Simon of Chicago. By *atemporal* foresight Professor Stark means that mental capacity or function which is involved in solving what I will call a fully posed problem, such as that of finding the shortest path to the centre of a maze. By *temporal* foresight he means that power or activity by which a man poses problems for himself to solve, so that the coming into being of the problem is itself for the decision-maker an event occupying a moment or moments, so that time relationships subsist between the elements of the problem. In schemes of thought of the Simon type the 'decision-maker' is faced with a choice among existents in a system which is already complete and *closed* in the sense that its structure, the set of relationships composing it, cannot be added to by the decision-maker himself, but must be accepted by him and made the best of. His task is to understand this structure and then, by the exercise of judgement only, to deal with it by *selecting* among the possibilities, already existent, which it offers. By contrast with this, in such a scheme of thought as my own the decision-maker's field of choice is created by himself so that he is faced, not with a set of relationships all simultaneously, and so in a sense timelessly, existing at each instant, but with a system which evolves from moment to moment in his own mind. Professor Stark's distinction of a temporal from an atemporal problem or situation thus makes use of the need, or the absence of need, for time-using activity to *pose* the problem, in order to label or mark the contrast which, from a different viewpoint, might have been referred to as subjective versus objective, or as creative versus judgemental.

The value of looking at the contrast under Professor Stark's temporal-atemporal aspect appears very impressively in the quotations he makes from Professor F. Bartlett, from whose book *Thinking** he reports the following passage:

The thinker in the closed system is in the position of contemplating a finished structure. Very often this may be exceedingly complex and elaborate and the rules of its construction difficult to appreciate. The thinker is, however, in the position of a spectator searching for something which he must treat as being in some way 'there' all the time.

'Time', Professor Stark proceeds, 'is not intrinsic to the [closed] system, only to the solution of it. The decision-maker is a system-solver or a solution-selector. Quite different is the situation of Bartlett's contrasting thinker in experimental science who' (he quotes again from Bartlett),

is in the position of somebody who must use whatever tools may be available for adding to some structure that is not yet finished, and that he himself is certainly not going to complete. Because the materials that he must use have properties of their own, many of which he cannot know until he uses them, and some of which in all likelihood are actually generated in the course of their use, he is in the position of an explorer rather than of a spectator.

Although Professor Bartlett is concerned with a different context from my own, I judge from these quotations (not being myself acquainted with his book) that he might feel some sympathy with my own attitude.

* F. Bartlett, *Thinking* (New York: Basic Books 1958) (quotations taken from Professor Stark's article).

As so often in the past, Professor C. F. Carter has compelled me to try out an idea in a new context. In a letter dated 31 January 1960 he writes:

I have two daughters, Mary and Lucy. Both of them are fairly bright, and if you ask me 'Do you expect M (or L) to pass the eleven-plus examination?', I should answer 'Yes'. Nevertheless the degree of my assurance is greater for L than for M. Am I right in thinking that, for you, this difference in degree of assurance can only be accommodated by attaching non-zero potential surprise to M's passing?...This still seems to me to use the word 'surprise' in a special sense—so special that it would be better to devise a new word for it. For although I do not think M is as bright as L, '*I shouldn't be surprised*' if M passed.

We referred Professor Carter to the first axiom of the axiom-system set out in *Expectation in Economics* (1949), final Appendix, and reproduced in chapter x of this book: 'An individual's degree of belief in a hypothesis can be thought of as consisting in a degree of potential surprise associated with the hypothesis, and in another degree associated with its contradictory.' The state of mind he describes can be faithfully stated in our terms as follows:

Hypothesis	Potential surprise
M will pass	$y_M = 0$
M will not pass	$y_{\overline{M}} = 0$
L will pass	$y_L = 0$
L will not pass	$y_{\overline{L}} > 0$

or it may be:

Hypothesis	Potential surprise
M will pass	$y_M = 0$
M will not pass	$y_{\overline{M}} > 0$
L will pass	$y_L = 0$
L will not pass	$y_{\overline{L}} > y_{\overline{M}}$

In the letter we have quoted, Professor Carter is, by implication, refusing to separate the question 'How much should I be surprised by event A?' from the question 'How much should I be surprised by event not-A?'. Now if we insisted (surely against reason) on speaking in terms of chances or odds, it would of course be true that to give L a smaller number of 'chances' of not passing (a lower probability of not passing) than M would be the same thing as to give L a larger number of chances (a higher probability) of passing than M. Do we want our uncertainty variable to be of such a character that it deprives us of the freedom to separate the two hypotheses and treat their respective uncertainties as independent of each other? We think that in expressing the matter in this way, we have isolated the real source of Professor Carter's repugnance against our use of 'surprise'. He thinks those ideas should not be separated, we think they should be separable. Mary, it seems to the observer, may perfectly well find in her examination paper questions which she can answer, for she has considerable and diverse knowledge and there are many such conceivable questions. But there are also many conceivable questions, quite appropriate to the level of this examination, which she would not be able to answer. It thus seems to the observer perfectly possible for her to succeed, perfectly possible for her to fail. With Lucy it is different. Her knowledge and abilities are such that the observer finds it difficult to imagine any set of fair and appropriate questions with which she could not cope. It is perfectly possible she may succeed, it is less than perfectly possible she may fail. *Possibility* is an entirely different idea from *probability*, and it is sometimes, we maintain, a more efficient and powerful uncertainty variable, able to perform semantic tasks which the other cannot.

XII

A COUNTER-CRITIQUE
ON PROBABILITY

In a profoundly interesting article on 'Probable Knowledge and Singular Acts' in the *Metroeconomica* symposium, Professor Richard S. Weckstein has pointed out the importance of considering separately each different conception of probability and of asking whether one or other of these distinct ideas may not be serviceable for this or for that one of all the different applications, including those of analysing decision. Professor Weckstein begins his article by listing the objections which have been raised against the use of probability, under various definitions, in the description of decision-making, and proceeds:

What makes a list of this sort unsatisfactory, it seems to me, is that it treats probability as though it were a single agreed upon concept. As in fact this is clearly not the case, the question arises, what part of the list is properly applicable to which conception of probability? How much of the list is properly applicable to all conceptions of probability? And, is it possible that from the point of view of the economic theorist the various conceptions of probability may be thought of as complementary goods? If so, does it turn out that we are left with a usable concept of probability for each of those applications to which probability is to be put?

In order to test this he divides concepts of probability under three main heads:

(i) Frequency probability, with two variants represented respectively by von Mises, who defines it as the frequency of favourable events in an infinite series of events, and by Reichenbach, who defines it as the frequency of favourable events in a class which need not be a series and need not be infinite.

(ii) Logical probability, or the degree of confirmation, represented by Keynes, Jeffreys and Carnap.

(iii) Subjective probability, represented by the views of Ramsey, de Finetti and Savage.

Professor Weckstein relates these concepts to each other in an exceedingly interesting way which also juxtaposes the two ideas, *probability* and *possibility*:

But what can be said of the situations in which so little is known about the possible outcomes, that all one can do is to hold open the mental *possibility* of the occurrence of those outcomes? Once the definition of probability relaxes the requirement of an infinite series, the size of the reference class seems to be left unspecified. Therefore, it is possible for us to envision a gradual approach to the absence of evidence without a jump into a situation where probability is totally inapplicable. The resulting broad range over which the frequency conception of probability may be applicable suggests the need for a measure of the reliability of the evidence on which probability is based.

Professor Weckstein in this passage comes very close to an explicit recognition of the distinct and basic role of *possibility* in the analysis of decision, and to treating it as a quite different and separate idea from that of probability. He does not, of course, follow us at all along the path which this recognition seems to us to open up, that of treating *uncertainty as a release of imagination*, as a positive *resource*, neutral in itself, which the human spirit can bend to its purpose of anticipative experience. Instead he draws back from the brink, and treats that situation, where absence of evidence allows many and widely diverse hypotheses all to claim what we have called *equal status*, as an exceptional and degenerate case defeating the individual's natural search for the outcome with the *best* status in the area bounded by certainty of wrongness and certainty of rightness. The need for 'a measure of the reliability of the evidence on which probability is based' finds two distinct proposals. Keynes suggested the idea of 'weight': 'new evidence will sometimes decrease the probability of an argument, but it will always increase its "weight"'.* Reichenbach's proposal, in Professor Weckstein's words, is that 'As the probability of an *event* may be calculated from the relative frequency of its occurrence in a class of similar events, so may the probability of a *statement of probability* be determined from the relative frequency of true statements in the class of similar probability statements'. Thus in Reichenbach's terms as Professor Weckstein explains them

---

* J. M. Keynes, *A Treatise on Probability* (Macmillan, London, 1921), p. 12. (Quoted by Professor Weckstein.)

we should say that 'the probability of Keynes's low-weight probability statements is less than the probability of high-weight probability statements'.

Readers of this present book will find in our chapter XXIV a discussion of how a related problem can be handled in terms of potential surprise. Given the degree of potential surprise which the decision-maker attaches to a proposition H, and given the degree he would attach to a proposition K if he attached zero potential surprise to H, then for some purposes it seems appropriate to assume that the degree of potential surprise he will in fact assign to K will be the greater of these two degrees. The contrast between Reichenbach's conception and our own, in so far as they are at all comparable and in so far as the respective problems they have in view are similar, seems to us to lie in this: that Reichenbach is prepared to let the influence of a proposition, on the decision-maker's mind, be lessened, not only by the consideration that this proposition cannot claim sufficient evidence in its favour to mark it 'certainly right', but also by the consideration that such merely 'probable' propositions have on the average proved untrustworthy in such and such a proportion of cases. Is not this as though a vagrant charged with theft should be convicted on the ground that besides the evidence against him personally there is a suspicion that vagrants are often thieves?

Amongst the objections to the use of one or another concept of probability in the analysis of decision, which Professor Weckstein systematically considers, one of the questions nearest to the heart of things is whether we can give meaning to the notion of the probability of a singular act (most especially, to what we ourselves have called a crucial act). Here I find it difficult to be sure just what his attitude is:

If the Mises definition of the frequency conception of probability is adopted, then probability in this sense cannot be applied to single cases. I can add nothing to this conclusion.... Reichenbach [however] justifies the transition from the probability of the class to the single case by the use of the concept of the 'posit'. Reichenbach uses the term 'weight' as the value of such a posit and 'a weight is what a degree of probability becomes if it is applied to a single case'.*

* Hans Reichenbach, *Experience and Prediction* (University of Chicago Press, 1935), p. 314. (Quoted by Professor Weckstein.)

Reichenbach's justification of this transference of probability from the class (what we ourselves have called a 'divisible experiment') to the single instance is, in the last resort, justified teleologically or pragmatically, by the claim that

...if decisions are made on the basis of the posit, a person will maximise his chances of success in the long run of all such one-time decisions.

In commenting on this contention, we feel bound in the first place to take issue with Professor Weckstein's wording. Perhaps he would be willing to write 'a person will maximize his success in the long run' and not 'his *chances of* success'. The latter phrase throws back the whole question into the melting-pot. For surely the point of Reichenbach's contention is that *the long run* composes something analogous to our 'divisible experiment' out of the dissimilar individual cases of decision. In so far as a man can really be consoled for the failure of his career by the success of his love affairs or vice versa, in so far as Reichenbach's 'long run' is long only in the number of its individual composing items and not in the time it is going to take to be gone through; in so far as the individual has no doubts that there will indeed be a long run; and finally in so far as none of the items required to compose the long run is *crucial* in our sense, then we can see force in Reichenbach's argument; but these many if's are a great difficulty for it. In so far as we accept it, however, the claim which can legitimately be made for it is that it maximizes the individual's success and not his chances of success.

Professor Weckstein's article, so perfectly and scientifically impartial in substance and so generously sympathetic in tone, contains amongst its wealth of argument one more point on which I feel bound to offer a somewhat different view. He says:

Next, consider the argument that the probability number assigned to the occurrence of an outcome must be changed whenever the number of outcomes considered changes, and that this adjustment of probability numbers has no analogy in the psychology of a decision-maker. This happens to the probability statements because of the formal requirement that the sum of the probabilities of all the possible outcomes equals one, and the probability of any particular uncertain event be expressed as a fraction of certainty.

When Professor Weckstein speaks of the '*formal* requirement' that probabilities should sum to unity, I feel that his words convey a suggestion that there might be some escape from this requirement without abandoning the essence of the notion of probability. Surely this is not so? Once we abandon the *distributional* character of probability we are in an essentially different scheme of thought, the conception of a non-distributional uncertainty variable of which potential surprise is an example.

XIII

UNCERTAINTY IN SUM

All the argument of these chapters on uncertainty has been concerned with thoughts or feelings. These are of necessity the thoughts or feelings of some one person in his particular circumstances of some one moment. By uncertainty we mean something in the character or in the circumstances of such thoughts: uncertainty is for us subjective. Uncertainty gives room or scope for the ordering, in a particular respect, of suggested answers to some question, or for the assigning to them of status in a particular respect. What is this respect? We define it by referring to a state of mind whence it is absent, to wit, the individual's feeling that some answer is *certainly wrong*. Other answers than this one can be more or less remote from its status of 'certainly wrong'. The degrees of this remoteness we wish to express as values of a variable, and our central task in these chapters has been to choose between two forms which this variable might take, the distributional and the non-distributional.

Much the greatest difficulty we seemed to encounter in writing these chapters lay in formulating our task, in reaching such a statement of it as we have just given. For we had to indicate in what respect a status is to be accorded to suggested answers, without using any term which might seem to favour a distributional or a non-distributional variable as the measure of this status. On this account it was not permissible to speak of the probability, likelihood or possibility of a suggested answer, and we were driven to a construction or indirect seizing of the idea. The word uncertainty itself has given us pause on similar ground, for it can convey either the mind's consciousness of ignorance and its consequent willingness to entertain an array of diverse hypotheses, or alternatively the mind's hesitant contact with any hypothesis which either has not a complete case in its favour or has some partial case against it. The diversity of the entertained hypotheses as a body or the poor attack of individual hypotheses against the mind's scepticism are two interpretations corresponding respectively to the phrases we used above: '...something in the circumstances (*videlicet*, the presence of a multitude of other hypotheses) or in the character (*videlicet*, the implausibility of a hypothesis itself),' and corresponding also to the two notions, distributional and non-distributional variable.

A distributional uncertainty variable takes the number unity to stand for the idea 'certainly right'. When an answer which is looked on as 'certainly right' can be seen as an assemblage of parts, each part seeming necessary to the completeness and the rightness of the answer, no one of these parts by itself can claim the number *unity* as the measure of its status, each must be content with a proper fraction. But since the assemblage of all the parts yields a subjectively 'complete', 'certainly right' answer, logical consistency requires that the summation of all the fractions shall come to unity, and this requirement imposes itself whether the parts are few or many and regardless of the status which it is desired to accord to any one of them. Thus the status of a suggested answer to some question, the remoteness of this answer from the status of 'certainly right' or 'certainly wrong', is a thing different in nature, when it is to be indicated by a distributional uncertainty variable, from status or remoteness indicated by a non-distributional uncertainty variable. For let us suppose that all the answers which have been suggested to some question are to be accorded equal status. Then this status will be lower, remoteness from 'certainly right' will be greater for each of them, the more of them there are. This is the inescapable logical consequence of using a distributional uncertainty variable. Do we desire this built-in characteristic?

In order that a distributional uncertainty variable may be used, it is necessary that the list of suggested answers should be *specific* and *complete*: specific, in the sense that every one of the answers must find a place in a system or taxonomic structure (even if this means no more than that they are values of a variable) and have this place or role properly stated, in equal detail and precision for each answer; complete, in the sense that there must be no *residual hypothesis* represented by some such form of words as '...some other answer', and meaning simply that the decision-maker's existing list of specific answers is liable to be added to by further, as yet completely unspecifiable, hypotheses.

The residual hypothesis is a closed box; but even if its contents cannot be discerned and distinguished from each other, cannot the share or proper fraction assignable to it be arrived at by observation of the statistical relative frequencies of the other, specific, hypotheses, the sum of these relative frequencies, each expressed as a proper fraction, or probability, being deducted from unity to give the aggregate probability of the hypotheses still hidden in the residual hypothesis? Cannot the decision-maker thus arrive at a frequency-distribution, or probability-distribution, which is valid though not fully detailed? One of our most basic assertions concerns the insidious fallacy concealed in this approach. This fallacy consists in confusing *substantial knowledge* afforded by a frequency-table about the outcome of a *divisible experiment*, with the assigning of a grade, or status, or judgement of remoteness from certainty, to each of a number of rival answers to a *non-divisible* experiment. It is as though one were unable to see any difference between the dried leaves of the tea-bush inside a casket of tea, on the one hand, and the marks on a label outside the casket saying 'Finest Quality' on the other. The frequency-table says what *will* happen, in an experiment *taken as a whole* consisting in many instances of a type of trial or performance. Each value of an uncertainty-variable says how difficult it is to use some particular hypothesis as the basis of an imaginative experience.

How important a part in life is played by non-divisible experiments? They are unavoidable, for no experiment can be repeated which by its nature necessarily destroys a condition essential to it; and no divisible experiment can be built up of trials or performances which cannot be repeated. Such *self-destructive experiments* are exemplified by every deed which will leave human knowledge and human memory of experience different from what it is; and what deed will not?

The status of an hypothesis we have defined as its relation to some standard which is itself a judgement made by an individual, such as 'certainly right' or 'certainly wrong', a judgement belonging to a class which is in some sense the same class for all individuals. This status we suppose the individual to indicate to himself by assigning to it a value of a variable. This variable may be distributional or non-distributional, but the kind of status indicated (the nature of the relationship to some standard and the identity of that standard) will not be the same in the two cases. We found that 'certainly right' was a suitable basis for the notion of a distributional uncertainty variable, since the whole or total itself, which is to be distributed, represents this status. A zero value of the distributional uncertainty variable represents 'certainly wrong'. Thus the kind of status we can indicate by a distributional uncertainty variable is that whose range stretches between 'certainly wrong' and 'certainly right'. In practice the only concrete example to be found of a distributional uncertainty variable is that of subjective, *a priori* probability. While various non-distributional uncertainty variables might perhaps be found, one in particular appears to have advantages. In contrast to the distributional case, its highest values represent 'certainly wrong'. Its least values, however, represent not 'certainly right' but 'perfectly possible'.

What has been regarded by a person as 'perfectly possible' is to him, when it does occur, perfectly unsurprising. An event which he had dismissed as wholly impossible will cause him the greatest surprise he is capable of experiencing. Between these two extremes, however, we say that there are other degrees, of mild, moderate, considerable, etc., surprise, and we define *degrees of possibility* as the subjective judgements which, if made by some individual about specified kinds of events, would, in case those events occurred, cause him those degrees of surprise. Such judgements can therefore be expressed in terms of *potential surprise*, and we think of a bi-unique correspondence between degrees of possibility and degrees of potential surprise, according to which zero potential surprise stands for perfect possibility and the absolute maximum of potential surprise stands for perfect impossibility, each of these being judgements made by an individual.

For any individual, a thing is possible so long as he is unaware of any incompatibility between that thing and the texture of the natural and the human world, and between that thing and the existing situation of that world with its not unlimited speeds of change. But there is no logical or formal limit to the diversity of things which can all simultaneously seem thus to be able to accommodate themselves to the nature and situation of the world, even when these things are mutually contradictory and mutually exclusive: possibility or potential surprise is non-distributional.

The usefulness of our concept of potential surprise has been questioned on the ground that probability and potential surprise can be mapped on each other. If such a mapping is to be bi-unique, it is inevitably misleading. What probability represents perfect possibility? Not a probability of one, for this stands for 'certainly right', and we cannot strongly enough insist that 'certainly right' and 'perfectly possible' are two ideas wholly distinct and remote from each other. But what particular probability, less than unity, has any special claim to represent perfect possibility? If *any* and *every* probability greater than zero can correspond to perfect possibility, which in terms of potential surprise can be stated only as zero potential surprise, then any bi-unique mapping of probability on potential surprise is purely arbitrary and artificial. This contention does not in the smallest degree conflict with the idea that recorded statistical frequencies may provide part or the whole of the basis of a judgement of possibility.

Potential surprise is a measure of possibility. Possibility of what? Possibility for the individual to attain some imaginative experience. Such experiences are inhibited or dimmed by a barrier of disbelief, of imperfect acceptance of the congruity of the imagined situation or chain of situations with what he knows of the nature and current state of the world. The part played by an uncertainty-variable in our scheme is as a measure of the strength of this barrier in certain directions, and a means of indicating which these directions are, so as to make possible a statement of the constraint subject to which the individual can create his imagined future. We therefore measure possibility in the reverse sense, by a measure of *disbelief* which stands at zero to indicate perfect possibility.

PART III

ASCENDANCY

XIV

A BASIC MODEL

Hitherto we have considered only one aspect of a hypothesis: the judgement made of it by an individual in comparison with such judgements as 'certainly right' or 'certainly wrong'. Were the question, to which various hypotheses are proposed as answers, asked purely out of idle or scientific curiosity, that aspect might be the only one that mattered. But when the question is: How shall I be affected by the consequences of such-and-such a proposed course of action of my own? it is plain that one suggested answer may name consequences which I more desire or more dislike than those of another answer. The decision-maker, imaginatively contemplating the suggested consequences of some one action-course, will be able to arrange these various hypotheses in order of his own preference from worst to best. Thus he would, in general, have at any rate two orderings of his hypothetical outcomes of any one course of action: the order according to possibility, and the order according to desirability. But before we consider this general case, let us consider the special one where it happens that all the hypotheses in an exhaustive set are accorded equal and perfect possibility. *Possibility* can then play no part in any selective act by which some hypotheses might attract special attention to themselves, and if any do so it must be in virtue of their desirability or undesirability in the eyes of the decision-maker. Now this exhaustive set of hypotheses is the answer he gives himself to the question: If I do so-and-so, what can happen as a consequence? The aspects of this answer that practically matter to him, however, are its *worst* and its *best* possible outcomes; and the question how possible these outcomes are does not arise, for, by our assumption, all hypotheses which he does not completely exclude as impossible are looked on as equally and perfectly possible. It follows, as I would claim, that the best and the worst hypotheses, the extremes in the desirability-undesirability ordering, are the only ones to which he need pay any attention. Why be concerned because the proposed action can bring moderate misfortune, if it can equally possibly bring great misfortune? It is the latter idea which will count with the decision-maker and preoccupy his mind. It is the great misfortune only that he need consider. Again, who will settle his hopes on a small prize when a big one can be brought equally within apparent reach by accepting, as the price of both these hopes, exposure to one and the same worst possibility? And again, what defence or comfort against the thought of 'perfectly possible' disaster, when exposure to that threat has been accepted as the price of high hope, is afforded by the thought that moderate and unexciting successes are also perfectly possible?

If the reader finds these propositions alien and hard to accept, I believe the reason is his training in the use of a distributional uncertainty variable, one by its nature incapable of handling the notion of possibility. When many different things are all equally and perfectly possible, it is the brilliant and the black *extremes* which hold our thoughts.

Thus we reach the simplest form of the idea of focus-hypotheses able, amongst all the hypotheses which spring up in answer to some question, to attract to themselves exclusively the decision-maker's attention. In this simplest model, all relevant hypotheses are perfectly possible. But if we suppose that at some other level of possibility, some level of potential surprise between zero and the absolute maximum, there is another set of hypotheses ordered, like the 'perfectly possible' set, amongst themselves according to desirability or undesirability, the same argument as before will apply: amongst this semi-possible set it will be the extreme members, the most brilliant imagined success and the worst imagined misfortune, that will exclusively command attention. We may continue to elaborate the model by as many similar steps as we like, and each possibility-rank will provide a pair of extremes capturing all the attention given to that particular rank of hypotheses.

In order to discuss conveniently the problem which the last paragraph has raised, that of the relation between hypotheses of different degrees of possibility, we must confine ourselves for the moment either to hypotheses of 'success' or to hypotheses of 'misfortune'; and further, we must leave aside for the moment the question of what test divides hypotheses into these two classes. Let us then assume for the time being that amongst the hypotheses standing on any one possibility level or rank, we are concerned only with those representing some degree of success. What, now, will be the relation to each other of the respective extreme favourable hypotheses of two different levels of possibility or potential surprise? We may suppose that usually a higher level of potential surprise will give scope for a freer flight of fancy, a greater imagined success, so that as we pass from the more possible to the less possible ranks of hypotheses, the extreme member of each rank will have a more interesting *content* or *face-value* but a less interesting degree of believability. Which of two hypotheses, occupying the favourable extremes of two different possibility-ranks, will be the more interesting *on the whole*, which will have the greater power to hold the attention of the decision-maker, will depend on the resultant of the opposed influences of these two differences. One such comparison between two hypotheses will be that between the extreme member, representing the highest imagined success, amongst the 'perfectly possible' hypotheses, and the extreme member of some less than perfectly possible rank. Then it may be that the latter will be the more interesting, and we have the result that in this more sophisticated model as in the simpler one, there will be just one hypothesis 'more interesting' than any other amongst the hypotheses of success, and that this 'most interesting' hypothesis will be one which is assigned more than zero potential surprise. Now we can state our problem. Will the 'most interesting' hypothesis have the power to concentrate the decision-maker's attention and interest upon itself to the exclusion of the other hypotheses each representing the highest success amongst those assigned one or other degree of possibility? Will it thus be able to shut out from his attention not only the 'best' hypothesis of the 'perfectly possible' rank, but also the best hypothesis of every other possibility-rank, both those whose content or face-value is less desired and those whose content is more desired than its own? Will it have this power, that is, in the same way as, in our simpler model where all hypotheses are perfectly possible, the one representing largest success has the power to exclude from attention all the other, equally and perfectly possible, hypotheses of lesser degrees of success? No cogent argument against the supposition that it will have this power to command special and virtually exclusive attention, in contrast to the neglect in which other hypotheses of lesser *or greater* success are left, seems to me so far to have been advanced.

'Or greater' success: we are supposing that the commanding position in the decision-maker's mind attained by one particular hypothesis is due to a resultant of influences: the bright hopes represented by its *content* are dimmed to some degree by the greater-than-zero potential surprise he assigns to it; but taking both these influences together, the result is an *expectation-element* of greater attention-arresting power than arises from other hypotheses, even some representing in their content even higher imagined success, but also carrying higher potential surprise.

We shall pass presently to a model of still greater refinement. But meanwhile we wish to show that, between our simplest and our more sophisticated model, there is less essential difference than might appear. There is nothing in the nature of our suppositions to exclude the notion that two, or several, hypotheses to which different degrees of possibility have been assigned might all be 'equally interesting' to the decision-maker. The lesser possibility of one hypothesis might be precisely compensated by the greater intrinsic brilliance of the imagined success it represented. Thus there is nothing in logic to forbid our supposing the decision-maker, when weighing some proposed course of action, to have in mind many different levels of possibility or of potential surprise, on each of which he orders a number of hypotheses according to their face-value desirability, or undesirability, and so obtains a set of extreme hypotheses each being the most desirable on its own level of possibility; and there is nothing in logic to forbid our supposing that all these extreme hypotheses, *including the one regarded as perfectly possible*, are to him *equally interesting*. Plainly in that case, no one of them can command his exclusive attention; but plainly also, there is no need for him to pay attention to more than one of them, and this one can be the *perfectly possible* hypothesis of most desired face-value. Thus, in a type of case to which there is no logical objection, the simplest model and the more sophisticated model are assimilated to each other.

One more step, and we have the complete basic conception of focus-hypotheses. In many cases it will not happen to be true that all the extreme hypotheses of success, one on each level of possibility, will be equally interesting to the decision-maker. One or other of them will stand out, and this one need by no means be the 'perfectly possible' extreme hypothesis. But it may still be within reach of the decision-maker's imagination to conceive a kind of success which, *if* it seemed to him perfectly possible, would be neither more nor less interesting than the actual 'most interesting' hypothesis. This specially conceived kind of success will be less brilliant, less attractive in face-value, than the actual 'most interesting' one, for it is supposed to have perfect rather than imperfect possibility, zero rather than greater than zero potential surprise. By thus supposing the decision-maker to transform his actual set of hypotheses into an *equivalent perfectly possible set* we enable our simplest model, in effect, to serve all our analytical purposes.

But we are not yet ready to establish this latter proposition completely. We must turn first to consider the hypotheses of misfortune. By the 'interestingness' of a hypothesis, as will be already evident to the reader, we do not mean the pleasure it gives in being contemplated, even when this pleasure is looked on as compounded of face-value and plausibility or possibility, but, in sharp distinction we mean as it were power of fascination. One can be fascinated by what is dangerous and threatening as well as by what is beautiful or pleasurable. Just as in our simplest model we regarded both extremes of the desirability-undesirability ordering as having special power to claim attention, and indeed as being the only two hypotheses in that ordering to which the decision-maker would pay any attention, so in the more sophisticated model we look for two *focus-hypotheses*, one of them a hypothesis of success and the other of misfortune. A few pages earlier we expressly confined our discussion to hypotheses of success, but we could equally well have confined it to hypotheses of misfortune and developed for them an argument precisely reflecting the one about success-hypotheses which we have just set out.

One further variant of this chapter's line of thought can find its appropriate place before we end. Suppose the decision-maker were able on any ground to regard one particular level of possibility or potential surprise as the most relevant or the best adapted to release him a little, but without too great an

exposure to the dangers of his ignorance, from the bonds of
'perfect possibility'. Then he might conceivably treat this
possibility-rank as the only one that mattered, and its two
extreme elements, one of success and one of misfortune, would
then be his focus-hypotheses for the action-course in question.
We are here introducing, however, an idea of the ranking of
possibility-ranks according to 'relevance' in some sense, an idea
standing somewhat outside our main scheme of thought.

We end this chapter by formally defining two concepts which
have already been named in the course of the foregoing. By
expectation-element we mean the combination of a suggested
answer to some question about the future, and the degree of
potential surprise assigned, at some one moment, to this hypothesis by some individual, whom we shall refer to in this capacity
as the decision-maker. By *focus-hypothesis* or *focus-element* we
mean an element, in the sense we have just given to this word,
which has some special and extraordinary power to command
and concentrate upon itself the decision-maker's attention. In
what we shall present as a centrally important group of cases,
there will be two focus-elements, one selecting itself from
amongst the hypotheses of success and the other from amongst
the hypotheses of misfortune.

We turn now to the essential problem raised by our division
of hypotheses into those representing success and those representing misfortune. By what test is this division to be made? Is
any such division, in any absolute sense, justifiable at all, or are
hypotheses merely more desirable or less desirable than others,
without being positively desirable or undesirable? For the
mathematician there is no such thing as a large number, but,
simply, some numbers are larger than others. Is a parallel
statement true for us? Or can we say that *for a particular person,
at a particular moment*, the division into the two classes is meaningful? This we examine in the next chapter.

XV

THE NEUTRAL OUTCOME

If we are to speak of outcomes as positively good or bad, and not simply as better or worse than each other, there must be some imaginable outcome which the particular individual, in his particular circumstances of some named moment, would consider to be neither good nor bad but *neutral*. In calling an outcome good or bad, we mean simply that it is so judged by the individual. A 'good' outcome, if in anticipation of our following argument we allow ourselves this expression, is one whose occurrence in actuality or in imagination gives him pleasure, it is one whose occurrence is desired; a bad outcome is one which gives him pain and whose non-occurrence is desired. Instead of pleasure and pain we shall often speak indifferently of enjoyment and distress, and of the outcomes which engender these as success or misfortune, or as favourable or hurtful, or as making the individual better off or worse off. There is a valuable purpose to be served by ranging side by side these many expressions with their essential common thread of meaning with various shades and associations. For by referring to particular shades of meaning and comparing these with our own feelings we may be able to solve some of the semantic-psychic problems which lie at the heart of our subject.

The argument we have advanced in the preceding chapter requires the assumption that hypotheses about the outcome of any action shall be able to be divided, by the decision-maker, into those that are hurtful or disliked and those that are successful and desired. Without this division we could not argue for two focus-hypotheses, one of success and one of misfortune, since if, for example, the perfectly possible outcomes when ordered according to desirability ran merely from less desirable to more desirable without any anchorage in a neutral outcome, we could claim at most that *either* the most desired *or* the least desired hypothesis would concentrate the decision-maker's attention upon itself, but we could not tell which of them would do this and we could not claim that *both* would have greater power to do so than the interior hypotheses of the ordering. The idea that the hypotheses, although they can be ordered amongst themselves, cannot each be looked on as either distressing or pleasurable in itself, arises I think from neglect of the fact that judgements concerning them are not made by a detached, impartial and uninvolved observer but by the individual who will himself be affected by the outcome and who makes such a judgement at some particular moment in his special circumstances of that moment. We shall argue that the idea that success and misfortune are merely relative to each other is contrary to common experience. Success and misfortune, as hypotheses about the future, are relative not to each other but to the individual's experience and knowledge of the past. At this threshold of our discussion, however, our concern is to admit that the idea of focus-hypotheses depends upon that of a neutral outcome, and this notion we proceed to develop.

The neutral outcome, neither enjoyable nor distressing to imagine, will surely be one which does not represent a decisive and dramatic departure from the position which the individual conceives himself to be in at his viewpoint. It is one which offers no change, either of improvement or deterioration, from his existing situation. An outcome will be neutral if the decision-maker judges that a shift in his ascription of possibility to it, from high to low potential surprise, or even from certainty of its impossibility to certainty of its unique truth, would leave him feeling neither better nor worse off than he does before this shift of belief. All three of these foregoing statements, which we mean to be essentially equivalent to each other, involve the notion of a present or 'viewpoint' position, a point of departure, an actual, attained and existing situation. It is the inevitable presence of such an actuality, as an inescapable and obvious standard of comparison, which forms the basis of our claim that outcomes are good or bad and not merely better or worse than each other. An outcome can seem such as would place a man in a worse position *than he is in now*, or in a better position than he is in now, and it is by comparison with this present actuality that the outcome will be judged positively good or positively bad. To claim that the idea of neutral outcome is meaningful is to claim no more than that a man can assess his actual viewpoint situation and compare it with other imaginable situations.

Let us pause for a moment to assess the present stage of the argument. We have in effect now given *two* definitions of neutral outcome. The first says that a neutral outcome is one whose occurrence gives the decision-maker neither pleasure nor pain to imagine. The second says that a neutral outcome is one judged by him to represent no change from his actual situation. The claim that these two definitions are compatible must rest on an appeal to the reader's own intuition or introspection. So also in the main must the first of two propositions which we claim to be true of a neutral outcome defined in either of these ways. This is, that such an outcome will seem to the decision-maker less interesting, it will have less power to arrest his attention, than any hypothetical outcome the imagining of which does positively please or distress him. When is life boring, insipid, unstimulating and lack-lustre? When it offers neither hope nor threat, when there is nothing, either of positive good to be attained or of positive bad to be avoided, that seems worthy of exertion, sacrifice and risk. The second of our two propositions involves something of a paradox and in itself throws light on the nature of the idea of neutral outcome.

We have suggested that a neutral outcome will be one which the decision-maker deems little more or less desirable than his viewpoint situation. This proposition asserts nothing as to whether there is any particular outcome, neutral in this sense, which he looks on as possible in any degree. At some named moment, in his particular circumstances of that moment, might he not consider all neutral outcomes to be impossible, might he not consider it certain that, for example, a great improvement in his fortunes was about to occur? Here is the critical and key point of the matter. We have to ask: a great improvement, *compared with what*? It cannot be denied that great shifts in a man's fortunes can suddenly take place. But what do these shifts consist in? Shifts *of what*? They are shifts of *his interpretation* of his apparent circumstances. New items of knowledge or belief may be added to those known circumstances, to cause such change of understanding or of evaluation. But essentially his fortunes change when his ideas about them change. There is a sense in which a man who discovers a gold field on his farm is not, objectively, richer after the discovery than before. No visible change may have taken place on his land, but simply the knowledge has come to him that a gold-bearing reef has been traced on the neighbouring farm right up to the edge of his own territory, into which it certainly continues. What, then, has changed? In what does his new-found sense of wealth consist? His expectations have changed, there now open before him action-courses which will realize great wealth. But the fact that this wealth is not yet realized does not keep him in a state and feeling of poverty.

Let us draw the implications of this train of thought for the concept of neutral outcome. We asked in the preceding paragraph whether a man might not on occasion think that no happening was possible which would constitute for him a neutral outcome; whether he might not suppose that a great improvement was certainly imminent; and we asked: a great improvement compared with what? The answer plainly is: a great improvement compared with what, until just now, he *had* believed his circumstances to be, *not* a great improvement on what he *now* believes them to be, for his present belief and evaluation of his position necessarily takes account of his expectations. It follows that not only do we define a neutral outcome as one which would make little change in the decision-maker's viewpoint situation, so far as its advantages, the degree of wealth, freedom, opportunity in a wide sense that it represents, are concerned, but we also assert that, reciprocally, any change of his system of expectations will affect his assessment of his viewpoint situation, so that if new and brilliant possible happenings come to seem within reach, the viewpoint situation itself will thereby be changed and made more agreeable.

The double link between, on the one hand, the decision-maker's viewpoint situation, and on the other the set of imagined situations which seem to him perhaps attainable from it, throws once more into relief the subjectiveness of the entities we are discussing. As a basis of his decision and action, a person's viewpoint situation is what he considers it to be, it has the character in detail which he imagines in it, it exists in his mind. The double link itself is complex. In one direction it is a matter of definition; we define the neutral outcome as the emergence of a situation which in at least one respect resembles the viewpoint situation; in the respect, namely, that the individual judges them equally agreeable and desirable. In the other

direction the link consists in the psychic impossibility of a viewpoint situation which is very much less agreeable and desirable
than the least agreeable and desirable one that seems perfectly
possible of attainment from that starting-point; and we can
equally say, the impossibility of a viewpoint situation which is
very much more agreeable than the most agreeable of those
which seem perfectly, or fairly, attainable from it.

The upshot of our discussions is as follows. Any happening or
course of events which suggests itself to the decision-maker as
an answer to his question: what consequences for me will flow
from such-and-such an action of mine? and which is neutral in
the several mutually compatible senses that we have indicated,
will be assigned by the decision-maker a low or zero degree of
potential surprise. Under the assumptions which constitute our
so-called basic model, where hypotheses of the outcome of any
action-course are supposed to be divided merely into the possible
and the impossible, the foregoing conclusion can be given its
strongest form, that any outcome which is neutral will carry
zero potential surprise. In this basic model, a state of mind in
which the decision-maker looked upon all neutral outcomes as
impossible and, accordingly, felt certain that his proposed action
could not fail to transform his viewpoint situation into something altogether better (or altogether worse) would be self-
contradictory; for that viewpoint situation takes its colour
largely from what it can lead to, and if what it can lead to has,
at worst, a particular degree of desirability, the neutral outcome
itself cannot have a much lesser desirability. Let us take it that
such degrees of desirability can not only be compared with each
other and ordered into greater and less, but that the *difference*
between any two such degrees can be compared with the difference between any other two degrees and these differences
themselves ordered. We can then assign to distances marked
along an axis the meaning of differences between degrees of
desirability of hypothetical outcomes of some action: a larger
distance will mean a greater difference. Points on the axis will
correspond to various hypothetical outcomes and we shall draw,
in Fig. xv 1, a segment of this axis containing all the points
belonging to hypotheses looked on as *possible*, all other hypotheses being looked on by the decision-maker as *impossible*, and
being represented by points on another straight line parallel to

the axis and separated from it by a gap indicating the distinction between the possibility and impossibility classes, or between the assignment of zero potential surprise and the absolute maximum of potential surprise.

In the resulting Fig. XV 1, where the desirability-axis is labelled G and the only two degrees of potential surprise recognized in the basic model are labelled $y = 0$ and $y = \bar{y}$ we

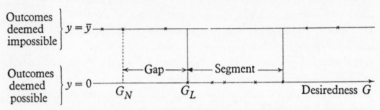

Outcomes deemed impossible $\Big\}\ y = \bar{y}$

Outcomes deemed possible $\Big\}\ y = 0$

$\leftarrow$ Gap $\rightarrow$ $\leftarrow$ Segment $\rightarrow$

G_N G_L Desiredness G

× stands for some outcome, deemed possible (if on G-axis) or impossible (if on line $y = \bar{y}$).

G_L stands for the least desirable amongst *possible* outcomes,

Fig. XV 1

are able to show a point G_N carrying the absolute maximum of potential surprise, that is, looked on as impossible, and representing a far less desirable outcome than the least desirable, G_L, of the 'possible' outcomes. When G_N is claimed to be the neutral outcome, its separation from G_L on the 'undesirable' side constitutes, we assert, a contradiction.

In chapters XVI and XVII we shall begin to develop a refined model where this contradiction, as we shall there show, would take a somewhat different form.

XVI

CARDINALITY

That he can *order* the intensities of the feelings, actual and imagined, by which he responds to an actual experience or judges that he would respond to one which he deems possible, is the only power of comparison or quantification of his responses that we need assume in the decision-maker as the basis of our argument of chapter xiv. That chapter contains (as we think) a self-sufficient core of our treatment of 'choice in face of bounded uncertainty'. Nonetheless, we should like the decision-maker to be able to say, in perfect generality: When I compare the feeling induced by stimulus A with that from stimulus B, the difference between them seems to contain so and so many steps, equal amongst themselves and each equal also to each of those I use in comparing my responses to stimulus C and to stimulus D. For if we could suppose him able to say this, we could bring a much greater refinement into our treatment of problems, and make a much greater diversity of problems amendable to analysis, than the argument of chapter xiv by itself allows. In the foregoing brief synopsis of the task and motive of this chapter we have, as it were, laid duck-boards across a conceptual quicksand by means of expressions which now need to be made precise.

We have defined an expectation as an imagined situation or event labelled with a particular calendar date and looked on as a possible sequel to some particular immediately available act. When, taking a further step in the decision-making process, the individual imagines himself committed to that act and thus is able to experience *by anticipation* some feeling connected with its imagined sequel, we have the special type of feelings whose compared intensities are relevant for the decision. It is the intensities of these feelings by anticipation, namely, the feelings of enjoyment and distress by anticipation and of potential surprise, which we must, in especial, suppose the decision-maker to be able to order, or to compare in some more sophisticated way. We must likeways suppose him able to order, or compare more subtly, the attention-commanding power of an expectation element composed of a face-value and the potential surprise associated with it. So much for what things are to be ordered or to be measured. What, now, do we need to mean, and what can we mean, by measurement of these things, and in what further freedom will the power to measure, rather than merely to order, the intensities of feelings result? This last question can illuminatingly be inverted: What operational or manipulative power do we ultimately seek, in desiring to *count equal steps between* any pair of intensities?

In Part II, although we spoke of potential surprise as a function of the face-value, or of the desiredness, of an hypothesis or expectation, we represented this connection by discrete points in a Cartesian plane and not by a continuous curve. We might, nonetheless, have drawn such a curve if we had been willing to suppose that the decision-maker's discriminable and orderable levels of feeling were infinitely many within the meaningful range of potential surprise and that of desiredness and covered densely the whole of each of these ranges. But so long as we suppose that the discriminated levels of any kind of feeling are merely orderable, we shall still be precluded from attaching any meaning to the relative steepnesses of such a curve at different points and to the convexity or concavity of its segments. Yet it is reasonable to ask whether such relative steepnesses and the resulting convexity or concavity might not be given some meaning which would add to the power of our tool: we wish to make sense and use of the particular shape which, in actually putting on paper a potential surprise curve or a ϕ-curve, we are bound to give these curves. It is for this that we need to be able to count equal steps from one level of feeling to another.

The notion of equal steps by which we can suppose that the decision-maker, examining his own thoughts, might proceed from any level to any other level of feeling, counting these steps in each case so as to turn the discriminability of the two levels of each pair from a mere unquantified divorce into a measured interval, seems to involve three questions:

(i) What is to be meant by equality of the steps?

(ii) How are we to suppose that the decision-maker recognizes and establishes this equality for himself in any concrete case?

(iii) On what principle are the steps to be subdivided so as to achieve measurement to any required degree of approximation?

In discussing what we are to mean by equality amongst the steps or units of feeling, and by what test we are to recognize this equality or its absence, we are freed by the nature of our main problem from a difficulty which confronts, for example, the economist seeking to cardinalize utility for the purpose of an exterior dynamics; for unlike the economist, we are not concerned with the 'constancy through time' of our step or unit. Our scheme of thought is about the solitary moment and cannot, by its basic pre-suppositions, be about 'several such moments at once'. Thus we are unaffected by any empirical findings of the detached observer which declare that individuals appear inconsistent when their judgement or behaviour at one date is compared with that at another date. Still more plainly, we are not concerned with inter-personal comparisons. We have, indeed, no escape from accepting the decision-maker's own judgement of what constitutes equality of any two steps, but we can show that he has available a unifying principle which unites into one thought his judgements of steps widely separated in his ladder of measurement of any variable.*

Let there be two distinct intensities A and E of some feeling or psychic response in the most general sense. Then if we can suppose the decision-maker to hold these in mind within his moment while he compares with them a third intensity B, he may be able to say that B is 'nearer to' A than to E or vice versa. If he can thus compare *differences* between intensities, as well as the intensities themselves, and judge that the 'distance' from A to B is greater or less than the distance from B to E, then if an intensity C is presented to him such that he cannot, in spite of his assumed power to discriminate in general between a larger and a smaller difference, declare the distance A to C to be greater, or less, than the distance C to E, we can claim, as a starting-point, that the whole interval A to E has now been divided into two *equal* sub-intervals.

---

* This conception of repeated halving first came to my notice in the classic article by Professor W. E. Armstrong called 'The Determinateness of the Utility Function' in the *Economic Journal*, vol. XLIX, no. 195 (September 1939). In writing that article he was unaware of a similar suggestion made by Professor Ragnar Frisch.

The idea has since been widely discussed by Sir Dennis Robertson and others.

So far as the meaning and principle of this *ordering of dif-ferences* is concerned, the intensities of feeling, between which the differences or distances appear, can be supposed to be either experienced or anticipated; for our purpose it is evidently feelings by anticipation, that is, by imagination of consequences, supposed possible, of an act to which the decision-maker imagines himself committed, that are relevant.

Now if the distinctness of two arbitrary levels or intensities of feeling can thus be given the meaning of an interval and this interval can be divided into two equal parts, each of these parts can be similarly divided into what will be two quarters of the initial interval; each of these quarters into two eighths and so on either indefinitely or down to some least discriminable difference. The ladder thus established is a unity in somewhat the same sense as a scale of physical length, or physical mass, dependent on a unique, identified specimen of length or mass. The unity is achieved in a different way, but there is no denying that if we define as equal the two sub-intervals, A to C and C to E, and if F, say, is in the same sense equidistant from A and C, and G is equi-distant from C and E, then the sub-sub-intervals A to F and G to E, and so on and so on, will in our sense be equal to each other. We have thus achieved a ladder of equal steps against which any arbitrary difference or gap between intensities can be 'offered up' (in the carpenter's sense) and measured. Moreover, we have at the same time answered our third question about a means of subdivision.

In admitting that there may be a least discriminable dif-ference betwen levels of feeling, we are in effect admitting that psychic variables of the kind we are seeking to use may not be strictly continuous. We shall, nonetheless, follow the examples of economics and other moral sciences in discussing their mutual relations in terms of the differential calculus. Neither popula-tion nor money values are indefinitely subdivisible, yet demo-graphers and economists treat them as if they were. So shall we treat our intervals of feeling.

In the matter of comparing amongst themselves the values of a variable, the primary distinction is between a variable whose values can merely be placed in order from less to greater and a variable whose values can be said to be separated by so and so many units of distance. This distinction is of concern to economists and they refer to the former class of variables as ordinal and to the latter class as cardinal. Within the cardinal class there are again several distinctions. Some economists have noted a kind of variable where differences, that is, distances, between levels or intensities of some psychic response (for example, utility) can be apprehended and can be ordered, but where, in their view, *differences of differences* cannot be ordered, so that it would not, presumably, be possible to get far in the discussion of these variables by means of the differential calculus; and where also there appears to be no question of a unit which could be counted, added and so on. However, Professor Ragnar Frisch and Mr W. E. Armstrong appear to us to have shown (independently of each other) that if differences are orderable we can construct a scale of equal steps which can themselves be chosen as small as we like, so that to any desired approximation such a variable is measurable in an ordinary sense of the word, though still, of course, in a manner quite private and personal to the individual concerned. In an extreme form of measurability a unique natural unit, and also a unique absolute zero, impose themselves. The unit of population, for example, is one person. But this kind of measurability really amounts to count-ability, and there is in these cases neither need nor possibility of sub-division of the unit (save perhaps in statistical averaging). Where, as with physical length, indefinite subdivision is not at odds with the meaning of the thing to be measured, we have the true and central meaning of measurability and we are also quite precluded from claiming pre-eminence for any special unit. The unit can in such cases be anything we like, and any measurement expressed in one unit can be re-expressed in another by merely doing a multiplication sum and, if the zeros of the two scales are different, adding a constant. Such an adjustment is called a linear transformation, and thus we say that length, mass and so on are variables measurable up to a linear transformation. In the earlier part of this chapter we claim to have shown, by the device of Frisch and of Armstrong, that such measurability is also available to our decision-maker and to us when, as a kind of *internal* observer, we place our-selves inside his mind and his temporal circumstances and identify ourselves with him.

The variables which, in order to replace our basic model of

chapter xiv by a sophisticated model, we wish to treat as measurable, are four: the face-value of a hypothesis, its desiredness, the potential surprise associated with it, and the ascendancy or attention-arresting power of an expectation element composed of a face-value or a degree of desiredness, on the one hand, and of a degree of potential surprise on the other. The use we need to make of the assumption that distances between levels of these psychic responses can be placed beside a scale of equal steps, does not involve us in wanting a unique absolute zero. It is interesting to notice, however, that at any rate with potential surprise not merely one but two 'fixed points', or particular levels whose special meaning is self-evident and, perhaps we might even say, the same for everybody, do offer themselves. For the entire absence of surprise, experienced or potential, is surely a thing recognizable by each person in himself and can be claimed to mean the same to everybody; while the absolute maximum of potential surprise, even if no comparison of the intensities of feeling of different individuals makes any sense, yet surely is the same for everybody in its *interpretation*, namely, absolute disbelief.

XVII

THE CARDINAL POTENTIAL SURPRISE CURVE

In constructing our basic model in chapter XIV we at first supposed the decision-maker to be able merely to classify the hypothetical outcomes, which he had conceived of for some action open to him, as either possible or impossible. Only the 'possible' outcomes were relevant to his task of choosing between this and other available actions, and all the 'possible' outcomes stood on the same footing as each other in their degree of possibleness. Later we supposed him able to discriminate between the degree of possibleness of this hypothesis and that, and thus to arrange the 'possible' hypotheses in a number of ranks of which he could say that the hypotheses in one such rank were more possible than those in another, but had no means of saying by how much they were more possible. In chapter XVI we went on to consider whether possibleness, as represented by potential surprise, could be thought of as a cardinal variable, that is, as measurable on a scale, in a manner having something in common with the way in which we measure physical distance. Having shown why we took this to be legitimate, we further concluded that when a number has been assigned to stand for the absolute maximum, $\bar{y}$, and another for the absolute minimum, y_0, of potential surprise, it is permissible for the purpose of theory to assume that potential surprise can range over all the real numbers between those two. Since we claim that the absolute minimum of potential surprise has a psychic reality and a meaning referable to experience, we stipulate that this absolute minimum shall always be represented by the number zero corresponding to an entire absence of surprise. What particular number is assigned to $\bar{y}$ will then depend on what unit is chosen for the measurement or expression of degrees of potential surprise, and the only constraint upon this choice will be the requirement for convenience that $\bar{y}$, which also we look upon as a psychic reality, shall be represented by a whole number. We shall express the foregoing claims by saying that potential surprise is cardinal up to multiplications by suitable coefficients.

Potential surprise can, of course, only serve a theoretical purpose if it is regarded as a function of some other variable or variables, and our assumption that there is nothing in its own nature to prevent it from ranging over all the real numbers within some interval does nothing to ensure that, in any concrete instance, potential surprise can in any sense be taken to assume all these numerical values. If, for example, the decision-maker has in mind, for some available action, just two distinct hypothetical outcomes, then, at most, just two distinct degrees of potential surprise will be involved. In chapter XIV we did in fact assume that the hypothetical outcomes which the decision-maker conceives of for some one available action are discrete and not infinitely many, and in such a case it is plain that we cannot draw a continuous potential surprise curve with all the analytical convenience that such a curve affords. The question what can best serve in our analytical models as the argument or independent variable on which potential surprises is supposed to depend must now be systematically studied.

By a hypothetical *outcome* of an action we mean in the first place an imagined segment of history; a segment confined indeed on all sides to what is interesting or of concern to the individual whose action it is, and limited by some time-horizon beyond which he does not care to let his fancy stray; but a segment whose description, in all those aspects and in such degrees of exactness as do interest the individual, would in general require a long and difficult verbal or statistical statement, presenting a richly complex picture. It is upon the character of this intricate entity, and its relation with what the individual knows or believes about the state of the world at his temporal viewpoint and about the nature of that world, including its human portion, in its physical and psychical constitution, that his judgements of potential surprise must be based. To present each assigned degree of potential surprise as depending formally on the whole of such a configuration would mean showing it as a function of an immense number of unspecifiable variables. To escape from this there are two routes. Either we can be content to say that the hypothetical outcomes are a finite set of discrete, individual entities, to each of which some degree of potential surprise will be assigned so as to turn each into an expectation-element thenceforward to be treated as a unified thing in itself; or we can seek some one feature present in different degrees in different hypotheses, and able, on the one hand, to epitomize all that character of a hypothesis upon which the potential surprise it earns is ultimately based; and also able, on the other hand, to be treated for analytical purposes as itself the immediate foundation or source of potential surprise judgements, so that the adjudged degrees of potential surprise can be looked on formally as functions of this single variable. In this chapter we are concerned with this second route, and our purpose in exploring it is to gain access in subsequent chapters to a systematic formal analysis by which insights otherwise difficult can be attained.

One candidate for this role has already been indicated. In chapter xiv we suggested that for any particular individual in his circumstances of a particular moment, there would be some level of desirability, and likewise some level of distastefulness, in the hypotheses he entertains about an action, such that beyond those levels, desirability or distastefulness could only further increase at an increasing sacrifice of possibility. So long as we assume that hypotheses are complex, discrete and individual, it will be convenient, when we need to string them, as it were, along an axis, to use *desiredness-distastefulness* as the label of that axis. But when desiredness-distastefulness itself depends monotonically upon some single other characteristic of the hypotheses, and when the degrees of desiredness-distastefulness of the hypotheses concerning some one action can be represented by numbers which constitute a segment of the real continuum, then it follows that numbers representing that other characteristic can also form such a segment, and we may just as easily use that other characteristic as the label of our axis.

We have justified the search for such 'other characteristic' as a means to a more powerful analysis. But there is one extremely important field of action where the continuous potential surprise curve is naturally appropriate. This is the field of business action in search of profit, and in especial that of decisions about the scale, character and timing of extensions and improvements of physical productive equipment aimed at making the largest possible *investment-gain*. Here the hypothetical outcomes are naturally valued in money terms, or even present themselves direct as sums of money, and this money value seems very exactly to fulfil our requirements for the 'argument' on which potential surprise may be deemed to depend. The hidden structure of enterprise from which, if at all, its success must arise will have itself to be in some directions magnified or hypertrophied, as compared with the mediocre enterprise, if that success is to be extraordinary. Within a certain range each such feature can vary without distinguishing this particular instance of enterprise from a crowd of others. Beyond those ranges both the features themselves, in their exceptional degree, and the success which springs from them, become potentially surprising. Thus the money measure of success can be said to epitomize what underlies that success, and to be the natural independent variable of the potential surprise associated with the various conceivable degrees of that success.

By investment-gain we mean the following. If in the Nth unit time-interval from his viewpoint the decision-maker, should he decide to construct some technically specified industrial plant, would have to make an outlay u as an instalment of its construction-cost, and if a market interest-rate $r(N)$ prevails at that viewpoint for loans of term N, then the cash equivalent at the viewpoint of the sum u deferred N time-units is, say, $s = u\{1 + r(N)\}^{-N}$, and the total discounted construction cost is, say, $S = \sum\limits_{N=1}^{M} s$, where construction will be completed in M unit-intervals. Similarly if, for the Qth interval $(Q > M)$, the decision-maker assumes that the value of the plant's output in that interval will exceed the cost of materials, power, labour and so on to operate the plant in that interval by an amount v whose discounted equivalent is $z = v\{1 + r(Q)\}^{-Q}$ then the total discounted value assumed for the plant is $Z = \sum\limits_{Q=M+1}^{T} z$ and the *investment-gain*, according to this particular set of assumptions or conjectures about construction-cost and future earnings, is $G = Z - S$.

We wish, then, to consider a continuous function $y = y(G)$ connecting cardinal potential surprise y with the (cardinal) amounts G, which are expressed in money value and may be positive, negative or zero, of gain from business ventures. This particular subject-matter or concrete interpretation of our scheme of thought has for us a number of practical conveniences. The idea of a zero gain may well seem to the decision-maker to mean no change from his viewpoint situation, and would thus afford a natural and concrete interpretation of the idea of neutral outcome according to our secondary definition of the latter. Our present more concrete and particularized subject-matter also provides us with more than one practical measure of the compactness or of the diversity of the set of 'perfectly possible', zero potential surprise hypotheses. When this set forms a single, unbroken range of a continuous variable, bounded by two particular values of that variable, we shall speak of it as the *inner range* of hypothetical outcomes. The distance between its two extremes, in comparison with the sum of money proposed to be invested in the venture, will indicate the diversity of the outcomes. We may call this comparison the diversity-ratio. In these terms, our contention is that an enterpriser whose mind is fully open to the character of his basis of expectation will adopt for any venture, where the investible sum is an important proportion of his total funds at command, a potential surprise curve with a large diversity ratio, and that the inner range will extend to considerable 'perfectly possible' losses as well as gains.

When, in chapters XIX and XX, we have developed the notion of focus-outcomes for a continuous cardinal potential surprise curve, we shall be able to define a *standardized diversity ratio* as arising from the comparison of the distance separating standardized focus outcomes* with the investible sum. There is, however, another set of comparisons which for some purposes may be looked on as more relevant, namely, the ratio of the 'loss' segment, and again of the 'gain' segment, of the inner range to the investible sum, or to the enterpriser's total funds at command; and ultimately the ratio of the standardized focus loss to the investible sum, ratios which play a central role in the theory of investment-decisions developed by Mr R. A. D. Egerton in his book on *Investment Decisions under Uncertainty*.

All these constructions, however, depend on our using the cardinality, which we have assumed for potential surprise, to

---

* This notion is described in chapter XX below. See also *Expectation in Economics* (Cambridge University Press, 1st ed. 1949, 2nd ed. 1952), pp. 24, 25.

trace out those portions of the potential surprise curve where hypotheses are regarded as imperfectly or doubtfully possible, that is, where they carry some degree of potential surprise between $y = 0$ and $y = \bar{y}$. Now when a larger hypothetical gain is compared with a lesser one which itself, however, seems to the decision-maker to call for the setting aside of slight obstacles if it is to be imagined as coming true, will he not in general discover more serious obstacles to his acceptance of the larger hypothesis? And as he passes to ever larger hypotheses of gain, will not one at last be reached which cannot be made to seem possible at all, no matter how he fills in by hopeful conjecture the gaps in his knowledge of the existing situation and the nature of the world? Hypotheses of loss will surely also seem increasingly difficult to regard as possible the larger they are, once a particular size is passed, and amongst these also there will be a largest hypothetical loss to which even the slightest possibility can be conceded.

According to these arguments the *y-curve* expressing potential surprise y as a function of positive or negative gain G will for most investment schemes conform to a specific 'shape-type' as follows. On a Cartesian diagram let the horizontal axis serve for values of G and the vertical for y. Then our shape-type will have a horizontal inner segment $y(G) = 0$ stretching on either side of the neutral outcome $G_N = 0$ to distances which are not negligible in comparison with the distance representing the investible sum. Beyond the upper extreme of this segment, that is, the largest positive value of G for which $y(G) = 0$, there will be a positively sloping segment where y and G increase together. This rising horn of the curve will at some finite value $G = \bar{G}$ attain the level $y = \bar{y}$ standing for absolute rejection of the possibility of the hypothesis concerned. Beyond this the curve will run out infinitely along the level $y = \bar{y}$ to indicate that all hypotheses of still larger gain than $\bar{G}$ are quite rejected. There is evidently no reason in general to suppose that the 'loss' branch of the curve will approximate at all closely to a mirror image of the 'gain' branch, but it will again have a sloping segment where y and the *numerical* size of hypothetical losses increase together. Over this segment y will accordingly decrease as G algebraically increases. Again there will be a largest barely possible hypothetical loss or, scarcely to be distinguished from it, a smallest impossible loss $\overline{\overline{G}}$, and beyond that an infinite range of losses all judged impossible. If, finally, we suppose the transition between the segments to be in each case a smooth bend rather than a cusp, we have for the shape-type of y-curves of investment-schemes a profile like a vertical section through an ordinary flat-bottomed enamel basin, as in Fig. XVII 1. Within this shape-type there can evidently be

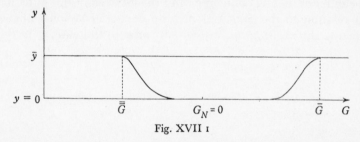

Fig. XVII 1

countless variants and modifications, each, perhaps, constituting a sub-type on its own. An obvious possibility is that the decision-maker may think it perfectly possible that the whole of his stake in the investment-scheme may be lost; or he may think such loss not impossible. In either case the 'loss' branch of the y-curve will be truncated where it meets a perpendicular to the G-axis erected at an amount of loss, say $G = S$, equal to the whole sum to be invested, as in Figs. XVII 2 A and B.

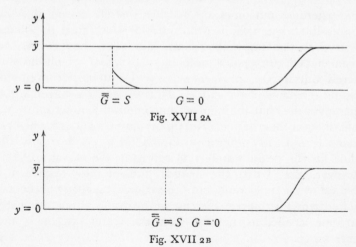

Fig. XVII 2A

Fig. XVII 2B

Our resolve to treat possibility and potential surprise as continuous variables, and accordingly to suppose that the potential surprise curve $y = y(G)$ can decrease and increase between zero and the absolute maximum of potential surprise by sloping segments instead of by jump discontinuities, requires us to modify the argument presented in chapter xv concerning the neutral outcome. An absolute contradiction between the meaning of 'neutral outcome' and the location of this outcome in relation to the potential surprise curves of action-schemes open to the decision-maker will only arise in this case, as in the

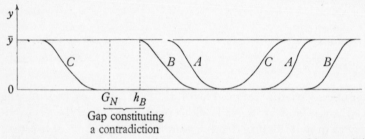

Gap constituting
a contradiction

The decision-maker will not concern himself with action-scheme C because it is manifestly inferior to A and B. If, electing B, he places his neutral outcome G_N to the left of the worst 'barely possible' outcome h_B of B, he will thereby involve himself in a contradiction.

Fig. XVII 3

case where all outcomes are classified merely as 'possible' or 'impossible', when the neutral outcome is assigned by all the y-curves to the 'impossible' class. But when these curves are basin-shaped, impossible outcomes are those which lie not merely outside the inner range, $y = 0$, but outside even the sloping segments of the curves. Thus we can no longer argue unequivocally that the neutral outcome must lie within some at least of the inner ranges of all those y-curves of action schemes, nested within each other as in Fig. XVII 3, which it is worth while for the decision-maker to consider. We can still claim, however, that when the neutral outcome lies outside the greatest of the inner ranges of these curves, the *degree* of contradiction grows with every increase in the distance separating the outcome labelled as 'neutral' from the nearer extreme of the inner range.

XVIII

THE ASCENDANCY FUNCTION

The conception we have now to put forward will not be rightly understood if it is thought of as an alternative account of a procedure by which the decision-maker is supposed to get in touch with some objectively existing future, a future which is there to be found if only our data are assembled with sufficient thoroughness and interpreted with sufficient skill. To postulate the attainability of such a contact with a future having existence and meaning of this kind is to reject completely the whole argument of this book. Briefly to repeat, we say that if such a future is within reach of the mind while that mind is still experiencing the actuality of a differently located moment, then *decision* in our sense has no place in the appropriate analytical scheme of thought. Decision in our non-empty sense, if there is such a thing, is creative. Not everything which can be seen in the happenings of a moment of decision, and in subsequent moments, can be accounted for by reference to earlier moments. Outcomes of *available* actions are not ascertained but created. We are not speaking, be it noted, of the objective recorded outcomes of actions which have been performed. Those actions are not 'available'. An action which can still be chosen or rejected *has no objective outcome*. The only kind of outcome which it can have exists in the imagination of the decision-maker. In choosing one action out of many available, he seeks to experience by imagination, in that highest degree achieved only when decision has committed him to one special action, some outcomes which he can create for that action within the constraint of the seemingly possible, which promise a more satisfying imaginative experience than any that he can create for any of the other actions. The imaginative experience (being the only attainable experience labelled with a future date) which is the most satisfying has, we thus assert, to fulfil the three conditions, first, that what is visualized is in some of its aspects desired for itself; secondly, that it is looked on as in some degree possible; and thirdly, that the action for which these outcomes are created is the one to which the individual's decision has committed him. Since the actions must be judged before the choice amongst them is made, we must suppose that the quality of an imaginative experience that will arise from a committed state of mind can be appraised before the commitment is made. This supposition is surely inescapable if we look upon choice of action as guided, in any sense which the nature of things allows, by the supposed consequences of actions. This, then, is the purpose in pursuit of which we conceive the decision-maker to choose his action. It would be a senseless negation of this purpose to combine into some weighted average the entire set of rival and mutually contradictory possible-seeming outcomes which he can imagine for any given act. His purpose will be served by selection. What we have to put forward in this chapter, in extension of chapter xiv, is an account of the means of that selection.

The account we shall offer proceeds by describing a function connecting the characteristics of an expectation-element with what we shall variously call the *attention-arresting power, interestingness or ascendancy* of that element. These three expressions are to be taken as indifferent names for the same idea. We thus look upon one element as having assigned to it a higher algebraic value of this function than another element. But this is not the end of the matter. The values of the function respectively assigned to this or that expectation-element merely serve to *select* the element or elements upon which the decision-maker's whole attention will be concentrated. A young man is attracted in various ways and degrees by various girls, but he can only experience a genuine and absorbing passion for one of them at a time. It would, perhaps, be conceivable for him to graph the intensity of attraction he felt for each girl as he became acquainted with her, but when he really fell in love, all points of the graph except one would become irrelevant.

What will give to one expectation-element ascendancy over another in the decision-maker's mind so that, if these two elements occupied the field alone, the former would capture and concentrate upon itself his whole attention to the neglect of the other? We say that such ascendancy will be the combined effect of the desiredness or distastefulness of the hypothetical outcome and of the potential surprise associated with it.

A hypothetical outcome loses ascendancy by seeming to the decision-maker less than perfectly possible, it gains ascendancy by representing a high degree of success or of misfortune. For some readers a different language may more acceptably convey this notion. Instead of ascendancy we might call this quality of an expectation-element 'relevance'. For we have argued that in default of knowing what outcome *will* flow from a given proposed action of his own, this knowledge being unattainable except when the question to be answered is trivial, the decision-maker is reduced to asking himself what, at best and at worst, *can* flow from it. 'What can' need not mean what is *perfectly* possible, it should surely mean what is sufficiently possible, when the hypothesis in question is of such-and-such a degree of goodness or badness in itself. And we have shown reason for saying that in face of an array of mutually rival and contra-dictory hypotheses about the consequences of a proposed action, the decision-maker must select rather than meaninglessly aggre-gate or average, since only by selection will he attain a basis of satisfying imaginative enjoyment.

In chapter xiv we proposed for his selective act a theory which requires few special assumptions and can be applied to decisions in many fields. By making this theory somewhat less general in application we can get from it deeper insight into some aspects of the selective act, especially those arising from the decision-maker's expectation of changes of his own expecta-tion. In that earlier chapter the hypothetical outcomes of an available act were looked on as discrete and individual, each consisting in the detailed statement of an imagined course of events or sequence of situations. In that chapter we spoke of the decision-maker as ordering these hypotheses according to their desiredness or their distastefulness, and of performing such ordering within each of a number of classes (of hypotheses) distinguished according to the greater or lesser degree of potential surprise assigned to them. What we did not do was to treat the hypotheses as mere scalar numbers; to treat these numbers as together constituting a segment of the real con-tinuum; to suppose that the variable thus formed, when associated with any given constant degree of potential surprise, could be treated as the sole argument on which the degree of desiredness, and also the degree of interestingness, arrestingness or ascendancy, of hypotheses depended; and to claim for potential surprise a similar quality of being measurable on a scale and of ranging over a continuous segment of the number-axis, as distinct from merely possessing distinguishable degrees of intensity. This last step, however, we took in chapter xvii, while in chapter xvi we had already argued for the legitimacy of treating human responses, such as feelings of enjoyment, distress or surprise, or such as the assigning of potential surprise, as measurable in their level or intensity by each person for himself on a personal and private scale. We shall refer to any set of numbers, employed to indicate the intensity of any such response, as a *psychic variable*, and we shall not feel it necessary, in using this term, to distinguish explicitly between the response itself and its intensity. It remains for us in this chapter and the next to complete, by the rest of the steps we have listed, the construction of a continuous model, as contrasted with our basic model, of the means of selection of expectation-elements.

In thus describing the programme of chapters xviii and xix we have uncovered a question which was already latent in chapter xiv and must now be explicitly dealt with. What is the relation between desiredness and ascendancy of hypotheses? Since we are assuming that desiredness and potential surprise are the only two characteristics of a hypothetical outcome which govern its ascendancy, there is nothing which makes it obligatory or convenient to distinguish at all between the desiredness and the ascendancy of a set of hypotheses all carrying one and the same degree of potential surprise. The need to distinguish between desiredness and ascendancy arises from the need to compare the ascendancy of several hypotheses carrying different degrees of potential surprise, since if these were all equally desired, their ascendancies would be different, and conversely. The units which measure ascendancy can be identified with those which measure desiredness or thought of as distinct from them: nothing hangs upon this. What we maintain is that in whatever units each of the two responses are measured, the relation between these responses or psychic variables, for any *given* associated degree of potential surprise, is one of proportionality.

Already in chapter xvii we have found and resorted to a field of action, important for its own sake, which fulfils the necessary conditions for the construction of a continuous selection-model. We there supposed the decision-maker to be a businessman choosing amongst business ventures and constructing for each of them a curve $y = y(G)$ expressing potential surprise as a continuous function of hypotheses about the gain or loss to be had from the venture, these hypotheses being each expressed in money and being together supposed (by a slight licence in spite of their monetary expression) to form a segment of the real continuum. In what follows we shall often refer to them as 'face-values' of the expectation-elements into which they enter, the effectiveness of these elements in gaining the decision-maker's attention depending not directly or merely on the face-values but on these after allowance has been made for the potential surprise associated with them.

Our purpose now is to set out some assumptions, each possessing, so far as may be, that intuitive cogency that would in former times have earned it the name of axiom, and none of them superfluous to the construction of a workable analytical instrument; and then to deduce from this set of assumptions the chief features of a surface $\phi = \phi(G, y)$ showing the manner in which the ascendancy ϕ of expectation elements depends on their face-value G and potential surprise y in any context which enables all three of these psychic variables to be treated as continuous. Besides deriving the general character of the ϕ-surface from some assumptions about human nature, we wish to show how various shape-types of this surface reflect varieties of human temperament.

ϕ, then, stands for the ascendancy, relevance or interestingness of expectation-elements (G, y). Since we give no meaning to degrees of potential surprise less than zero or greater than the absolute maximum $\bar{y}$, the surface is defined only for the closed interval $0 \leqslant y \leqslant \bar{y}$. Hypothetical outcomes which the decision-maker looks on as impossible will have no interest or relevance for him in his task of decision, and so we can say that ϕ will be zero everywhere on the line $y = \bar{y}$. Since we are in effect assuming that interest or relevance attaches to the *possibility of change* in the decision-maker's situation, and if a given positive or negative gain which in the decision-maker's judgement cannot happen is, for that reason, of no interest, will not a zero gain or loss which can happen be equally of no interest? Change is equally excluded, whether he thinks of change which cannot happen or of no-change which can happen. At first, then, we shall assume that ϕ will be zero also everywhere on the segment $G = 0$, $0 \leqslant y \leqslant \bar{y}$. With these two assumptions, $\phi \equiv 0$ defines a T-shaped figure with its foot at the zero value of G and of y, and its arms running out infinitely along the line $y = \bar{y}$.

Our assumptions that a larger hypothetical gain is more interesting than a smaller one, that a numerically larger hypothetical loss is more interesting (has a heightened concern and relevance for the decision-maker) than a numerically smaller one, and that a more possible hypothesis is more interesting than a less possible one, can for the purpose of our next investigations be summarized:

$$\frac{\partial \phi}{\partial G} > 0 \quad \text{for } G > 0, \tag{i}$$

$$\frac{\partial \phi}{\partial G} < 0 \quad \text{for } G < 0, \tag{ii}$$

$$\frac{\partial \phi}{\partial y} < 0 \quad \text{for } 0 \leqslant y \leqslant \bar{y} \text{ and for } G \neq 0. \tag{iii}$$

The basic character of the surface indicated by our assumptions can best be visualized by tracing in the Gy-plane the 'level curves' or 'contour lines' $\phi \equiv$ constant for a series of equally-spaced values of ϕ. $\phi \equiv 0$ has already given us a T-shaped figure. Each expression $\phi(G, y) \equiv$ constant > 0 implies some relation between y and G which, taking u as an alternative name for y in order to avoid confusion with the potential surprise curve of some venture, we may write $u \equiv u(G)$. Differentiating $\phi\{G, u(G)\} \equiv$ constant we have

$$d\phi \equiv \frac{\partial \phi}{\partial G} dG + \frac{\partial \phi}{\partial u} du \equiv 0$$

so that

$$\frac{du}{dG} \equiv - \frac{\partial \phi}{\partial G} \Big/ \frac{\partial \phi}{\partial u}. \tag{iv}$$

On the 'gain' side of the diagram (Fig. XVIII 1) that is, where G is positive, the partial derivatives of ϕ with respect to G and y are, by assumptions (i) and (iii), of opposite sign to each other, and so in the positive range of G, by (iv), du/dG is everywhere positive, that is to say, every move along a curve $u = u(G)$ towards increasing values of G will also be a move towards increasing values of u, and this will be true no matter how far along the G-axis we move. Nevertheless, since u is another name for y, it is also true that $u(G)$ can never exceed $\bar{y}$. But something much more interesting is true. Each curve $u = u(G)$ is a contour-line obtained from the condition $\phi \equiv$ constant > 0, while everywhere on the line $y = \bar{y}$ we have

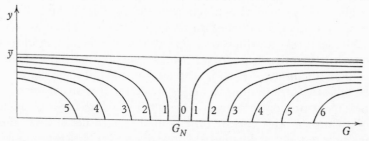

Curves numbered 1, 2, ..., are contours or equal-ϕ-lines, $\phi \equiv$ constant of the surface $\phi \equiv \phi(G, y)$. Contour number 0 is T-shaped; the others, $u_i \equiv u_i(G)$, represent $\phi \equiv$ constant > 0.

Fig. XVIII 1

by definition $\phi \equiv 0$. It follows that no contour-line $u = u(G)$ representing a greater-than-zero level of ϕ can anywhere *attain* the line $y = \bar{y}$.

An argument identical in form with the above will apply to the other half of our diagram if we everywhere write 'loss' instead of 'gain' and use, say, L to mean a variable measured on the G-axis from the same origin but increasing in the opposite sense. We shall continue to illustrate our arguments by reference to the gain side, but everything to be said applies also to the loss side by mere substitution of L for G.

The two conditions which each contour-line $u = u(G)$ is bound by our assumptions to fulfil for all $G > 0$, that every increase of G must carry it nearer to $y = \bar{y}$ but no increase of G can carry it up to that line, can only be simultaneously fulfilled by a curve which, *in broad character*, approaches $y = \bar{y}$ asymptotically. But the fulfilment of these two conditions gives no guarantee that $u = u(G)$ will be everywhere differentiable (smooth) nor even that it will be everywhere concave to the G-axis. If we wish to have it so, we must fall back on the principle that coherence and simplicity are a guide to truth, an argument which has, of course, played a large but mostly unacknowledged part in economic theory ever since the invention of indifference curves.

Fig. XVIII 1 is meant merely to illustrate those characteristics which, according to the foregoing argument, we shall expect to find in every instance of a surface representing the ascendancy, interest or relevance of hypothetical outcomes of a business venture as a function of the face-value and of the potential surprise attached to those hypotheses. These are the 'chief features' to which we referred near the beginning of this chapter, together with two features which can by no means support themselves on basic assumptions having some claim to be self-evident, but must rest on those considerations of smoothness in nature, or perhaps of mere intellectual aesthetics, which economists at any rate are frankly unable to dispense with; the features namely of downward convexity and of differentiability of the curves $u \equiv u(G)$, which we shall hereafter always call 'contour lines'.

Another mode of representing in two dimensions the three-dimensional surface $\phi = \phi(G, y)$ is by means of *profiles* $\phi = \phi(G, y \equiv \text{constant})$, that is to say, diagrams each showing one of the curves in which the ϕ-surface meets a plane parallel to the G-axis and perpendicular to the Gy-plane. Such profiles draw attention to a group of problems which we have not yet considered.

It cannot be true that ϕ increases indefinitely with increase in the numerical size of gains and of losses. For even amongst gains there will surely be for each individual some size which represents all he could ever want or use, so that the ideas of still greater gains would have for him no greater interest. Amongst losses it is still more plain that there will be for each person with his given fortune or his given amount of funds at command some size representing complete and final ruin, so that nothing worse has any meaning. The level of interestingness or ascendancy corresponding to a perfectly possible outcome of this kind must in logic be taken as an absolute maximum $\bar{\phi}$ delimiting at one end the meaningful range of ϕ, so that the latter will be defined only in the range $0 \leqslant \phi \leqslant \bar{\phi}$. Thus on the loss side the profile $\phi = \phi(L, 0)$ is anchored, as it were, at two determinate points. It will, according to our assumptions, be zero at the neutral outcome $G = L = 0$. And it will be at an absolute maximum $\bar{\phi}$ at that value of G or L which represents the loss of so large a part of the sum to be invested as to constitute ruin in a financial or personal sense. Between these two points, how will the segment be shaped? It is plausible that over some range of hypothetical losses, bearing a small ratio to the investible sum, the decision-maker's concern will deepen only slowly; as he approaches and enters a middle range of losses, however, his anxiety will increase

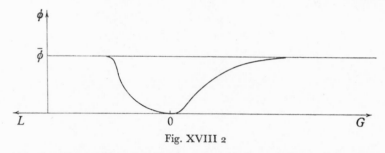

Fig. XVIII 2

more rapidly with each step towards larger suppositions of loss and will finally rush steeply up towards the absolute maximum. If so, the profile $\phi = \phi(L, 0)$ will be convex towards the axis of L and G. On the gain side it seems natural to suppose that when the profile $\phi = \phi(G, 0)$ has already climbed most of the way from zero to the absolute maximum of ϕ, the remainder of its approach will be much less steep than this earlier part, or that some real vagueness in the size of gain corresponding to the absolute maximum of ϕ can be well represented by a last segment having a slope which is very slight in comparison with that needed to attain the beginning of this last stage. If so, the gain profile will, in contrast to the loss profile, be broadly concave to the G-axis, and the two profiles will together produce the shape-type illustrated in Fig. XVIII 2. However, this apparent contrast, if we look at the matter somewhat differently, appears to conceal a harmonious unity of the profile as a whole.

Hitherto in this chapter we have thought of ϕ as increasing with increase of positive G and also as increasing with numerical increase of L or negative G. This has always seemed and still seems to us natural. For let us remember that what ϕ means is not pleasure or pain, nor even encouragement or inhibition, but the power of expectation-elements to command attention, to focus upon themselves the decision-maker's concentrated interest and appraisal. I can be interested, engrossed, as well by the imagination of disaster as by that of triumph, and the part played by this response in our scheme of analysis does not seem to require or justify any distinction between the cases where it is a response to the one or to the other. But if for any reason we do prefer to treat ϕ as negative when it measures the

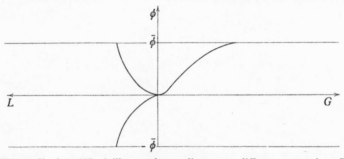

The profile $\phi \equiv \phi(G, \text{o})$ illustrated according to two different conventions. The 'gain' branch $(G > \text{o})$ is the same in both. The 'loss' branch, according to one convention, is in the positive, and only, range of ϕ. According to the other convention, the loss branch is in a negative range of ϕ.

Fig. XVIII 3

response to the idea of loss, then the convexity, towards the G-axis, of the loss branch of the ϕ-profile, viz. $\phi = \phi(L)$, and the concavity, towards the G-axis, of the gain branch $\phi = \phi(G)$, combine to produce a single sweep of curve with an everywhere decreasing slope. Such a treatment was proposed by Mr J. Mars* in his review article in 1950, and Mr Mars's diagram makes a strong claim for it on aesthetic grounds. Mr Mars does not, however, propose to confine ϕ, as we do, within bounds set by the notion of an absolute maximum. In Fig. XVIII 3 the profile is illustrated according to the just-discussed convention.

Whichever we prefer of these two ways of visualizing the

* 'A Study in Expectations: Reflections on Shackle's *Expectation in Economics*', Part I. *Yorkshire Bulletin of Economic and Social Research*, vol. II, no. 2 (July 1950). See diagrams X and XI, pp. 87, 90.

ascendancy function $\phi = \phi(G, y)$, this function has a special and particular shape for each particular decision-maker. This detailed form expresses an aspect of his own peculiar temperament and personal character, just as the particular shape of a potential surprise curve belongs to and expresses his view of the possibilities of a particular specified action scheme. The business of the next chapter is to show the effect of bringing these two statements, one a statement of his general mode of response to situations, the other a statement, formulated by himself, of a particular situation, into relation with each other.

The ascendancy function or ϕ-surface which we have described in this chapter is a second step, following on that of the cardinal potential surprise curve, carrying us towards a sophisticated or refined decision-model from the starting-point of the basic model described in chapter XIV. That basic model, however, is not to be looked on as merely a crude prototype. It contains the justification of our whole procedure. Our third step is to combine the cardinal potential surprise curve with the ascendancy function in an account of the meaning and determination of focus expectation elements.

XIX

FOCUS ELEMENTS

If, for some business venture, the potential surprise y assigned by the decision-maker to hypotheses G of the size of gain or loss of money from this venture can be looked on as a continuous function $y = y(G)$ of these outcomes, then in the expression $\phi = \phi(G, y)$ of the decision-maker's response to expectation-elements (G, y) we can insert the constraint $y = y(G)$ and thus obtain the expression of a twisted curve, or 'space-curve',

$$\phi = \phi\{G, y(G)\}.$$

We now, in the first place, define focus elements as the maxima of this twisted curve, and it is the task of this chapter to investigate the whereabouts of these maxima and to study their meaning.

The formal test for a maximum

$$d\phi \equiv \frac{\partial\phi}{\partial G}\,dG + \frac{\partial\phi}{\partial y}\,dy = 0,$$

whence
$$\frac{dy}{dG} = -\frac{\partial\phi}{\partial G}\Big/\frac{\partial\phi}{\partial y}$$

shows us that at any such point the y-curve is tangent to one of the contour-lines given implicitly by $\phi(G, u) \equiv$ constant > 0 and explicitly written, say, $u = u(G)$ where u is another name for potential surprise. For from $\phi(G, u) \equiv$ constant we have

$$d\phi \equiv 0 \equiv \frac{\partial\phi}{\partial G}\,dG + \frac{\partial\phi}{\partial u}\,du,$$

so that everywhere on such a contour-line

$$\frac{du}{dG} \equiv -\frac{\partial\phi}{\partial G}\Big/\frac{\partial\phi}{\partial u}.$$

We are not troubled by the need to discriminate between maxima and minima, since although there can be points of tangency between the y-curve and a contour-line which are minima, there are necessarily also maxima, and it is the latter only that we are for the present concerned with. The inevitable occurrence of maxima follows from the facts that the twisted curve $\phi = \phi\{G, y(G)\}$ passes through the neutral outcome $G = 0$, where $\phi = 0$, and also attains, at two points, the line $y = \bar{y}$ on which ϕ is everywhere zero, and that between the neutral outcome $G = y = \phi = 0$ and these other points where $y = \bar{y}$, $\phi = 0$ it traverses a part of the ϕ-surface where ϕ is greater than zero.

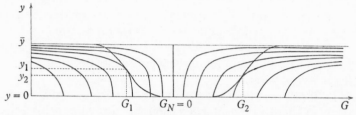

G_N neutral outcome. (G_1, y_1) primary focus loss. (G_2, y_2) primary focus gain.

Fig. XIX 1

All these relationships, as well as the next questions which must be raised in their regard, become vividly apparent when we superpose the diagram of the y-curve upon the contour-map of the ϕ-surface as in Fig. XIX 1. When as in Fig. XIX 1 the mainly convex-downwards y-curve is combined with contour-lines which are concave-downwards throughout, the twisted ϕ-curve $\phi = \phi\{G, y(G)\}$ has one maximum on each side of the neutral outcome. These two maxima we call *primary focus-elements*. A conspicuous and essential truth about these elements considered as a pair is the absence of any reason why they should be equal to each other in their values of any one of the three variables G, y, ϕ. This fact offers us both a difficulty and a number of advantages in the solution of our next problem, which is how we should suppose the decision-maker to effect decisive comparisons between the available business ventures, or investment schemes, when each is represented by such a pair of primary focus-elements.

Four answers to this question, broadly, have been proposed. One of them suggests that a second stage of selection will result in the complete eclipse of one of the focus elements by the other, the latter then serving as the decision-maker's effective assumption about the outcome of the venture. This was my own earliest view,* later independently advanced again by Mr J. Mars.† This view pursues to the end the line of thought on which we are launched by our claim that a man cannot base a satisfying imaginative experience on a multiplicity of mutually rival and contradictory suppositions. Must then these suppositions be reduced to one? Must the uncertainty, which we have asserted to be part of the meaning of the word decision, play its part wholly in the intermediate stages of the act of decision? Or can we allow it to remain even in that final experience which is the goal and purpose of decision? The supposition of a final, committed experience based upon two focus elements is the simplest means of retaining in the whole act of decision a formal role for uncertainty.

If both of the primary focus elements are to be thought of as present in the decision-maker's thoughts throughout his act of decision, this presence could take either of two forms. Interpreting ϕ as the measure of an element's power not simply to command the decision-maker's attention but even directly to influence him for or against the particular action-course, and treating ϕ as negative when it arises from a hypothesis of loss, as Mr Mars had already done, we could, with Mr Mars himself and Professor B. R. Williams, suppose the decision-maker to form the algebraic sum of the ϕ-values of the two primary focus elements. That sum when obtained for each of the available action-courses, ventures or investments, would show which of them most strongly attracted him. (It follows from our discussion of the meaning of 'neutral outcome' in chapter xv that at least one and usually several of the available ventures would seem to offer an improvement on his existing situation, unless indeed all seemed the precise equivalent of it, pull being in every case exactly balanced by push.) This method has a formal simplicity which must be weighed against what we may call the psychic simplicity of our own alternative. But the scheme of

* See 'The Nature of the Inducement to Invest' and 'A Reply to Professor Hart', *Review of Economic Studies*, vol. VIII, no. 22 (October 1940).

† See 'A Study in Expectation', *Yorkshire Bulletin of Economic and Social Research*, vol. II, no. 2 (July 1950), p. 81, where Mr Mars refers to the need for a 'singularization process' to follow the 'polarization' or dual focusing process.

thought to which ϕ belongs when interpreted as a direct pull or push on the decision is an essentially different one from our own. ϕ for us is not the attractiveness or repulsiveness itself of an expectation-element, but the relevance or attention-arresting power which belongs to a highly attractive or highly repellent hypothesis not too much enfeebled by an air of unreality. In the simplest of all our models we supposed the decision-maker to be able only to classify hypotheses as possible or impossible, and to be concerned, accordingly, with only the best and the worst among the possibles. These two focus elements thus differed from each other in only one respect or dimension, they occupied different positions on the axis of success-misfortune which in our present context is the axis of gain and loss of money. For the decision-maker choosing amongst business ventures these focus elements would, in fact, simply be sums of money. An elaboration of our continuous model capable of restoring this concreteness and simplicity has something to give in exchange for being formally more complex.

Our line of thought having led us to the notion of focus-elements, there is from that point a fourth divergent path which can carry us to a complete theory of decision. This fourth solution, proposed by Mr J. J. Puthucheary of the University of Malaya, rests on a special view of how the potential surprise curve comes into being and of the meaning it has for the decision-maker, and we shall give Mr Puthucheary's own account of it in a later chapter.

We begin our account of the third of the above-mentioned solutions, which reduces the focus elements to a mere pair of money sums, one a gain and the other a loss, by returning to Fig. XIX 1 and describing afresh in terms of visual geometry the determination of a pair of primary focus elements. Let us trace the twisted curve $\phi = \phi\{G, y(G)\}$ from a starting-point at the origin, $G = y = \phi = 0$, at first through increasing values of G. If the Gy-plane be regarded as horizontal, the twisted curve lies everywhere vertically above the potential surprise curve $y(G)$ of the venture or action scheme in question. Where $y(G)$ coincides with the G-axis the ascendancy ϕ of expectation-elements (G, y) will, by the argument of chapter XVIII, be proportional to G, so that the twisted curve will rise in a straight segment from the origin (0, 0, 0) to a point vertically above the upper extreme of the inner range of $y(G)$, that is, the highest value of G for which $y(G) = 0$. At this upper extreme of its inner range, $y(G)$ begins to diverge from the G-axis, and the twisted curve will in consequence begin to be influenced by increasing values of y. As we continue to move through successively higher values of G, the potential surprise curve $y(G)$ will approach the line $y = \bar{y}$ and eventually attain it at some finite value of G, and at this point the twisted curve $\phi = \phi\{G, y(G)\}$ will evidently again reach zero having necessarily descended from some highest level attained between this point and the origin. Instead of tracing the twisted curve itself we could have traced its vertical projection or 'shadow' on the horizontal Gy-plane. Imagine the twisted curve to be represented by a wire. Then light falling vertically will throw on the horizontal plane a shadow of this wire, and this shadow will be simply the potential surprise curve $y = y(G)$. As we move to the right along the positive part of the inner range $y(G) = 0$ of this curve, we pass in succession the points of the G-axis whence spring, at non-zero angles to this axis, contour-lines $u(G)$ corresponding to successively higher levels $\phi \equiv$ constant > 0, and we may say, therefore, that we cross successively higher contour-lines. Where $y(G)$ swings away from the G-axis we shall at first perhaps continue to cross successively higher contour-lines, for at first the influence of increasing values of G may outweigh that of the increasing associated values of y. But since the potential surprise curve $y = y(G)$ does, while the contour-lines $u = u(G)$ do not, attain the line $y = \bar{y}$ at some finite value of G, it follows that somewhere $y(G)$ must begin to cross successively lower contours in order to reach a zero value of ϕ at $y = \bar{y}$. Since we think of the contour-lines as covering densely the whole zone $0 \leqslant y < \bar{y}$ (an interval open at one end unless we include the T-shaped curve $\phi \equiv 0$ as one of the contour-lines) and since no two contours represent the same level of ϕ, it follows that, if the potential surprise curve $y(G)$ crosses any contour, it will come to, or leave behind, a higher contour than the one it is crossing. Thus the highest contour which $y(G)$ encounters will be one which it does not cross. If the potential surprise curve and this highest attained contour are both of them smooth and continuous, and if they have only one point in common, that point will be a tangency between them. By a like argument in which we merely substitute for G the variable L, measured along the G-axis in the opposite sense to G, we can trace the potential surprise curve towards the left from the origin and thus determine the loss or negative value of G to which there will correspond the other constrained maximum of ϕ.

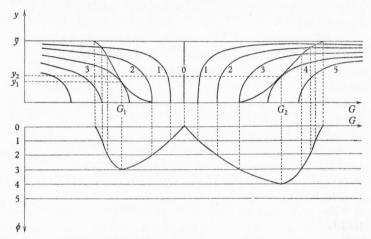

Diagram to illustrate *primary focus outcomes*. 1, 2, ..., 6 are levels of ϕ, shown in upper part of figure as contours of the surface $\phi \equiv \phi(G, y)$; in lower part, as ordinates of the profile $\phi \equiv \phi(G)$. (G_1, y_1) primary focus loss; (G_2, y_2) primary focus gain.

Fig. XIX 2

In Fig. XIX 2 we again imagine the twisted curve

$$\phi = \phi\{G, y(G)\}$$

to be represented by a wire, and we suppose the shadow of this wire to be thrown, first by a vertical light on to the Gy-plane where the shadow coincides with the potential surprise curve $y = y(G)$ of the venture, and secondly by a horizontal light on to the $G\phi$-plane where the two constrained maxima can be seen, as it were, in a profile of the twisted curve. In this Fig. XIX 2 the $G\phi$-plane is supposed to have been rotated through one right angle about the G-axis so that points on the $G\phi$ projection of the twisted curve lie on the page directly below the points of the curve $y(G)$ to which they correspond.

The two points of tangency which, in a central type of case, the potential surprise curve $y(G)$ of an action scheme or venture will have with contour-lines $u(G)$, or $\phi \equiv$ constant > 0, of the ϕ-surface are examples of what we have called primary focus elements or primary focus outcomes of this action-scheme or venture. The one which falls in the positive or 'gain' range of the outcome variable G we shall call the *primary focus gain*, and the one in the negative or 'loss' range of G the *primary focus loss*. We shall not confine the use of these terms to our cardinal or most sophisticated model, since the need to determine, for each primary focus outcome, an equivalent *standardized* outcome will arise equally when we carry out our analysis in its other, ordinal, form where we do not assume that the psychic variables y and ϕ are measurable, even on the decision-maker's private and subjective scale, but treat their intensities as merely orderable. In the ordinal model the primary focus outcomes will, of course, not be tangencies, since no significance (relevance) can be attached to the smoothness or otherwise of the curves when the variables can be subjected to monotonic transformations without affecting the meaning of the tale they have to tell. Nonetheless, the differences between our cardinal and ordinal models are in no way fundamental, and indeed an ordinal treatment has already been exemplified, in chapter xiv, in what we called our basic model. Meanwhile in the next chapter we shall complete our apparatus in its cardinal form.

XX

CHOICE AMONGST ACTIONS

There is nothing but accident to make equal the degree of potential surprise belonging to the primary focus loss and that belonging to the primary focus gain. In order, then, to give to our sophisticated model the simplicity of our basic model, where, since all relevant hypotheses are assigned zero potential surprise, the degrees belonging to the two focus outcomes are necessarily equal, we must find for each primary focus outcome of the sophisticated model an *equivalent* outcome carrying zero potential surprise. Whereas the primary focus elements of a venture are, say (G_i, y_i) and (L_i, y_i) we need expectation elements $(G_m, 0)$ and $(L_n, 0)$ which can validly replace, as the decision-maker's basis of imaginative experience, those primary elements. What is the appropriate test of equivalence for this purpose? It is surely the possession of an equal power to command attention; $(G_m, 0)$ will be equivalent to (G_i, y_i) if $\phi(G_m, 0) = \phi(G_i, y_i)$. In visual terms the procedure for finding a *standardized* focus gain, equivalent in the above sense to the primary focus gain, will be extremely simple, and will consist in tracing the contour line $u(G)$ on which the primary focus gain lies, down to its meeting with the G-axis. The two intercepts on the G-axis, G_m and L_n, thus obtained are evidently scalar quantities in contrast with the primary focus outcomes which are points or vectors. In what we have called the basic model, where all hypothetical outcomes of an investment scheme would be supposed to be divided by the decision-maker into the two categories of 'possible' and 'impossible', there would evidently be no distinction between primary and standardized focus outcomes, since the primary focus gain would be the largest amongst the hypothetical gains regarded as 'possible' and all of these would carry an equal degree of potential surprise which, since at least one hypothesis in an exhaustive set must carry zero potential surprise, would be zero; and no standardization would thus be necessary.

We see, then, that the effect of standardizing the primary

focus outcomes is to secure for the sophisticated model a simplicity as great as that of the basic model. Now in that basic model certain things are inescapable. There are, if our argument of chapter XIV be accepted, only two hypothetical outcomes to which the decision-maker will have cause to pay attention; and it will by no means make sense for him to compare different investment schemes by simply finding, for each of them, the algebraic sum of its focus gain and focus loss. If one focus loss is ten times as large as another, the large loss cannot be compensated, in its influence on decision, by a focus gain ten times as large as the one which would just compensate the small loss; for the large loss, if suffered in fact, would bring irretrievable ruin, the small focus loss would not. Such adding together of the focus outcomes of the basic model would be no more sensible than the proposition that, if a consumer's monthly intake of butter is reduced by a kilogram, his contentment can always be restored by giving him an extra kilogram per month of sugar. Moreover the solution of our problem is suggested by the method which makes possible the consumer's analysis, that of the indifference map.

On a Cartesian diagram, let distances rightward from the vertical axis stand for standardized focus losses of the sophisticated model, or for focus losses, *simpliciter*, of the basic model; and let distances upward from the horizontal axis likewise stand for focus gains. Then any combination of a focus loss and a focus gain, and thus the decision basis of any investment scheme, can be represented by a point on what we shall, in this book as elsewhere, call the gambler indifference map. Any point on the positive-positive quadrant of the map being arbitrarily chosen, the decision-maker, interpreting his own personal temperament and tastes, can find other points, and in principle an infinity of other points, such that investment schemes represented by these points would be to him no more nor less attractive than one represented by the arbitrary first point. When he is thus indifferent between the points of such a set, it is natural to suppose that these points will form a smooth continuous segment of a curve, and we shall call such a segment a gambler indifference curve.

From the formal meaning of gambler indifference curves, from an obvious fact of the investing decision-maker's situation, and from some assumptions about human nature which very readily suggest themselves and have long been accepted in those parts of economic theory which neglect uncertainty, we can derive some ideas upon which our use of the gambler indifference map will rest. First, the gambler indifference curves are taken to cover densely the whole positive-positive quadrant of the $G_m L_n$-plane from $L_n = 0$ up to, but not always including, an abscissa $\bar{L}_n$ representing the decision-maker's whole 'fortune', so that any arbitrarily chosen point in the zone so defined will be contained in some one (and only one) of the gambler indifference curves. No two points belonging to different curves are equally attractive to the decision-maker, whence it follows that no two curves can have any point in common, no two curves can intersect or touch each other. Since, if two points are to be equally attractive, the one implying the larger standardized focus loss must also imply the larger standardized focus gain, it follows that each gambler indifference curve must slope upwards to the right. If two points having the same ordinate are compared, the one lying farther to the left is preferred because it represents the same focus gain and a smaller focus loss. If two points having the same abscissa are compared, the one having the larger ordinate is preferred, because it represents a larger focus gain for a given focus loss. It follows that if point B lies in a gambler indifference curve lying above and to the left of the curve containing point A, point B will be preferred. When the action-schemes being compared are investment schemes, the decision-maker will have in mind some definite available sum of money which is the most he can dispose of on behalf of himself or those who have placed their wealth at his discretion. This sum we shall call his fortune, for even if it belongs legally to a company of which he is merely the manager, we shall suppose (realistically, we believe) that he identifies his own success with that of the firm. This sum is the most that he can lose. He may, indeed, borrow money at fixed interest and embark it along with his fortune in some investment scheme. But if the outcome of that investment scheme is a loss greater than his fortune, the excess of the loss over the fortune will be suffered by his creditors. Thus at that point on the loss axis which corresponds to the decision-maker's fortune we erect, perpendicular to that axis, a barrier to the right of which the gambler indifference curves would have no meaning and are not drawn. We have to consider what will be the relation between the gambler indifference curves and this barrier.

There are no doubt people, each with a considerable fortune at command, for whom possible doubling, trebling, ..., of that fortune would make a venture seem worthwhile even if it also held the possibility that the fortune would be entirely lost. For others the fear of losing all they possessed would not be compensated by the hope of any gain however great. To these two temperaments there correspond two sharply distinct types of

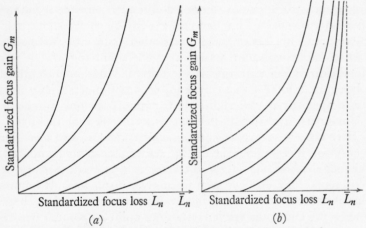

$\bar{L}_n$: the decision-maker's fortune or maximum amount he can lose.

Fig. XX I A   Fig. XX I B

gambler indifference map. For the more cautious temperament, any point which threatens total ruin as one of its possibilities, that is, any point on the 'barrier' erected at an abscissa equal to the decision-maker's fortune, is more repellent than any point whose worst threat is less then total ruin. No point on the barrier, that is to say, can be contained in any of his gambler indifference curves, which therefore must approach the barrier asymptotically as they rise from left to right but can never reach it. For the headlong gambler, on the other hand, there is no such restriction, his gambler indifference curves can meet the barrier at finite ordinates. The two types of map are illustrated in Fig. XX I A and B.

Such a gambler indifference map can illustrate the comparison of action-schemes of the most general kinds. But when these action-schemes are investment schemes each proposing the exchange of some of the decision-maker's assets for others, each such scheme must prescribe the form to be taken after such exchange by every part of the decision-maker's fortune. This necessity hinders very little the use of the map. When the question is whether some specified part of the decision-maker's total collection of assets (say, a given sum of money which he is holding as a bank balance) shall be exchanged for some specified piece of concrete equipment, then the exchange of these two assets for each other will leave the rest of the decision-maker's fortune unchanged in form and amount, and thus the two points on the gambler indifference map, one standing for his existing collection of assets and the other for that same collection when a particular equipment system or machine has been substituted for a particular quantity of cash, can legitimately be compared. The only complication arises when what is to be received, or what is to be parted with, consists of two or more objects to each of which *separately* the assignment of focus gain and loss would naturally be made. For then it is necessary for these pairs of focus gain and loss to be combined into a pair belonging to the two objects in combination. Thus if the choice open to the decision-maker is between three or more sets of assets, one being a sum of money which he at present possesses and could retain, another being a concrete equipment system A on which the whole of this money would have to be spent, and the third consisting of (i) a different equipment system B which would cost only a part of the money, together with (ii) the cash remainder thus to be left in his possession, he will have to arrive at a focus gain and loss for equipment system A and a focus gain and loss for the combination of equipment system B with a certain quantity of cash.

Money held otherwise than as part of the necessary apparatus for the day-to-day conduct of a business or a private life, money used as a store of wealth, has a very special character. Whereas when the decision-maker invests in a system of concrete equipment he may be supposed to be primarily concerned with the possibilities of gain or loss from using this equipment itself and to relegate to secondary importance the question of how any wealth released from this use in the form of gross earnings shall, when the time comes, be reinvested, or even to draw his expectational horizon so that this question lies mostly beyond it, we cannot suppose him to be thinking in this way when he decides to hold a stock of money. For this money will not, in money terms, yield any gain or loss, and thus unless his only desire is to feel sure that he will not suffer any loss in terms of money, we must suppose him to be waiting, in the manner which we shall analyse in Part IV, for some future answering of questions which will clarify his expectations and enable him to choose amongst investment opportunities available at that deferred date. Thus unless his desire is purely to avoid loss in terms of money, his election of money as an asset must look to the possible answers to some questions which only events themselves in their own time can resolve, and to the gain and loss possibilities which those answers may allow him to imagine for some equipment system then to be constructed. Money's essence is to allow deferment of choice amongst complex alternatives, and the focus gain and loss to be assigned to a holding of money thus depend on the possibilities of gain and loss which the decision-maker, at his viewpoint, ascribes to those deferred alternatives, and to the freedom, which by holding money he preserves, to look forward to making a deferred choice amongst them.

However, a set of questions each sufficiently clear cut and simple, and also sufficiently independent, in its potential effect upon the outcomes of investment in particular types of equipment, from all the others, to enable the decision-maker to imagine clearly a complete set of such different deferred investments amongst which he would choose when the questions should be answered, may be impossible for him to formulate. In such a case, he will not be able to assign to a holding of money anything except a zero focus gain and loss of money, and if he looks on money as having an unchanging purchasing power, or if he is satisfied to measure his gain and loss in terms of it without considering its purchasing power, we may say that he assigns to a holding of money a complete freedom from the possibility of gain or loss. Suppose that in these circumstances, having a certain fortune which he can realize in cash or which he already holds as cash, he is engaged with the question how much of this fortune he shall embark in constructing a plant of given technical design and purpose, for which he can choose a smaller or larger *scale* within some range of continuous variation, and how much of the fortune he shall retain in cash. By assumption, if he holds the whole of his fortune in cash its representative point will lie at the origin of the gambler indifference map. If, instead, he decides to use part of the fortune to construct a plant of given scale, the focus gain and loss of the *whole* fortune will be those attributable to this plant.

By plants (equipment systems) of given technical design in a variety of sizes we cannot in general mean geometrically similar plants. Geometrical similarity might apply to the hulls of different sized ships, but it is difficult to think of more than one or two such examples. By plants of similar design it will be natural to mean plants which use the same physical, chemical or electrical processes by means of machines operating on the same principles and organized in one particular way. When a series of points is plotted on the gambler indifference map, each representing the proposal to construct a plant of different scale but of given technical design in the above sense, what curve to contain these points is likely to suggest itself?

Two sets of circumstances, distinguishable but inter-acting, seem to bear on this question. Market conditions on one hand, and technical economies of scale on the other, will enter the decision-maker's reckoning when he seeks to trace what we will call, as elsewhere we have done, the scale opportunity curve. The economist is here inevitably drawn to his great solvent assumption which brings order into so immense an area of problems that else is chaotic. If the firm buys its factors of production, and also sells its product, in markets which are perfectly competitive in the economist's technical sense, and if also there is an absence of technical economies and diseconomies of scale, so that the 'production function', linking the quantities of the means of production used with the quantities of product which they yield, is linear and homogeneous, so that a doubling of every one of the means of production doubles the product, a trebling trebles it, and so on, then there seems no reason why such a doubling or trebling of the *scale* of the plant should not double or respectively treble both the focus gain and the focus loss so that the scale-opportunity curve would be a straight line which, if extended, would pass through the origin.

Our purpose here, however, is merely to show how our scheme of thought may be used to analyse the link between size and uncertainty and enable new questions to be framed about it. The effect of geographical market imperfections, of monopoly and monopolistic competition of various degrees founded on this or that circumstance of an industry's technique or of its historical organization, and perhaps especially of duopoly or oligopoly, in bending the scale-opportunity curve out of the straight line which perfect competition might give it; and the influence, inter-penetrating and combining with that of market forms, which economies or diseconomies of scale might similarly have; could well form the subject of a study in its own right. These questions would lead us too far into the special concerns of the economist for us to pursue them here. The notion of the scale opportunity-curve has, however, given rise to an extremely interesting criticism which we must consider in conclusion of this chapter.

With great kindness, Mr Richard Blandy of the University of Adelaide wrote to propose a more general use of the scale-opportunity curve, in which we should imagine the decision-maker to have one such curve for each of a number of different industries, or stages or techniques of industrial production, in which he might consider embarking his capital. There is, in general, Mr Blandy points out, nothing to prevent such scale-opportunity curves from intersecting each other, and at any such point of intersection the decision-maker could obtain no guidance from his map as to which of the two industries in question he should favour; or rather, there is nothing in the lines of thought which we picture by means of the gambler indifference map and the structure of concepts on which it rests, to show how in such a case the decision-maker would elect one industry rather than another. It is, in fact, evidently true that whether we confine ourselves to a single variable by which we claim that the attractiveness of different action-schemes can be compared, as those do, for example, who suppose the decision-maker to calculate a mathematical expectation of the profitability of each action-scheme; or whether, as in our own scheme, we endeavour to show that the whole reach and scope of ideas comprised under the heading *uncertainty* can be handled entire without abandoning the simplicity of a two-variable apparatus; or whether we are willing to employ more and yet more variables until all possibility of concrete and particular results escapes us; still there can be no guarantee that two or more action-schemes, as assessed by our chosen apparatus, will not appear equally attractive and leave the decision-maker apparently indifferent between them. In raising a question leading to this line of thought, Mr Blandy's letter has been most valuable.

We have now completed the essential description of our model of decision. We claim for the thread of thought that we have traced thus far a certain strength and continuity in the sense that, if one accepts certain premises about human nature and the nature of conscious life, there seems to be no obvious escape from the path that we have followed. All rests, however, on acceptance of the basic model of chapter XIV. In this present chapter we claim to have shown that, if the notion of focus elements is accepted within the confines of that model, the natural and perhaps the inevitable means of completing a decision model based upon them is the gambler indifference map. The final step, carrying us through chapters XVIII, XIX and XX to our present point, is the proposition that in seeking to refine the basic model we must adhere to its essence, to the notion of a pair of focus expectation elements whose meaning requires them to be held separately in existence, in the decision-maker's supposed thoughts, throughout.

XXI

CRITICS OF FOCUS ELEMENTS

Criticism of the scheme of thought that we have described under ASCENDANCY can be systematized as follows. Four main divisions are respectively concerned with the essential notion, detailed character or process of formation of the continuous potential surprise curve; with the question whether the use made of this curve by the decision-maker in reaching a decision must be supposed to employ every part of the curve in an active role or whether it is selective; with the conventions to be adopted in specifying the ascendancy-surface and the question whether the variables involved in the potential surprise curve and the ascendancy-surface are to be looked on as cardinal or ordinal; and with the interpretation of the focus elements and the propriety of introducing yet another psychic 'space' in the form of the gambler indifference map.

One aspect of the difference between the two ways of thinking, the way which expresses itself in a subjective probability distribution and the way which is embodied in a potential surprise curve, is the tendency of the former to suppose that one hypothesis, or a compact group of closely similar hypotheses, will seem to the decision-maker more remote from 'certainly wrong' than any others, so that the probability curve has a distinct mode. In contrast to this definite location of a 'most probable' hypothesis, the potential surprise curve has by its nature, critics might say, a formal bias in the opposite direction. No critic so far as we know has put the point in this way, but one of the most interesting suggestions for amending our conception of the potential surprise curve maintains that the very process by which the decision-maker reviews, grades and assembles his data must by its nature lead to, or essentially depend on, the establishment of a 'primary hypothesis' upon which the evidence will seem to converge. He will seek and select one line of explanation or interpretation of his mass of evidence by the test that if this were the drift of things, the strongest suggestions arising from his data would find a place while those which could not be fitted into the picture would be those of lesser sharpness or internal consistency or apparent relevance or obvious meaning. Thus the potential surprise curve would have at most a very short inner range of hypotheses carrying zero potential surprise and the location of this definite trough would be its most important feature. The author of the line of thought which I have here sought to condense and interpret is Mr J. J. Puthucheary, whose own words are as follows:*

It is necessary first of all to distinguish the importance of the difference between expectations and possibilities. Action or decision is based on expectations rationally formed or otherwise, while possibilities express the uncertainty of the outcome. In situations of uncertainty, it is conceivable that the outcome is so indeterminate that both gains and losses are treated as possibilities. But as long as they are considered possibilities, the situation is one of indecision. Decision can only take place when one of the possibilities is transformed into an expectation.... What probably happens is that one of the outcomes is transmuted into an 'expectation' and the other into a 'possibility'.... I think it would be correct to say that the distinction between an expectation and a possibility is due to the psychological attitude to the focus outcomes. This psychological attitude is generally based on the difference in degree of potential surprise associated with focus values but not necessarily so.

The term 'transmuted' is not intended to convey the idea that the distinction between expectation and possibility is a secondary process; something extraneous to the original hypotheses. The distinction is a part of the hypotheses and I think it would be correct to say that where the primary hypothesis† postulates a gain income, it would be an investment from which gains are expected and losses are possibilities. The secondary hypotheses on the gain side will help to determine the final value of the gain on which the expectation of the entrepreneur will be focused. Consequently, the primary hypothesis helps to determine the general shape of the y-curve and which of the focus-values is the expectation....

If the discussion up to this point is valid, then two changes must be made to Shackle's model. First the general shape of the y-curve must be changed....

* 'Investment Incentive and Income Tax', *Public Finance*, vol. xiv. See also, by the present writer, 'The Nature of the Inducement to Invest', *Review of Economic Studies*, vol. viii, no. 22 (1940).

† I would again remind the reader that Mr Puthucheary's 'primary hypothesis' is a wholly different idea from my 'primary focus element' defined in *Expectation in Economics*, chapter ii, and in chapter xix of this book.

On the assumption that there is a primary hypothesis and all secondary hypotheses are related to it, it seems legitimate to suggest that the shape of the y-curve would be more like a wedge than a bell....

The actual shape of the curve [?detailed and particular shape of the curve G.L.S.S.] is unimportant. Its general characteristics are that the apex of the curve (zero potential surprise) would be at some point away from the neutral [outcome].

I think the essential difference between Mr Puthucheary's views and my own is the following. Whereas he supposes that the decision-maker will always contrive to gather materials sufficient to compose a complete argument in favour of one specific hypothesis of the course of events which would flow from some proposed action, my own assumption is that the decision-maker will be aware that his expectation-forming materials can never be known to be adequate, and that he will be conscious of the infinitely many ways in which their gaps can be filled by conjecture. Mr Puthucheary may believe that those materials, where gaps appear amongst them, will be supplemented by a more or less arbitrary *tour de main* of assumption, so that the primary hypothesis is reached by fair logical inference from a set of postulates only some of which can be called facts. Mr Puthucheary's decision-maker, I would say, opts for 'rationality' at all costs, even when it can only be artificial.

It must be admitted that much empirical evidence seems to favour Mr Puthucheary's view. When asked how they reach investment-decisions, businessmen often name a single figure for the profit-earning performance which they require of an investment before they will undertake it. This figure is ordinarily expressed as a percentage which the extra yearly profit, due to the new productive facilities proposed to be created, is required to bear to the sum of money to be laid out on those facilities. The percentage named is often between 33 and 50, the number of years during which such a rate of earning is to persist not being specified. Alternatively, the businessmen sometimes express the required performance as a rate of earning sufficient to amortize the investment in about three years. Net profits of 33 % per annum are evidently equivalent to amortization of the investment in about three years, and the special relevance of this period has long seemed to me to lie in its being the longest which the decision-maker's knowledge of his viewpoint situation can have any power to illuminate. What a man knows of the situation existing today can tell him much about what will be the situation in three months' or six months' time, for there is, even in these days, some limit to the speed at which the world-picture can be transformed. In some respects today's circumstances shed light on those of a year or even two or three years hence. But a very striking fact shows also that they are not felt to throw light on the situation ten or fifteen years hence. When we study the curve which expresses the yield of fixed interest securities as a function of their remaining life to maturity, we find, in times when the bill-rate is low, that this curve rises steeply as we pass through maturities increasing from zero to five years and less steeply thereafter. The transition is, of course, a part of the smooth course of the curve, whose gradient decreases throughout, but rather markedly so around five years. What can this course of the curve mean, if not that five years is long enough to import into the question of the future of interest-rates (that is, of security prices) most of the uncertainty that any period however long could bring in? If it is true, then, that the businessman takes into account only the profits which his knowledge of the circumstances existing at his viewpoint entitles him in some degree to count on, we have, in his apparent practice of testing these profits against a single figure of required performance, a piece of evidence strongly favouring Mr Puthucheary's view.

It is possible, however, to interpret the businessmen's statement rather differently. The buildings which they erect or the machines which they instal will certainly remain physically capable of performing their tasks far longer than three years. The danger to their economic usefulness lies in obsolescence, which, however, in so far as the new equipment does not, even when ordered, already lie under the shadow of existing fresh discoveries or inventions, is something entirely beyond worthwhile conjecture. Thus to construct a new plant embodying the latest knowledge is to open the possibility of many years' profitable operation, and the businessman can surely 'hope' for profits whose present value would amortize the investment not just once but many times over. And yet, can one man have such gains in sight without these opportunities being apparent to many others? If too many embark too extensively on ventures aiming to exploit the same new market or the same new technique, the gains may prove illusory. One step further: this danger may well be recognized by the businessmen. If so, they will have in mind the possibility of loss as well as of great gain.

An extremely interesting question about the nature and use of the potential surprise curve has been posed by Professor Richard S. Weckstein in his article on 'Probable Knowledge and Singular Acts':*

Another way of describing a lack of evidence is to say that on the basis of that evidence the outcomes can only be partially ordered (at least one of the possible outcomes is not known to be more or less probable than others),† which makes it difficult to place the alternative acts in a complete order. This kind of ignorance is likely to produce confusion and lack of confidence. Three ways of reacting to such situations occur to me: postpone or avoid a decision, if possible; obtain more information if it is feasible to weigh the gains from doing so against the costs; if forced to choose, resort to a rule appropriate to a state of ignorance of outcomes. But I am not aware of any positive theory of choice which properly applies to these situations, nor of any experiments which shed light on actual behaviour when people are faced with such partially ordered alternatives. I do not consider that Shackle's theory deals with these cases either, as Shackle assumes a person attaches a *complete* weak ordering of potential surprise to the possible outcomes in arriving at a stimulation function.

Let us admit at once that the decision-maker, proposing to himself various hypothetical outcomes as candidates for the status of expectations, may find, in seeking to imagine these outcomes as possible, that different objections or difficulties obstruct his vision of different outcomes, and that it may be a hard task or even an impossible one for him to assign relative degrees to these qualitatively different kinds of difficulty. From other sources too, let us admit, such a breakdown of the attempt to order different hypotheses completely may arise. (A weak ordering, where two or more hypotheses may be assigned equal

* *Metroeconomica*, vol. xi (April–August 1959), p. 109.

† [Professor Weckstein's footnote] 'Odds, Possibility and Plausibility in Shackle's Theory of Decision', by G. Gould and G. L. S. Shackle. *Economic Journal*, vol. lxvii (December 1957), pp. 659–64.

degrees of potential surprise, is evidently no less vulnerable in this regard than a strong ordering where every hypothesis is placed as either more or less potentially surprising than any other.) In this matter both distributional and non-distributional uncertainty-variables seem to be on the same footing. The question, then, is which of the constructions, which can be built on one or other type of uncertainty-variable to provide a description of the act of decision, can best explain how the decision-maker copes, as he must, with this confused situation by some such policy as those Professor Weckstein has listed.

'Postponing' decision, or rather, deciding upon those immediate and intermediate actions which seem to promise the availability, at some deferred date, of the greatest diversity of choice amongst courses of action for the further future beyond that date, is perhaps a necessary condition for adopting Professor Weckstein's second policy of seeking more information, so that we might say his first and second policies are two aspects of the same idea. His third policy refers to 'a rule appropriate to a state of ignorance of outcomes'. Here we can claim that our scheme of thought contains as part of its structure the notion that such a rule will be followed when there is far-reaching uncertainty in the decision-maker's mind. For when he feels that extremely diverse outcomes, including large losses or serious misfortunes as well as large gains or striking successes, are all *perhaps* deserving of low potential surprise, then he will assign to the action-scheme in question a numerically large focus loss (or whatever, in other contexts than the economic, corresponds to a large loss) as well perhaps as a high focus gain. When the two resulting focus outcomes are plotted on his gambler indifference map, the point representing this pair of values will, if he is a cautious man rather than a reckless gambler, lie below and to the right of his origin indifference curve, since the latter will be convex to the loss axis, and he will reject the action-scheme in question in favour of one concerning which his expectations, in both our own and Professor Weckstein's senses, are 'clearer'; one, that is to say, whose focus loss is numerically smaller and therefore also its focus gain.

The notion of focus elements has been criticized along several lines. Their selective aspect is objected to by those who, while perhaps accepting the idea of potential surprise, say that to base decision, in effect, on only two points of the potential surprise curve of an action scheme is to 'waste information'. In our view, this is much as though a railway traveller, wishing to go to York, should be accused of wasting travel facilities because he did not take the trains to Birmingham, to Bristol and to Brighton as well as the one to York. This criticism betrays, indeed, a radical misconception of our whole approach and of the purpose which we conceive the act of decision to serve and of the conception we have adopted (we claim no power to prove it true, but merely choose it as our assumption) of what the human situation is in respect of the nature of time and the non-emptiness of decision. In brief, we say that the hypotheses whose assigned degrees of possibility are expressed by the potential surprise curve are mutually contradictory and that therefore it is as senseless to try to follow all of them as it would be to book tickets for trains travelling simultaneously in divergent directions; that because of this uselessness of aggregation, because of the need for selection which the very nature of things imposes, the decision-maker is free, and is bound, to select rather than add together the unaddable; that the desired experience which the act of decision can afford him is that of committed anticipation, an experience by imagination, and that therefore he may as well select those hypotheses, amongst the many mutually contradictory ones which offer themselves, which give him the best of the available experiences of this kind.

It is, in our view, not only legitimate but essentially necessary, in basing decisions on that form of uncertainty judgement which the potential surprise curve expresses, to use the curve as a means of selection and not as a means of averaging. By contrast a probability distribution, legitimately used to discover uniquely the (undoubted) outcome of a divisible experiment, must of course be used in its entirety, since every one of the contingencies represented in it will, if the distribution is correct, help to compose the total outcome of the divisible experiment. All that appertains to this proper use of a probability-distribution is quite irrelevant, as we have urged at length in chapter VII, to the question how uncertainty judgements can be expressed in contexts where true uncertainty is present, and how those judgements are to be applied to the making of decisions. To lop off part of a probability-distribution and neglect it, in seeking to determine the outcome of a divisible experiment, would plainly be not merely to waste information but grossly to distort and invalidate the information contained in the distribution as a whole. Of the potential surprise curve nothing of the sort would be true, if the lopping off were performed *after* the curve had been applied to its selective task, and it is only *after* the performance of that task that any part of the curve is treated as irrelevant; for when the focus elements are being determined, the whole curve, *ex ante facto*, must be brought into confrontation with the ϕ-surface. Once the selection of the focus elements has been performed, the legitimacy of discarding the rest of the curve, the fact that this relegation leaves the meaning of the focus elements unaffected, springs from the non-distributional nature of potential surprise.

As this book was being set up, I had the opportunity of showing chapters VII and IX to Monsieur Guy Devillebichot, who was already acquainted with earlier versions of my scheme. In an exceedingly interesting letter he has written in part as follows [M. Devillebichot uses x to stand for face-values of hypotheses, as we formerly did]:

Ne faut-il pas reconnaître la difficulté, dans certains cas concrets, à savoir ce que représente la variable continue x: on peut s'interroger sur la possibilité d'états du monde discontinus, la variable continu x n'étant pas la *conséquence* d'un choix possible de la nature; on voit mal comment on peut assigner à chaque x *directement* un degré de possibilité.

In this book we have tried to emphasize sufficiently, as we did not in earlier versions, that in all aspects of the scheme continuity is a special case. Monsieur Devillebichot's comment is just. There is a great deal to be said for proceeding entirely in terms of discrete actions and imagined outcomes. My scheme of thought is perfectly amenable to this.

La surface ϕ et sa relative stabilité dépend de la stabilité du tempérament du 'decision maker'. Une étude des différents types de surface ϕ serait un moyen d'examiner le comportement du decision-maker. Ne serait-il pas possible de dégager à partir de là, des types de surface ϕ homogènes selon les branches de l'activité et d'en induire l'existence d'une structure rationelle, moyenne, raisonable

dans chaque branche, et pour des problèmes comparables. Autre-
ment dit, au delà des multiples variétés individuelles, ne peut-on
aboutir, par des comparaisons interpersonelles, à la construction de
structure ϕ types? Ne peut-on mettre en evidence aussi l'evolution
dans le temps des fonctions ϕ pour une firme, voire une branche de
l'activité, dont le dynamisme est croissant ou décroissant.

Mr H. R. Parker of Liverpool University has indeed suggested
that there is a pattern of evolution of an enterpriser's response
to uncertainty: at early stages of his career, before he has
reputation and fortune to lose, he is bold, but later becomes
cautious. An evolutionary study of the ϕ-surface greatly appeals
to us.

Monsieur Devillebichot comes next to a consideration which
seems to us to throw light on the basic difference between the
probability approach and our own, and to suggest some answer
to the question raised, in her exceedingly interesting editorial
comment in *Expectations, Uncertainty and Business Behaviour*, by
Dr Mary Jean Bowman.* She asks how those decisions are to be
analysed, where there is some similarity between a number of
recorded experiments of the kind the decision-maker is contemplating, so that we are in a no-man's land between divisible
and non-divisible experiments. Monsieur Devillebichot writes:

L'existence d'une partie commune entre ϕ = constante = ϕ_0 et $y(x)$
n'est pas gênante puisque les *standardised* focus points ne sont pas
modifiés. Néanmoins si la tangence est très etendue, dans le cas
particulier où les deux courbes sont partout presque confondues,
alors ϕ étant presque partout identique, son rôle s'efface ou du
moins est moindre.

On se rapprocherait alors de la thèse probabiliste où l'on s'efforce
d'attacher autant d'intérêt à chaque hypothèse, la seule différence
se manifestant dans la probabilité affectée à chacune.

A minor but distinct objection to the probability approach
is its need to treat as deviations, and handle by a separate step,
cases where the decision-maker gives to a hypothetical outcome x, having probability p, a greater or less importance than
xp. Our own approach accepts all such cases as perfectly
normal and provides a general frame within which they are on
the same footing as those (from our point of view) special cases

* Social Science Research Council, New York, 1958.

which are the only ones conceded by the probability approach to be 'rational'. Monsieur Devillebichot's comment indirectly draws attention to this, and he continues:

Ainsi votre thèse s'opposerait à la thèse classique de deux façons principales:

(1) par le nature différente de la variable mesurant l'incertitude: variable non-distributive;

(2) par la prise en considération de la troisième dimension ϕ dans votre thèse, les deux optiques se rapprochant à cet égard lorsque, à la limite, ϕ est presque constant.

The criticism to which he attaches most importance, however, brings us to the heart of the whole matter. He argues against the use of a non-distributive uncertainty-variable on the ground that it leaves the decision-maker without *a complete and coherent case for taking one action rather than another*:

L'incertitude se manifeste, je crois, essentiellement par l'incapacité où l'on est de dresser une liste complète des hypothèses qui peuvent se produire. Nous pouvons toujours redouter d'oublier une hypothèse importante qui serait parfaitement possible. Ainsi a priori, une variable non-distributive semble s'imposer. Mais en y réfléchissant, si une telle variable laisse toujours 'la porte ouverte' à de nouvelles hypothèses parfaitement possibles, elle n'elimine pas le problème. A l'inverse une telle variable nous prive de la *cohérence axiomatique* que détient la notion distributive de probabilité. Or, lorsqu'il s'agit *d'agir*, n'est ce pas surtout de cette cohérence que nous avons besoin?

One of the contrasts which it is the purpose of this book to bring out, is the cleavage between the view which supposes that a complete, coherent case for acting in one way rather than another is always attainable, and the view that there is in life an *essential* uncertainty. It is not, I would say, the adoption of one kind of uncertainty-variable rather than another, but on the contrary it is the nature of things, which robs us of the power to calculate.

XXII

MR EGERTON'S THEORY OF ASSET PORTFOLIOS

In his brilliant book *Investment Decisions under Uncertainty**
Mr R. A. D. Egerton has examined, as a question of basic
relevance to his theme, the relation between the number of
distinct kinds of asset which it will seem to the decision-maker
advantageous for him to hold, and the number of particulars,
that is, of values of variables, or vector-elements, by which he
expresses to himself the relevant character of each asset. We will
use the word *asset* to mean a stated quantity or number of a
stated type of objects. We suppose the decision-maker at his
viewpoint to find himself in possession of a given set of assets
having then a given market value. He must decide for what set
of assets of equal market value he will exchange his existing
set, and it is of course open to him to retain that existing set
unchanged. He will choose a *portfolio*, or set of assets, in view of
the outcomes which he can envisage from so doing; such outcome may consist in the instalments of income to be received at
future dates and the market values to be attained by the various
assets at future dates. The choice of portfolio is thus a choice
amongst available action-schemes made in view of uncer-
tainly expected outcomes, and is accordingly typical of our own
theme.
Mr Egerton reaches the conclusion that

...the existence of a general law can be asserted; namely, that when
the valuation of a holding is determined by n factors, the most
attractive portfolio will contain not more than $n+1$ assets, and may
well contain less.

Mr Egerton is here using the word 'factor' for what (in order
to avoid confusion with the arithmetical sense of 'factor') we
have called values of variables or vector-elements; he speaks of
the valuation, that is, the degree of attractiveness, of the

* Liverpool University Press, 1960.

holding or portfolio being 'determined' by so and so many elements where we have preferred to think of these elements or values as expressing the relevant character of the portfolio; all these things are mere matters of words. In stating the law, however, Mr Egerton has omitted to mention a necessary condition for its truth, namely, that the vector-elements relating to the portfolio must be obtained by simple summation from the corresponding elements of the assets composing the portfolio. Thus, when he applies the law as a criticism of our scheme of thought which makes the attractiveness of a portfolio to depend on its focus gain and focus loss, Mr Egerton is adopting that one of the infinitely many ways in which the focus gain and loss of a portfolio could be derived from those of its composing assets, which consists simply in *adding* the focus gains of the assets to obtain that of the portfolio, and in likewise adding the focus losses of the assets to obtain that of the portfolio. We ourselves adopted that method, with due indication of the possibility that other methods might, instead, be appropriate, in chapter IV of *Expectation in Economics*. What Mr Egerton has done, in chapter VI of his book, is to show that in many circumstances, and those especially realistic, the additive method of combination is quite inappropriate. His criticism bears, therefore, not against our concepts of potential surprise and focus values, as he thinks, but against our choice of method of combining the focus values of individual assets into those of a portfolio. The great service rendered by Mr Egerton's chapter VI is to have shown, with a commanding argument of great incisiveness, that the additive method is unrealistic in most cases. By abandoning the additive method, as we have done, for instance, in chapter XXIV of the present volume, we turn aside Mr Egerton's shafts from our concepts.

We shall now present a formal example, simplified but not so as to lose generality, showing how a number of assets much greater than two or three might be required by a decision-maker who described each asset to himself in terms simply of focus loss and focus gain, in order that his resulting portfolio might have a satisfactory pair of focus outcomes. He may wish to reduce the focus loss of the portfolio below that numerical size which would result if he invested his whole fortune in a single type of asset; he may be able to achieve this desire with less sacrifice of focus gain by means of a portfolio, than if he chose the single asset-type with smallest focus loss per unit market value of asset. All this may be true for a decision-maker who characterizes all his individual asset-types and his portfolios as a whole by means simply of focus gain and focus loss.

Let us suppose that at some viewpoint

(i) There are n different types A, B, ..., E of assets, all having the same market price per unit.

(ii) The decision-maker is free to buy any n units comprising j units of A, k units of B and so on, each j, k, ... being equal to or greater than zero and less than or equal to n, provided $j + k + ... = n$. That is, the decision-maker is free to spend a given sum in any way on the assets of types A, B, ..., E in whole units.

(iii) When he considers singly a unit asset of any type, the decision-maker assigns zero potential surprise to one particular gain and to one particular loss, and the absolute maximum of potential surprise to all other outcomes. The two outcomes for which $y = 0$ will then be the (standardized) focus outcomes of a purchase of this asset.

(iv) The focus gains of unit assets of all types are equal, and each is an amount g; and the focus losses of unit assets of all types are equal, and each is an amount h.

(v) The decision-maker envisages n different and mutually exclusive sets of circumstances (a), (b), ..., (e) such that (a) would ensure the focus gain of A and the focus loss of each other type of asset; (b) would ensure the focus gain of B and the focus loss of each other type of asset; and so on. He assigns zero potential surprise to the occurrence of each of (a), (b), ..., (e).

(vi) $g = (n-1)\,h$.

Then a portfolio consisting of n unit assets all of different types will have a focus gain and a focus loss each equal to zero, while a portfolio consisting of n specimens all of one type will have a focus gain of ng and a focus loss of nh. A portfolio having n unit assets of more than one but fewer than n different types will have a focus gain greater than zero but less than ng and a focus loss numerically greater than zero but less than nh.

The special assumptions which we made in order to simplify the foregoing argument do not prevent its qualitative conclusion from being applicable in perfect generality to all cases where the decision-maker has in view diverse assets each specially adapted to one or other of a number of sets of circumstances which are rival possibilities in his mind. Amongst Mr Egerton's contributions to the analysis of decision in face of uncertainty, the one which I most warmly acknowledge as an essential part of the scheme of thought which I am seeking to construct, is his pointing out precisely in what the unrealism of the extreme position underlying the main argument of chapter IV of *Expectation in Economics* consists. In the following passage from *Expectation in Economics** I indicated that, if we assume that the focus outcomes of a portfolio of assets are *not* to be reckoned by simply adding the corresponding focus outcomes of the component assets, then we shall *not* conclude that a portfolio cannot advantageously consist of more than two assets:

If, then, combinations of more than two goods are ever chosen, one or other of two things must in such cases be true: either some qualities of the combination besides its focus gain and loss are being taken into account; or else the assumption that the focus gain and loss of such a combination can be obtained from the potential surprise functions for the ratios of price change of the individual goods in the direct way we have described does not always hold.

Although I thus directed attention to other possibilities than the simple adding of the focus gains (or losses) of the component assets in order to obtain the focus gain (or loss) of the portfolio, I thought it important to study the consequences of the simple additive reckoning, because my whole construction was founded on the assumption that the decision-maker concerns himself with the best and the worst that *can happen* as a consequence of this or that decision; and I interpreted this attitude (wrongly, as I now think) as meaning that he would always consider it possible for two or several assets all to yield their respective focus gains, or all to yield their respective focus losses. But evidently, if one asset depends for its success on the very circumstances which must ensure another's failure, that interpretation cannot be sustained. Mr Egerton has pointed out the fact, and

* *Expectation in Economics*, 1st ed. (Cambridge, 1949), p. 90.

the reason, that it cannot be sustained. And I might well have thought of this for myself, if, in writing chapter IV of *Expectation in Economics*, I had looked back at chapter III or appendix D to chapter II of that book, where I had developed in detail another consequence of the decision-maker's supposing that at some intermediate date he would know which of several possible sets of circumstances was going to prevail.

Mr Egerton's treatment of asset portfolios really falls into two parts. In the first he has shown, as we showed in chapter IV of *Expectation in Economics*, that so long as we reckon the focus gains (or losses) of a portfolio by simply adding the focus gains (or losses) of the component assets, there will be no advantage to the decision-maker, faced with gambler indifference curves convex to the loss axis, in holding more than two assets. (Save only, let us add, when one asset is money held, on the principles set out in chapter XXIV of the present book, to give freedom of choice amongst deferred blueprints.) Mr Egerton has generalized this principle to cover 'two value' or 'two element' asset characterizations of a more general kind, including, for example, those which speak of 'yield' and 'risk'; in fact, any pair of values which are used to plot a point, representative of the asset, on a Cartesian diagram. Secondly, however, Mr Egerton has turned to an entirely different task, and having advanced his first argument as a criticism of our scheme of thought, he has then proceeded to show just why this criticism is quite irrelevant to the concepts of potential surprise and focus values, and applies instead to the direct additive procedure for obtaining the focus values of a portfolio.

The question how a portfolio of assets should be chosen, in face of uncertainty about the future incomes and market values of each available asset, so as to make the owner safe against disabling loss, has been investigated mathematically by Mr A. D. Roy.* Amongst a large collection of assets it is statistically unreasonable to assume that all movements will be favourable or all unfavourable: this is the basis, as we understand it, of Mr Roy's discussion. He has shown how the decision-maker by relying on this principle of randomness can guard himself

---

* 'Safety First and the Holding of Assets', *Econometrica*, vol. XX (July 1952), and 'On Choosing Between Probability Distributions', *Review of Economic Studies*, vol. XXII (3), no. 59 (1954-5).

against catastrophe. It is in essence the same argument which relieves us of concern about the availability of air to breathe; if all the oxygen molecules, in their random dance, happened to move in the same direction at once, we should suffocate. However, there are more oxygen molecules than available assets and the molecules are not subject to business cycles, wars, politics or human infatuations.

XXIII

ASCENDANCY IN SUM

Three tasks have been reserved for this chapter. Whereas our basic model could be presented in a few pages, the sophisticated version has been developed over many chapters and we wish first to epitomize that argument. Secondly, the relation of that model to the basic model is to be briefly restated, and the nature and purpose of the conception which embraces both these models is to be re-expressed in terms which the completion of the second model has made possible. Thirdly, we must show the relation to each other of a number of ideas and propositions which have been separately put forward in different chapters and which may in consequence appear at present as loose ends.

Five structures or ideas compose the sophisticated model. There is first the replacement of a simple possible-impossible dichotomy by the notion of a continuous psychic variable allowing many, or perhaps all conceivable, degrees of possibility to be distinguished, named and ordered, and even perhaps located against a fixed background scale or grid of accepted fixed levels so as to be treated as measurable. This continuous uncertainty-variable was selected from amongst two candidates for the office, a distributive variable representing degrees of positive belief and a non-distributive variable representing degrees of doubt or disbelief.

Next we made two assumptions about the basis upon which the decision-maker judges the degree of potential surprise to be assigned to each of his imagined outcomes of some action scheme. This basis was assumed, first, to be some one characteristic possessed in common, in varying degrees, by all those outcomes. If the real basis of assessment is more complex, then we suppose that some single characteristic, a variable whose degrees can be distinguished and ordered, depends upon all the ultimate features composing the basis of judgement and exactly interprets the power of each to raise doubts about the outcome's possibility. Secondly, we assumed this basis-variable to be, in fact, desiredness, so that in the upshot of our argument, potential surprise would be assigned to an imagined outcome in a degree dependent on its desiredness for the decision-maker. Now the question may at first sight occur to the reader whether we are justified in assuming in one and the same variable both the above-mentioned attributes, namely, that it should accurately reflect the imperfection of possibility of the outcome and *also* its desiredness. But upon reflection it will be seen that what we are really doing is to treat both desiredness and possibility as functions of some underlying set of characteristics and then to turn our attention to the functional connection which must therefore exist between desiredness and possibility. As a separate matter, we shall usually assume that potential surprise is a single-valued function of desiredness; though the converse, of course, is not true so long as the potential surprise function contains, as we shall usually suppose it to, an 'inner range' $y(G) = 0$. Because hypothetical outcomes can be assigned less than perfect possibility, we have sometimes called their degrees of desiredness face-values.

Degrees of desiredness by their nature can be ordered. In our sophisticated model we treat degrees of desiredness, or face-values, as able to compose a continuous variable. Thus looking on potential surprise as continuously variable we can treat it as a continuous function of the continuously variable desiredness. The second of our component structures is the potential surprise curve or y-curve which expresses one of these variables as a function of the other.

The question next arises whether the variables which express possibility and desiredness are to be regarded as *measuring* or merely as *ranking* the intensities of these responses. In this matter our refined model has two alternative levels of sophistication. The main lines of our analysis remain unaffected by the election of cardinal or of ordinal variables, for as has been shown elsewhere,* if we look upon one or both of these variables as subject to monotone transformations without alteration of their essential meaning for our purpose, then when any such transformation is applied, the form of the function connecting the

* G. L. S. Shackle, 'Expectation and Cardinality', *The Economic Journal*, vol. LXVI, no. 262 (June 1956), W. M. Gorman, 'A Note on "A Revised Theory of Expectations"', *The Economic Journal*, vol. LXVII, no. 267 (September 1957); G. L. S. Shackle, 'Decision in Face of Uncertainty: Some Criticisms and Extensions of a Theory, *De Economist* (Amsterdam) 1958.

variables must also, in logic, be suitably altered, and thus the focus-element determined by one pair of variables will retain its identity when the responses, of desiredness and potential surprise, to which that focus element corresponds, are renamed, by transformation of the variables, without any change in their real and felt intensities. Indeed, we showed that when some objective or public measure is available of the feature underlying the desiredness of an outcome; for example, the size of the money gain from an investment; then the very same size of gain will be indicated as corresponding to a focus element, after a monotone transformation has been applied to the potential surprise variable, or to the desiredness variable, or both, as before that application; for the entities really involved are intensities of actual feeling and not the numbers arbitrarily tied to these intensities to label them; and the essential linkage is between the felt intensities of response, on the one hand, and the attention-commanding power of an expectation element, on the other, and not the formal algebraic expression of a function, for that expression itself must alter its form when the 'numbers on the labels' are changed.

What we lose, if cardinality is judged inadmissible, is the right to speak of the convexity or concavity of the y-curve or of the contour-lines of the ϕ-surface or of the profiles $\phi = \phi(G, y = \text{constant})$, and the right to think of the focus elements as points of tangency. These rights add to the power and efficiency of our tool but they are by no means indispensable to its main purpose.

In our basic model the attention paid to a hypothetical out-come depends on whether or not it belongs to the class of possible outcomes and, if it does, on whether, when the hypo-theses of that class are ordered according to desiredness or face-value, it is one of the two extreme members of that ordering. Unless it is one of these extremes it claims no attention. In our sophisticated model we consider many or infinitely many degrees of possibility and within each of the corresponding classes we suppose the hypotheses to be ordered according to their desired-ness. Thus ascendancy, the power of a hypothesis to command the decision-maker's attention, comes to depend on possibility as well as on desiredness. In our sophisticated model, then, the thing which exerts ascendancy is a vector associating a degree of desiredness (a face-value) with a degree of possibility or potential surprise. Such a vector (G, y) we call an expectation element. In the sophisticated as well as in the basic model, ascendancy is as it were polarized, or concentrated upon two elements which are in some sense opposites of each other. That sense is that while one of the two poles represents gain or success the other represents loss or disaster. We have to answer the question: Why may not all the hypotheses in any one possibility rank be desired, or all be disliked? Why may not all of them appear as successes, or all of them as disasters? Our third construction, that of the neutral outcome, therefore proposes that success or disaster must be interpreted as change in one direction or the other from some 'existing situation' which the decision-maker conceives to be his. But the character of this existing situation depends, itself, largely on what it is imagined to be able to lead to. Thus it must of its nature inevitably be somewhat centrally placed between notions of something much better and of something much worse than itself. If the best that can be hoped from the most favourable of the available action schemes is suddenly found to be worse than the hitherto-supposed 'existing situation', the decision-maker must revise downwards his conception of the latter. Or if there are no actions available to him, except those from which the worst outcome he need fear is better than his hitherto-supposed existing situation, he must revise his notions of it upward. He will not in any case consider action schemes whose best outcomes are worse than the worst outcomes of others, and even amongst those whose y-curves are related like links of a chain, only the topmost link will be considered (see Fig. XXIII 1 A). Only those actions will effectively compete with each other whose y-curves are 'nested' as in Fig. XXIII 1 B. The decision-maker's 'existing situation' will correspond to some point in the middle of this nest, and it follows that there will be for him a neutral outcome, identical with or closely resembling his existing situation thus located, such as to divide hypothetical outcomes into the positively, rather than relatively, good or bad.

The polarization of ascendancy and the weakening of ascendancy as possibility gets less are the two clues to the shape-type of the ascendancy function or ϕ-surface, $\phi = \phi(G, y)$. Instead of a continuous surface, the reader may prefer to think of discrete levels of possibility and discrete sizes of gain or loss. Then the function can best be visualized as a rectangular table or matrix with a row for each possibility level and a column for each face-value, the number entered under any row and any column denoting the ascendancy of the expectation element denoted by the combination of that row and column. Now we are to think of a row as an entity able to be interchanged bodily with any other row, carrying with it, nevertheless, its meaning

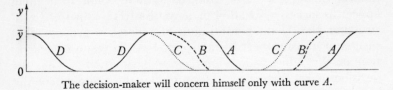

The decision-maker will concern himself only with curve *A*.

Fig. XXIII 1 A

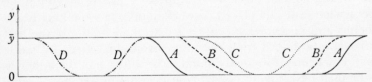

The decision-maker will dismiss curve *D* and make deliberate choice amongst the 'nested' curves *A, B, C*.

Fig. XXIII 1 B

of a given level of possibility. As we move it from one place in the table to another, all the numbers standing for degrees of ascendancy will move with it, and will remain the same numbers in spite of this change of mere physical position; for each such number, still in the same column and therefore representing the ascendancy of the same face-value or hypothetical outcome, will still assume that outcome to be accorded the same degree as before of possibility. Likewise we may suppose each column to be able to exchange its position bodily with that of any other column, carrying its meaning and its ascendancy-numbers with it; and again those numbers will not change their numerical values or their meaning. Indeed we can simultaneously shuffle both rows and columns in any way, subject to the understanding that each row or column carries the same meaning as it had before to its new position. What is the purpose of such an exercise? We intend it as a means of uprooting the idea that

cardinally measurable variables *or even ordered classes* are essential
to the notion of focus elements. For instead of labelling the
rows with the meaning of different levels of possibility, we could
in a mood of fantasy label them, for example, with colours or
with meaningless but distinguishable hieroglyphs; and we could
similarly label the columns with signs or names possessing no
natural order of their own. Still, the combination of any two
signs or names, one attached to a row and the other to a column,
would stand for a given expectation element, and would have
in the appropriate place in the table, where this row and column
intersected, the sign standing for the same real and felt
ascendancy as before. Possibility classes need not be thought of
as ordered classes but only as distinguishable and identifiable
classes; face-values need not be thought of as ordered but only
as distinguishable and identifiable; then each pair of distinct
and identifiable classes, one a possibility class and the other a
face-value class, will determine an ascendancy class. When any
action-scheme has had its imaginable outcomes distributed over
the two sets of classes, its focus expectation elements will have
been determined.

In the discrete model we have just described, as in the continuous model, it is evidently possible that two or many expectation elements on, say, the gain side may claim equal ascendancy,
for higher face-value may precisely compensate higher potential
surprise; but this possible plurality of *primary* focus gains in no
way embarrasses us, for an element can be found, or imagined,
whose degree of potential surprise is zero and whose ascendancy
is equal to that of the one or the many primary focus gains.
This *standardized* focus gain will be unique for any one action
scheme, and so likewise will be the standardized focus loss
similarly determined. The ascendancy function, its constrained
maxima or primary focus elements determined by its combination with the potential surprise curve, and the standardized
equivalents of these focus elements, together make up the fourth
of the structures composing our decision model in its sophisticated form.

The last of these structures is the indifference curve system
by which we represent the decision-maker's basis of choice
amongst action-schemes offering various pairs of standardized
focus outcomes. Here once more the loss and gain aspects of

our diagram are rendered asymmetrical by the fact that, quite plainly when we are concerned with investment schemes, and surely also, if perhaps in a less clear-cut way, in other contexts, there is some amount of loss which is completely and finally ruinous so that any notion of still greater loss is in effect meaningless for the particular decision-maker in his particular viewpoint circumstances. This idea needs to be expressed with slight modifications of wording according as we are speaking of the potential surprise curve, the ϕ-surface or the gambler indifference map. In the potential surprise diagram, the notion of a larger loss than the decision-maker's whole resources, whether these be an investible fund, a means of conducting a battle, a political reputation or what not, must evidently be associated with the absolute maximum of potential surprise, and so a perpendicular to the outcome axis (face-value or G-axis) must be set up at that outcome which represents this total destruction of the power to act further. In the ϕ-surface diagram as we conceive it, the hypothesis of the total destruction of resources sets a bound to the meaningful part of the diagram. To the left of this bound the hypotheses mean nothing and the ascendancy surface has in consequence no existence. In the gambler indifference map losses or misfortunes increase towards the right along the horizontal axis, but here again there is some absolute maximum possible loss which cuts off the meaningful part of the diagram. It is to be noted that points plotted on the gambler indifference map must refer to what we may call a total action-scheme, that is to say, one which prescribes the use to be made of the whole of the decision-maker's powers of action, the whole of his resources at command; in the case of an investment scheme, the whole of what we have called his fortune.

Two action-schemes may evidently differ only as to the disposal of a part of his total resources or fortune, the use to be made of the rest may be the same in both; but the hypotheses involved in the determination of the standardized focus gain and loss represented by any point on the map must refer to the outcome from some application of every part of the total resources. In the context of economic investment, for example, this means that if the choice which the decision-maker is about to make is between several investment schemes each requiring the same investible sum, and if this sum is only a part of the

decision-maker's 'fortune' in our sense, then he must be supposed to intend one and the same use, in each case, for the
rest of that fortune. This will be the most natural and usual
situation, for an enterprise will be newly founded only once,
and entirely transformed in purpose, organization and equipment hardly ever, but it may many times call for extension or
the re-equipment of one division or component plant. In such
a case there will be no question of altering the deployment of
most of the net value of the firm's possessions; this part of its
'fortune' will remain embodied in the equipment or the paper
assets in which it is; the question to be decided is simply the
destination of the remainder of that 'fortune'. One more rather
trivial complication may be worth a moment's mention. Two
investment schemes may involve different investible sums. Then
plainly, when on the gambler indifference map a point is
plotted corresponding to the less costly of the two investment
schemes, that point must be based on some explicit assumption
as to what will in this case be done with the difference between
the investible cost of the two schemes, and on expectations about
the possible outcomes of that use of that difference.

PART IV

EXPECTATION OF CHANGE
OF OWN EXPECTATION

XXIV

EXPECTATION OF CHANGE
OF OWN EXPECTATION

Can a decision-maker's viewpoint expectations, bearing on some outcome the truth about which will be known at the later of two future dates, include the idea that at the earlier of those dates he will entertain a different system of expectations from the one he entertains at his viewpoint? Can he expect a change of his own expectations?

If there can be expectation of change of own expectations, what constraint does logic impose on its form? That is, what kind of changes in his own expectations can a man expect without involving himself in logical contradiction? How will the selection of the focus elements of an action-scheme be related to an expectation of change of own expectations? How, in consequence, will choice amongst available actions be related to expectation of change of own expectations? Involved in these questions is the basic question, how are the degrees of potential surprise respectively assigned to event E, and to event F on the supposition that E is perfectly possible, to be combined into a degree to be assigned to F given the degree actually assigned to E?

Expectation of change of own expectations calls for a unified theory embracing answers to all the above questions. In this chapter we shall outline a theory which first enables those questions to be made more specific and then offers a solution of them. We shall assume as in Part III that each hypothetical outcome of each action scheme can be expressed as an algebraic value of a continuous variable G, and that by applying some standard of comparison such as the 'investible sum of money' required when the action scheme is an investment scheme, we can give meaning to such expressions as a *high* standardized focus gain or loss.

In our scheme of thought, the decision-maker can in all circumstances choose amongst the action-schemes which have presented themselves to him by comparing, in a manner pictured by the gambler indifference map, their respective pairs of standardized focus outcomes. Each envisaged action will have one and only one standardized focus gain, and one and only one standardized focus loss. But if between his viewpoint and the outcome date itself there is an intermediate date whose events, according to his viewpoint expectations, will afford him new knowledge and insight so that he will then adopt new expectations about the outcome, it is plain that his viewpoint conception of what these new expectations could be, on the one hand, and his viewpoint assignment of standardized focus outcomes to the action itself, on the other, must be intimately and systematically related. This relationship is what we now wish to study.

Instances of this relationship are of two types. In what we shall call type 1 the decision-maker supposes that the intermediate date will afford him knowledge beyond what he possesses at his viewpoint, but that it will not afford him any choice between available paths along which the action-scheme can be developed. In type 2 the decision-maker does suppose that he will be able at the intermediate date to choose amongst different forms which the still-future part of the action-scheme can then be given, and that he will make this choice in the light of new knowledge which some events at the intermediate date will afford. Type 1 is evidently involved and included in type 2, and we shall, therefore, first study type 1.

In our theory the expression of the decision-maker's expectations about any action-scheme is a potential surprise curve $y = y(G)$ which assigns to any hypothetical outcome G of the action-scheme a degree y of potential surprise. For any contemplated action-scheme he will have in mind at the viewpoint one and only one such curve. A supposition entertained by him at the viewpoint that at some intermediate date he may change his expectations about the action-scheme must in our theory take the form of a supposition that at that intermediate date he will adopt for the action-scheme a different y-curve from the one he entertains for it at the viewpoint. He cannot, however, specify at the viewpoint the unique form of any such new y-curve, for to be able to do so would be to have already adopted that new form at the viewpoint. It follows that an expectation of change of own expectations about the outcome of an action-scheme implies the entertaining of more than one possible form, a set or spectrum of possible forms, from amongst which the decision-maker supposes that, when the intermediate date shall have been reached, he will select one as the new form of the y-curve of the action-scheme. The members of such a set of y-curves we shall call conditional y-curves. Now there is plainly some systematic connection between the character of the spectrum of conditional y-curves and the form of the unique y-curve which, at the viewpoint, the decision-maker assigns to the action-scheme. As the basis of any suggestion about the nature of this connection, we need a rule by which, if two y-curves, and two only, both refer to one and the same action-scheme, and if it is true of each of these y-curves that its deferred adoption carries some degree, zero or greater than zero, of potential surprise, we can say what degree $y(G)$ of potential surprise will, at the viewpoint, be assigned by the decision-maker to any outcome G of the action-scheme. In what follows we shall propose and seek to justify such a rule, using for its expression a notation whose essential simplicity of meaning will quickly emerge from a first-sight complexity.

G, then, stands for some outcome or event imagined for the more remote of two specified future dates, and $y(G)$ is the potential surprise assigned by the decision-maker at his viewpoint to G. E_i is an exhaustive set of rival hypotheses about what may happen at the nearer of the two future dates, and $y(E_k)$ is the decision-maker's viewpoint potential surprise assigned to a member E_k of E_i. Each E_i is to be thought of as a *route* to G, and we shall discuss this notion below. $y_{E_i}(G)$ is the potential surprise assigned at the viewpoint to G *by route E_i*. That is to say, when the decision-maker imagines G as a sequel to a particular E_i only, and takes account both of the possibility of this E_i itself, and of the degree of possibility which G would claim in his mind if he supposed this E_i to be *perfectly* possible, then the degree of possibility he assigns to G is in our notation $y_{E_i}(G)$. The second of these two bases or constituents of $y_{E_i}(G)$, *videlicet*, the potential surprise that *would be* assigned *at the viewpoint* if the potential surprise $y(E_i)$ assigned at the viewpoint to E_i were zero, we write $y\{G, y(E_i) = 0\}$. Then our rule consists of the two following assertions:

$$y_{E_i}(G) = \max [y(E_i), y\{G, y(E_i) = 0\}], \tag{i}$$

$$y(G) = \min y_{E_i}(G). \tag{ii}$$

In words: We are proposing to assume that the degree of potential surprise assigned by the decision-maker at his viewpoint to an outcome or event G will be the *least* degree which any one of, in general, many *routes* to that outcome (a *route* being any sequence of events or situations which he might imagine as leading to it) would make appropriate; and we take, as the appropriate degree of potential surprise corresponding to a route containing only one intermediate event, the *greater* of two degrees, namely, the degree assigned at the viewpoint to the intermediate event itself, and the degree which would be assigned at the viewpoint to the ultimate event G, if the degree assigned to the intermediate event were zero.

In this basic form our rule stands in sharp contrast with the rule for calculating the *probability* of the combined occurrence of two events. If the probability of event B, when A's occurrence is taken as a fact, is $p(B \mid A)$, and if the probability of event A is $p(A)$, then the probability that A and B will both occur is $p(AB) = p(A) \cdot p(B \mid A)$. Unless either $p(A)$ or $p(B \mid A)$ is equal to unity, the probability of the combined occurrence of A and B is less than the probability of A alone and is less than the probability of B when the occurrence of A is taken as a fact. If we supposed the decision-maker to base his assignment of potential surprise upon probability, and if we were to regard lower probability as essentially associated with higher potential surprise, we should have to suppose that the decision-maker will attach higher potential surprise to the idea that event E might occur and be followed by event G, than he will to the mere occurrence of event E, or than he will to event G in case he attaches zero potential surprise to event E. However, what is in question for us is not probability but possibility. The question whether I can pass a series of examinations is the question whether I can pass the hardest of the examinations.

There is another aspect of the 'multiplication rule' for the probability of the joint occurrence of two or more events which disqualifies this rule for our purpose. With the notation used above, the probability $p(AB)$ that two events A and B will both occur is

$$p(AB) = p(A) \cdot p(B \mid A)$$
$$= p(B) \cdot p(A \mid B)$$

so that

$$\frac{p(A)}{p(B)} = \frac{p(A \mid B)}{p(B \mid A)}.$$

The relative probability of the two events A and B is one and the same no matter whether we think of these events as each occurring in isolation or whether we suppose that they occur in association with each other. The probability rule, that is to say, is concerned with the mere association of the two events, the idea that they occur together, and not at all with the notion of a *sequence* in which these events might be imagined to occur. Examples such as that of 'successive' drawings of cards from a pack without replacement need not deceive us. When each card drawn is laid aside instead of being replaced, the drawings, though they may be performed one after the other, are essentially simultaneous. The essence of the matter is that non-replacement of a card which has been drawn implies non-availability of that card when the other draw is made. This non-availability is equally achieved by dipping both hands into the pack at once and drawing out, simultaneously, a card in each.

The probability rule, then, is not concerned with the sequence in which joint events occur. Yet the idea of event A being followed by event B is a different idea from that of event B being followed by event A. Each of these two ideas can be thought of as the image of a unified event, and the two unified events thus pictured will in general be quite different from each other. They will, moreover, in general differ in their respective degrees of plausibility or possibility. A brilliant lightning flash quickly followed by a loud clap of thunder is one event; an isolated thunderclap, not preceded but *followed* by a flash of lightning, is a different event. The former on a cloudy day might seem perfectly possible, the latter extremely surprising. The multiplication rule treats sequence as irrelevant, and in other words is concerned not with two unified events (A followed by B) and (B followed by A) but with one unified event (A and B).

What we have called a route by which the decision-maker can imagine his viewpoint situation being carried into a situation where event G could occur, is, then, something entirely different from the notion of the joint occurrence of several events.

$y\{G, y(E_i) = 0\}$ is not the degree of potential surprise he attaches to the occurrence of G on the supposition that event E_i is a fact; it is the degree he would attach to G if he thought that E_i was perfectly possible. Again we meet the contrast between certainty on the one hand and on the other perfect possibility. When E_i seems perfectly possible, the decision-maker assigns $y\{G, y(E_i) = 0\}$ to the subsequent occurrence of G. If he thought G perfectly possible, we might suppose him to consider an imaginary event E_i', formally and technically identical with E_i but assigned to a date following instead of preceding G, and to assign to E_i' a degree of potential surprise $y\{E_i', y(G) = 0\}$. For two reasons, we cannot assume that $y\{G, y(E_i) = 0\} \equiv y\{E_i', y(G) = 0\}$. In the first place, why should event E_i be no more nor less effective and powerful in, as it were, preparing the way for event G than event G is in preparing the way for event E_i? Why should it not be much more, or much less, effective? If E_i is a shower of rain and G is my carrying an umbrella when, a few minutes afterwards, I go out to keep an appointment, and if E_i' is a shower of rain occurring just after I have returned home, there is no ground in general for supposing that $y\{G, y(E_i) = 0\}$ is equal to $y\{E_i', y(G) = 0\}$. In the second place we are not justified in treating E_i and E_i' as in every relevant sense identical. The most we can assume is that they are 'formally and technically' identical. But since they are assigned to different calendar dates their respective sets of circumstances will be different. We require an essentially different set of ideas from those provided by the theory of the counting of cases, the theory of probability. This necessity appears clearly in the fact we have just come across, that probability concerns the results of a series of 'random experiments' every member of which series is, as part of the very meaning of randomness, looked upon as not *a priori* distinguishable from any other member. To a series of random experiments, only those circumstances are regarded as relevant which are either part of the specific and express conditions which every member of the series must fulfil, or else are hidden within the randomness itself and are *ipso facto* and by definition undetectable and incapable of being differentiated as between different members of the series. For us each imagined event is in greater or less degree recognizably special and *sui generis*, its particularity arising from the circumstances which are supposed to surround and merge into it and to form for it an inseparable context or frame. The word 'route' thus involves the idea of sequence while the term 'joint events' ignores it.

When, out of some set S of cases, we take the proportion in which event A occurs, and out of the subset S' of cases in which A occurs we then take the proportion in which B occurs, and multiply these two proportions together, we get the proportion of S in which A and B both occur. If in this statement we interchange the letters A and B the statement will still be true. In the notion of the probability $p(AB)$ of the joint occurrence of two events A and B, no part is played by the notion of a temporal sequence in which A and B might be imagined to occur. In reckoning $p(AB)$ we are engaged merely in counting cases. In so far as that counting reveals a structure in the material, the phenomena or the history we are studying, that structure is non-temporal. Thus in the concept $p(AB)$ there is no place for the notion that a different quantitative value might be assigned according as A, or as B, was given its status ('perfectly possible', 'certainly true' or what not) before a status was assigned to the other event. The probability of joint events is a single idea, whereas our notion of the degree of potential surprise accorded to one event when another event is regarded as perfectly possible comprises two ideas, since either of the two events can be supposed to be accorded its status first. The status of the other event need *not*, then, be the same in both cases. It is the neglect of this difference between the notion $p(AB)$ on the one hand, and the pair of notions $y\{B, y(A) = 0\}$ and $y\{A, y(B) = 0\}$ on the other, that has led Mr W. M. Gorman to make what we believe to be an invalid criticism of our rule $y_{E_i}(G) = \max [y(E_i), y\{G, y(E_i) = 0\}]$.

In an extremely thought-provoking article* Mr Gorman says:

We will show that this rule implies that, if a pair of hypotheses mutually support one another in the sense that a knowledge of either would make the other less surprising, then they have the same degree of potential surprise.... Suppose that A and B are two hypotheses of this type; ... we may write a for the potential surprise of A, a' for

* 'How Surprising is a Chain of Co-incidences?' *Metroeconomica*, vol. IX, no. 2 (August 1957).

that of A if B were known, b for that of B, and b' for that of B were A known. Then, by assumption:

$$a' < a; \quad b' < b. \tag{1}$$

According to Shackle, the degree of potential surprise associated with the joint occurrence of A and B is the larger of a and b', that is, max (a, b').
Similarly it is max (b, a'). Hence

$$\text{max } (a, b') = \text{max } (b, a'). \tag{2}$$

We will now show that this implies that $a = b$. Suppose first that $a < b'$. Then, by (1)

$$a' < a < b' < b. \tag{3}$$

Thus

max $(a, b') = b'$

max $(b, a') = b,$

and so

$b = b'$ by (2) which contradicts (1).

Hence

$b' \leqslant a$ and $a' \leqslant b.$

Then

max $(a, b') = a,$

max $(b, a') = b,$

and so

$a = b$ [as was to be proved].

Mr Gorman's argument rests on the assumption, which he takes so much for granted as to leave it virtually unstated, that the potential surprise assigned to the sequence of events {A followed by B} is necessarily equal to that assigned to the sequence {B followed by A}; this assumption plainly arises from that train of thought, along probability lines, which leads him to refer to the 'joint occurrence' of A and B. Since for us the association of A and B in the decision-maker's mind can take two entirely different forms with quite different meanings and supporting, in general, diverse degrees of potential surprise, the lines of the answer we should make to Mr Gorman will be plain: equation (2) does not hold.

   Suppose that an explorer, in order to pass from point K to point L, must cross a line of mountains and a swamp. He will not be much surprised if a practicable route can be found on the mountain, but very much surprised if he succeeds in crossing the swamp. Our rule in these circumstances says that his potential surprise for the successful completion of the whole journey is equal to his potential surprise for the crossing of the swamp, and that it would accordingly be no lower than it is even if there were no mountains. Our rule thus bounds a range of diverse conceivable rules of which the other extreme might perhaps consist in *adding* the degrees of potential surprise respectively assigned to the crossing of the mountain and the crossing of the swamp. But this other extreme rule, opposite to ours, would surely be unrealistic, and much more so than our own rule. The boxer who wonders whether he can become champion of the world does not *add together* the prowess of this opponent and that to reckon the strength of the opposition. He may have many rivals, but it is the most formidable of these who measures, for him, the difficulty of attaining the championship. We claim three things for our rule: first, that of the two extremes of the range of diverse conceivable rules, it is the less remote from reality; secondly, that it has greater simplicity than any other rule; and thirdly, that this simplicity is not bought at too high a sacrifice of realism.

Our rule can be seen to imply that if at his viewpoint the decision-maker imagines some question being answered at the nearer of two future dates, bearing on the possibility of an outcome G_i imagined to occur at the more remote of those dates, and if at the viewpoint he asks himself whether he may not, when the intermediate question shall have been answered, assign to G_i a smaller degree of potential surprise than he assigns to it at the viewpoint, then he is logically bound to attach to the idea of such a reduction some greater than zero degree of potential surprise. For such a reduction would mean a switch, imagined to occur at the intermediate date, from one route, say E_f, to another, say E_k. That is to say, whereas, at the viewpoint, the decision-maker is basing his assignment of potential surprise to the particular outcome G_j on the supposition that the intermediate event will be E_f, the idea that at the intermediate date he might assign a new, and lower, potential surprise to G_j involves the idea of his basing this new assignment on a different intermediate event E_k. Then $y(E_k)$ is the degree of potential surprise assigned at the viewpoint to the idea that at the intermediate date there will be adopted a new route E_k to which there corresponds, at the viewpoint, a new and lower degree $y(G_j)$ of potential surprise assigned to G_j. Let us now adopt the following shorthand for some of the symbols involved in our rule:

$$y(E_f) = A \text{ or, } y\{G_j, y(E_f) = 0\} = B,$$
$$y(E_k) = A' \text{ or, } y\{G_j, y(E_k) = 0\} = B'.$$

All that we require to prove is that $A' > 0$ ('...he is logically bound to attach to such a reduction some greater than zero degree of potential surprise'). We have:

$$\max(A', B') > \max(A, B) \qquad \text{(i)}$$

(since otherwise the degree of potential surprise assigned at the viewpoint to G_j would be that appropriate to route E_k instead of that appropriate to route E_f);

$$B' \nless 0 \qquad \text{(ii)}$$

(since no meaning is attached to a degree of potential surprise less than zero);

$$B' < \max(A, B) \qquad \text{(iii)}$$

(the new degree of potential surprise which might be assigned at the viewpoint to G_j via route E_k is to be lower than the degree in fact assigned via route E).

Since $\max(A', B') > \max(A, B)$ by (i), and

$\max(A, B) > B'$ by (iii), it follows that

$\max(A', B') > B'$ so that

$\max(A', B') = A'$ and

$A' > B' \nless 0$ so that $A' > 0$, which was to be proved.

In a subsequent paragraph the argument we have just set out will be illustrated with diagrams. Meanwhile our conclusion, that a reduction of the potential surprise to be assigned to an outcome must, when imagined to occur at a future date, itself carry greater than zero potential surprise, can be reached directly as follows: A man cannot without logical contradiction say to himself: 'I should be greatly surprised if event F occurred. But there is an event E which, if it were to occur intermediately, would make me feel that event F would be very little surprising; and moreover, I shall not be at all surprised if event E does occur.'

We turn now to this chapter's ultimate objective, to employ our rule for combining the degrees of potential surprise assigned to, and assigned by, contingent y-curves, in order to answer the question posed on p. 199 above: 'There is plainly some systematic connection between the character of the spectrum of conditional y-curves and the form of the unique y-curve which, at the viewpoint, the decision-maker assigns to any deferred blueprint.' We shall show what this connection is in what we may call the continuous case, the one, that is, where the word 'spectrum' is justified by the supposition that there is an infinite family of conditional y-curves so that every degree of potential surprise, between and including zero and the absolute maximum, is assigned to each single particular outcome G_j by some one member or other of this infinite family of curves.

For simplicity we will apply our argument to those branches of the conditional y-curves and the viewpoint y-curve where G is positive. Over this range of G we assume $y(G)$ to be zero or increasing. To apply the argument to the negative range of G we need only alter the wording to allow for the negative (or zero) slope of the y-curves over this range.

Suppose that for every outcome G_j and for every preassigned degree Y of potential surprise, there is some curve $y = y(G_j; E_i)$ which assigns potential surprise Y to G_j. Suppose also that some degree $y(E_i)$ of potential surprise is assigned at the viewpoint to the adoption, at the intermediate date, of each of these curves. Suppose further that for any G_j there is a bi-unique correspondence

$$0 < y(G_j; E_i) \longleftrightarrow y(E_i) < \bar{y}$$

between the greater than zero degrees assigned by, and the degrees assigned to the adoption of, these curves, such that decreasing degrees $y(G_j; E_i)$ are associated with increasing degrees $y(E_i)$. Then we assert that the viewpoint potential surprise curve $y(G_j)$ will, according to our rule, intersect each curve $y(G_j; E_i)$ at that point where $y(G_j; E_i) = y(E_i)$. We will first explain the justification and the bearing of the assumption that increasing degrees of potential surprise are associated with the adoption of curves E_i which assign decreasing degrees of potential surprise to any outcome G_j, and then show the proof of our assertion. The assumption is a natural extension of the idea that according to any one curve $y(G_j; E_i)$ or according to the viewpoint curve $y(G)$ itself, higher face-values G will, beyond some point, be associated with higher degrees of potential surprise. For we are thinking of a family of curves $y(G_j; E_i)$ in which each member curve is such that $\partial y/\partial G > 0$. This association, on any one curve, of higher values of y with higher values of G is the natural concomitant of the association, for any one value G_j of G, of higher values of $y(E_i)$ with curves E_i which assign a lower value of $y(G_j; E_i)$ to this particular value G_j of G.

The proof of our assertion is as follows. We first express our rule with a slight change of notation but no change of meaning by substituting $y(G; E_i)$ for $y\{G, y(E_i) = 0\}$. The rule then reads

$$y_{E_i}(G) = \max [y(E_i), y(G; E_i)], \tag{i}$$

$$y(G) = \min y_{E_i}(G). \tag{ii}$$

Let us consider two curves E_f and E_k such that

$$y(E_f) < y(E_k), \tag{iii}$$

and correspondingly $y(G; E_k) < y(G; E_f)$. $\hspace{2em}$ (iv)

Suppose at first that $y(G; E_k) = y(E_k)$. $\hspace{3em}$ (v)

Then by (iv) and (v) $y(G; E_f) > y(E_k)$ $\hspace{2em}$ (vi)

and by (iii) $\hspace{4em} y(G; E_f) > y(E_f).$ $\hspace{2em}$ (vii)

By (i) $\hspace{3em} y_{E_f}(G) = \max [y(E_f), y(G; E_f)]$

which by (vii) $\hspace{3.5em} = y(G; E_f)$

and $\hspace{3em} y_{E_k}(G) = \max [y(E_k), y(G; E_k)]$

which by (v) $\hspace{3.5em} = y(E_k) = y(G; E_k).$

Then by (ii) $\hspace{2em} y(G)$ cannot be $y_{E_f}(G)$ for

$$y_{E_f}(G) = y(G; E_f) > y(G; E_k) = y_{E_k}.$$

Secondly, suppose that

$$y(G; E_f) = y(E_f). \tag{viii}$$

Then by (iii) $\hspace{2em} y(E_k) > y(E_f) = y(G; E_f),$ $\hspace{1.5em}$ (ix)

and by (iv) and (ix) $\hspace{1em} y(E_k) > y(G; E_k),$ $\hspace{2.5em}$ (x)

so that $\hspace{3em} y_{E_k}(G) = \max [y(E_k); y(G; E_k)]$

$$= y(E_k).$$

But $\qquad y_{E_j}(G) = \max\,[y(E_f)\,;\,y(G\,;\,E_f)]$

which by (ix) $\qquad = y(G\,;\,E_f) = y(E_f) < y(E_k)$

so that $y_{E_k}(G)$ cannot be min $y_{E_j}(G)$. We have thus proved that any curve E_i for which $y(G\,;\,E_i) > y(E_i)$ or $y(G\,;\,E_i) < y(E_i)$ gives $y_{E_i}(G) > y_{E_m}(G)$ when $y(G\,;\,E_m) = y(E_m)$, as we set out to do.

This result is illustrated in Fig. XXIV 1.

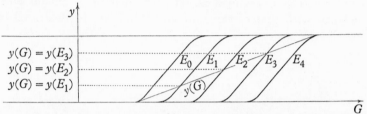

The curves labelled E_0, E_1, ..., E_4 are members of an infinite family or 'spectrum' of conditional y-curves. The idea that at the intermediate date curve E_i will be adopted as the unique y-curve of the action-scheme carries, at the viewpoint, potential surprise $y(E_i)$. The viewpoint potential surprise curve, $y(G)$, of the action-scheme intersects each conditional y-curve E_i at that point (G, y) where, according to that particular conditional y-curve, the outcome G would carry potential surprise $y(G, E_i)$ equal to the potential surprise $y(E_i)$ assigned at the viewpoint to the adoption, at the intermediate date, of that conditional y-curve.

Fig. XXIV 1

When we consider the whole of each of the conditional y-curve sbelonging to some one action-scheme, instead of merely the 'gain' branches or merely the 'loss' branches of these curves, the ways in which these curves can be related to each other are infinitely various, but two types of such arrangements may be noticed. In one we find the 'gain' branches of all the curves arranged as we have supposed in the argument of the immediately preceding paragraphs and as illustrated in Fig. XXIV 1, where if the adoption of curve E_j carries a higher degree of potential surprise than the adoption of curve E_i, then the gain G_j to which any given degree Υ is assigned by curve E_j is greater than the gain G_i to which that same degree Υ is assigned by curve E_i. In other words, curves whose adoption carries a higher degree of potential surprise have their 'gain' branches farther to the right along the G-axis. If the 'loss' branches of the conditional y-curves are arranged in a fashion which reverses the order of the gain branches, so that in a very loose sense we could say that the arrangement of the 'loss' branches mirrored that of the gain branches in a plane cutting the G-axis somewhere within the inner ranges $(y(G) = 0)$ of all the conditional curves, then we have the first of the two types of arrangement of the conditional curves each in its entirety, that we wish to consider. The loss branch of the viewpoint curve $y(G)$ will in this case be related to the loss branches of the conditional y-curves in a pattern which is qualitatively symmetrical with that of the gain side. This case is illustrated in Fig. XXIV 2 A.

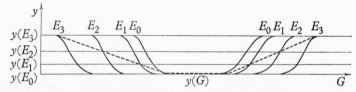

The viewpoint potential surprise curve $y = y(G)$ shown thus – – – assigns to any outcome G the degree $y(E_i)$ of potential surprise assigned at the viewpoint by the decision-maker to his adoption, at the intermediate date, of the conditional y-curve, labelled E_i ($i = 1, 2, ..., n$), which the curve $y(G)$ intersects at the abscissa representing the outcome G in question.

Fig. XXIV 2 A

The second type of arrangement has one conditional curve, say E_D, whose adoption carries at the viewpoint zero potential surprise. Those other conditional curves, say E_P, E_Q, E_R, whose gain branches lie to the right of the gain branch of E_D, have their loss branches also to the *right* of the loss branch of E_D. There are yet other conditional curves whose loss branches lie to the left of the loss branch of E_D and whose gain branches lie to the left of the gain branch of E_D. We suppose also that as we move away from the gain branch of E_D towards the right or the left we come successively across branches of curves whose adoption carries successively higher potential surprise; and similarly that as we move away from the loss branch of E_D towards the right or the left we come successively across branches of curves whose adoption carries successively higher potential surprise. If, now, we trace a curve on the principle that it shall intersect each branch of each conditional curve at an ordinate, y, equal to the potential surprise carried by the adoption of that curve, we obtain a W-shaped curve like that shown in Fig. XXIV 2 B. Can this be the shape-type of the viewpoint potential surprise curve $y(G)$ of the action-scheme? No. For our rule tells us, when locating the viewpoint curve $y(G)$ for any particular outcome G_j, to look for that one amongst all the conditional curves which affords to G_j the lowest degree of potential surprise; where, by the degree which it 'affords', we mean the greater of two degrees, namely the one carried by the *adoption* of this particular conditional curve and the one *assigned by* it to the particular G_j; and it is plain that, in Fig. XXIV 2 B,

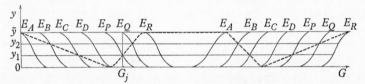

The degrees of potential surprise assigned to the adoption of the conditional curves E_A, E_B, ..., E_R are respectively

$$y(E_A) = \bar{y}, \quad y(E_B) = y_2, \quad y(E_C) = y_1, \quad y(E_D) = 0$$
$$y(E_R) = \bar{y}, \quad y(E_Q) = y_2, \quad y(E_P) = y_1.$$

Why does the viewpoint curve $y(G)$ *not* take the form shown by the broken line? Because at, for example, G_j we have max $[y(E_D), y\{G_j, y(E_D) = 0\}] = 0$ (since both elements within the square brackets are zero], and so min $y_{E_i}(G_j) \not> y_{E_D} (G_j) = 0$. The fact that max $[y(E_P), y\{G_j, y(E_P) = 0\}] = y_1 > 0$ is irrelevant.

Fig. XXIV 2 B

a zero degree of potential surprise is thus afforded to G_j, which lies within the inner range, $y = 0$, of a conditional curve, namely curve E_D, whose adoption carries zero potential surprise. The fact that curve E_Q assigns to G_j a degree y_2 which is greater than zero is thus irrelevant. In our second type of arrangement of the conditional y-curves, as in the first, our rule gives us for the action-scheme a viewpoint curve, $y(G)$, which conforms to the central 'flat-bottomed basin' shape-type of y-curves.

We turn now to type 2 of the two types of relation, which we distinguished above, between, on the one hand, a spectrum of conditional y-curves, from amongst which the decision-maker supposes at his viewpoint that he will at some intermediate date select one as the unique expression of his expectations about the outcome of some action-scheme, and on the other the unique y-curve which he assigns at his viewpoint to that action-scheme. The mark of this second type of relation is that the intermediate date is imagined not only to provide extra or clarified knowledge and insight, but also to offer a variety of courses which action beyond the intermediate date can follow, and amongst which the decision-maker, according to his viewpoint expectations, will then be free to choose.

We can evidently think of the decision-maker in a type 2 situation as looking forward to a date at which there will again be available to him a number of rival action-schemes. The character of this range of action-schemes having deferred availability; the exact description of each member of the set of schemes from amongst which he will, at that future date, be free to choose; depends upon which immediate action-scheme he will choose from amongst those available at his viewpoint. It is in this sense that the particular set of deferred action-schemes, which the decision-maker imagines to be made, at some future date, available by a given choice of immediate action-scheme, can be said to form part of that immediate scheme.

It will be convenient to have a name for an action-scheme of expected and deferred availability which is thought of as one of several rival forms which an immediate action-scheme can take in a part of the calendar lying beyond some specified future date, and we shall call such a deferred action-scheme a deferred blueprint or simply a blueprint. We are to think, then, of the decision-maker as looking forward from his viewpoint and supposing that at some future date, which we have in the foregoing been referring to as the intermediate date, some one or other of a set of events E_i (the 'intermediate event') will occur and will render available some one or other of several sets of blueprints (these sets perhaps overlapping each other by having one or more blueprints in common), and that at the same time the intermediate event will select, for each of the blueprints it has made available, a unique y-curve out of several conditional y-curves which the decision-maker may at the viewpoint entertain for that blueprint. Now, for any intermediate event E_i there will be, amongst the set of blueprints which it will make available, a preferred blueprint, B_i. Amongst the *set of preferred blueprints* B_i, one for each E_i, there will be one which has a higher standardized focus gain than any other. This standardized focus gain will be the standardized focus gain which the decision-maker will, at his viewpoint, assign to his immediate, general, action-scheme. Again there will be one amongst the B_i which has a numerically larger standardized focus loss than any other of the B_i. This standardized focus loss will be that, also, assigned at the viewpoint to the *immediate* or *viewpoint* or *general* action-scheme. One more matter in this connection remains to be clarified, or shall we say, one loose end remains to be tied up. When we speak of the preferred blueprint, B_i, out of the set of blueprints which would become available if E_i were to turn out to be the intermediate event, we mean of course the blueprint preferred in the light of the expectations held by the decision-maker *at his viewpoint*. His judgement of each blueprint, the exact form of viewpoint y-curve assigned to it, will (according to our theory) be based upon the set of conditional y-curves, which the decision-maker at his viewpoint entertains for it, in just the way we have described in the earlier part of this chapter. It is in this sense that we earlier said that the relation of type 1 was involved in the relation of type 2.

We can imagine a rather special, but central and illuminating, manner in which the two types of relation might be associated with each other. Suppose the decision-maker to have in mind at the viewpoint a set B_k of blueprints, choice amongst which will be open to him at the intermediate date, and suppose also that for each of these blueprints he has in mind at the viewpoint n conditional y-curves, one corresponding to each of the hypotheses E_i about what the intermediate event will be. Then E_0, for example, might give to B_0 a high focus gain and a numerically small focus loss, but E_2 might give B_0 a numerically very large focus loss. In this case the viewpoint standardized focus gain and loss of B_0 would both be numerically large. The same might be true, for a similar reason, of every one of the entire set of blueprints B_k. Yet it would not be true that the viewpoint action-scheme (the general, immediate action-scheme), whose adoption would promise to make available the choice amongst the B_k, would necessarily have a numerically large standardized focus loss. For the decision-maker at his viewpoint intends that when the intermediate date shall have been reached and one or other of the E_i has become the truth to the exclusion of the others, he will choose that one amongst the B_k to which this intermediate event gives a high focus gain and a numerically small focus loss.

We have been considering the nature of the link which, if the decision-maker's thoughts are orderly, must exist between the viewpoint y-curve, the one according to which at the viewpoint he assigns degrees of potential surprise to hypothetical outcomes of an action-scheme, and the array of conditional curves, one for each of the hypotheses he entertains concerning an intermediate event, some state of affairs which will become known at an earlier date than that of the outcome itself. A question which may occur to the reader must now be answered. We have referred to the decision-maker as 'supposing' that some event, the emergence and the becoming known of some state of affairs, at a stated intermediate date may afford him extra enlightenment about the later state of affairs in which he is practically and emotionally interested, the 'outcome'. We could (as elsewhere we did) express this idea differently by saying that the decision-maker expects that at the intermediate date some question, bearing on the outcome, will be answered. But, it may be objected, may he not doubt whether this question will be answered on the specified occasion? Can he not entertain the idea that the intermediate date can go past without vouchsafing any answer? To think on these lines is to use the words 'event' and 'answer' in a somewhat different and narrower way than we intend. At the specific intermediate date *some* state of affairs will prevail and the decision-maker will then have some knowledge or conception of it. The array or spectrum of conditional y-curves must provide one for each of the states of mind, that is, of knowledge concerning the intermediate event or state of affairs, which at his viewpoint the decision-maker looks on as in any degree possible. If one of these possible states of mind is in all relevant respects identical with his viewpoint state, and represents no enlargement of knowledge, bearing on the ultimate outcome, whatever, then this state also must have its conditional y-curve, and that y-curve will (with one proviso) be identical with the viewpoint y-curve.

Thus the theory we have advanced in the preceding paragraphs embraces all aspects and sources of doubt as to whether a particular conditional curve can at the intermediate date be adopted as the unique y-curve of the action-scheme. Let us take a concrete example. There are, in the early summer of 1959, two kinds of reason for doubting whether a Conservative government will be returned at a General Election in October 1959. One is the doubt whether, if a General Election is held in October 1959, a Conservative government will emerge from it; the other is the doubt whether a General Election will be held in October 1959. According to our 'rule', it is the greater of these two doubts which will be the effective degree of doubt concerning the election of a new Conservative parliamentary majority in October 1959. Any conditional y-curve concerning a blueprint dated October 1959 will have, attached to its then adoption, a degree of potential surprise which not only takes account of a variety of possible answers to the question 'What would be the result of an election?', but also takes account of the possible non-answering of *that* question through the emergence of a particular answer to another question: Will there be an election or not?

XXV

THE BASIS OF CHANGE
OF EXPECTATIONS

The judgement by which the decision-maker assigns degrees of potential surprise to hypotheses concerning the value which some variable will assume at some specified future date is necessarily based on values which he knows this or other variables to have assumed in the past. Let us call these latter values, basis values, and let us suppose the decision-maker to be looking forward to two future dates, at the nearer of which he expects that a basis value will become known to him on which he will found a potential surprise curve and focus values concerning some variable which will be observable at the more remote date. And let us also suppose that he has already, at the viewpoint, provided this latter variable with a viewpoint potential surprise curve. We will distinguish these various ideas by calling the basis-variable x and by writing $\mathcal{J}$ for the variable, called the outcome variable, in which the decision-maker is ultimately interested. $y_{0,2}(\mathcal{J})$ will stand for the viewpoint potential surprise curve formed at date 0 concerning the value which $\mathcal{J}$ will assume at date 2, and $y_{1,2}(\mathcal{J})$ for the potential surprise curve, of shape unknown at the viewpoint, which he will form concerning $\mathcal{J}$ when the value of x becomes known to him at date 1. We will also write $y_{0,1}(x)$ for the potential surprise curve which, at the viewpoint date 0, the decision-maker forms concerning the value which x will assume at date 1. The problem which we now wish to study is the following: When a new viewpoint is reached at date 1 a recorded value x_1 of x will become known and will be related in some way to $y_{0,1}(x)$. At this new viewpoint also, $y_{1,2}(\mathcal{J})$ will be given a unique and specific form. What will be the relation between the two ideas:

(i) The relation of recorded x_1 to $y_{0,1}(x)$.

(ii) The form (that is, shape and position on the $\mathcal{J}$-axis) of $y_{1,2}(\mathcal{J})$.

The first proposition we shall advance is that if x_1 falls outside the inner range, $y_{0,1}(x) = 0$, of the potential surprise curve which, up to date 1, has been entertained concerning x, then $y_{1,2}(\mathcal{J})$ will not be identical with $y_{0,2}(\mathcal{J})$. For when, at date 1, x_1 is seen to be outside the inner range, and to have registered a value which has hitherto been looked on by the decision-maker as potentially surprising, his judgement will by this event be shown to have been at fault. The data or the structures of inference, or the intuitive assessments, upon which his curve $y_{0,1}(x)$ was based, have proved in some respect faulty. But since x is a basis-variable for expectations concerning $\mathcal{J}$, it is almost inevitable that doubt should be cast, in the decision-maker's mind, on the validity of the structure of assumption, inference and intuition on which he has formed his curve $y = y_{0,2}(\mathcal{J})$. For a basis-variable must itself have a basis, and so long as the value of the basis-variable is still unknown, the basis of the decision-maker's judgement and expectations concerning this unknown value of the basis-variable will plainly have much in common with that of his judgement and expectations concerning the outcome variable itself. $y_{0,1}(x)$ and $y_{0,2}(\mathcal{J})$, that is to say, will stand largely upon common foundations, and if these foundations are seen to have been unsound in one case they are likely to be reconstructed in the other. Thus we take it as an axiom that if the particular degree of potential surprise, $y_{0,1}(x_1)$, which has up to date 1 been associated with the particular value x_1, is greater than zero, then the curve $y_{0,2}(\mathcal{J})$ will at date 1 be reconsidered and given a revised form as $y_{1,2}(\mathcal{J})$.

There is a temptation at first sight to suppose that whenever x_1 does fall inside the inner range of $y_{0,1}(x)$ the decision-maker will not feel any need to revise $y_{0,2}(\mathcal{J})$. But this is a fallacy. For $y_{0,2}(\mathcal{J})$, the potential surprise curve for $\mathcal{J}$ formed at the original viewpoint 0, may well have been based, in the manner we have discussed in chapter XXIV, on a spectrum of conditional curves, selection amongst which was looked forward to, from date 0, to be effected at date 1 by the event consisting in the emergence of an observable value of x. Now it is perfectly possible that various values of x lying within the inner range of $y_{0,1}(x)$ are each linked with one member of such a spectrum of conditional y-curves of $\mathcal{J}$. If so, it may evidently be the case that revision of $y_{0,2}(\mathcal{J})$ is bound to occur *whatever* value x_1 is registered by x at date 1. It is, however, equally possible that every value within some range of x is regarded as compatible with every one of the conditional y-curves of $\mathcal{J}$ in the entire spectrum, and that thus the occurrence of any value of x within this range will make *no selection* amongst the conditional y-curves of $\mathcal{J}$. If x_1 falls within such a range it will evidently make $y_{1,2}(\mathcal{J})$ identical with $y_{0,2}(\mathcal{J})$ and the latter can be said to be left unrevised. In such a case we shall call the relevant range of x the *range of non-revision*.

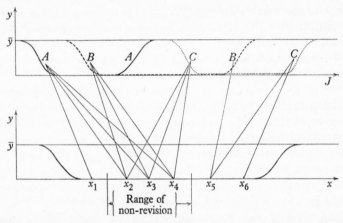

$x_1, x_2, \ldots, x_6$ are specimen hypothetical values of the basis-variable x. Should x register such a value as $x_2, x_3,$ or $x_4,$ within the range of non-revision, no selection will thereby be indicated between the conditional curves $y = y(\mathcal{J})$ (labelled A, B, C). Points x_2, x_3 and x_4 are shown *each* linked with *all* the conditional y-curves, $A, B, C,$ of variable $\mathcal{J}$. Should x register a value such as x_1, x_5 or $x_6,$ outside the range of non-revision, a selection will be possible amongst the conditional y-curves of $\mathcal{J}$ and so the viewpoint y-curve of $\mathcal{J}$, based, at any viewpoint, on those condit'onal y-curves which at that viewpoint have not been rejected, will undergo revision.

Fig. XXV 1

The idea of a range of non-revision, not coincident with the inner range, of a basis-variable is illustrated in Fig. XXV 1. The upper part of this figure shows a set of conditional y-curves of the variable, $\mathcal{J}$, in which the decision-maker is ultimately interested. We will refer to $\mathcal{J}$ as the outcome variable. The lower part of the figure shows a single y-curve for the variable, x, on which his judgement concerning the form* to be given to

---

* Let us repeat that we give to the expression 'the *form* of the curve $y = y(x)$' a meaning such that if the value of y assigned to *any* particular value of x is changed, we consider the form of the curve to have been changed.

$y = y(\mathcal{J})$ partly depends. Should the basis-variable x register a value within its range of non-revision, such as x_2, x_3 or x_4, no selection amongst the conditional y-curves will thereby be indicated. But if the recorded value of x falls outside the range of non-revision, for example at x_1 or x_5, some of the conditional y-curves A, B, C of $\mathcal{J}$ will thereby be rejected and the viewpoint y-curve $y_{1,2}(\mathcal{J})$, now that the viewpoint is at date 1 at which x becomes known, will be different, and more compact, than $y_{0,2}(\mathcal{J})$ which was the viewpoint curve at date o.

It thus appears that the extremes of size between which the range of non-revision can vary are zero, when every point in the inner range of the y-curve of the basis-variable is linked with less than the complete spectrum of conditional y-curves of $\mathcal{J}$, and the full inner range of the y-curve of the basis-variable, when every point in this inner range is linked with the whole of the spectrum of conditional y-curves of $\mathcal{J}$. The notion of the range of non-revision of the basis-variable is thus intimately linked with that of its potential surprise curve and of the latter's inner range, since this inner range sets bounds to the range of non-revision. Moreover, the two ranges, being judgements made by one and the same mind in one and the same moment and being thus based on the same knowledge, will presumably be somewhat similarly affected by any piece of news, so that when, taking up the stand of a detached observer, we compare their relation to each other at one date with their relation to each other at another date separated from the former by the decision-maker's receipt of news, we shall expect to see some stability in this relation. Nevertheless, for some purposes the idea of the range of non-revision can be used independently, and it is, indeed, in the context of comparison of the situations at successive dates that it forms the core of the argument.

The scheme of ideas comprising a basis-variable, its range of non-revision and the outcome variable whose potential surprise curve is formed by the decision-maker in the light of the recorded values of the basis-variable, provides us with the materials for an insulated dynamic mechanism within the meaning given to this term in chapter iv. A special case of the relationship between basis-variable and outcome variable arises when these two variables are the same in name though differently dated, and when the range of non-revision, say $\overset{\text{\tiny H}}{x_{1,2}}$, formed at date 1 and prescribing the bounds within which x has to fall at date 2 if it is not to engender revision of expectations concerning date 3, is formed in the light of the relation which has emerged at date 1 between the value, x_1, then assumed by x and the range of non-revision $\overline{x}_{0,1}$ which was entertained up to date 1. Now if x is a market price, we can make assumptions about the particular reaction (to buy or to sell specified quantities, or neither to buy nor sell) of every member of the market, given the relation between the emerging price x_1 and his hitherto entertained range of non-revision $\overline{x}_{0,1}$; we can infer the new ranges of non-revision $\overline{x}_{1,2}$, one for each member of the market, to which x_1 will give rise, and can also infer the price which will be established at date 2. Then we can suppose the viewpoint to be at date 2 and can observe the new, date 2, relation between price and previous range of non-revision for each member of the market; we can again infer his selling or buying reaction and his new range of non-revision $\overline{x}_{2,3}$; and so on.

PART V

SOME ECONOMIC ILLUSTRATIONS

XXVI

HORIZON, INTEREST AND INVESTMENT

The word *horizon* is used in economics to mean the most distant future date with which, in some particular matter, the decision-maker concerns himself. How does it come about that a given individual, in his circumstances of a given moment, sets his horizon at such and such a distance? In what various ways can we interpret his choice of a particular horizon, near or far, or, what features of the world can we suppose him to be reducing to manageable and explicit shape, when he thinks of an horizon? What economic phenomena are we to associate with the nearness of the horizon to the viewpoint? In brief, how can a near or remote horizon be explained, and what can it in turn explain? These are the questions with which this chapter is concerned.

Why should a decision-maker, in forming his expectations, ignore all future dates beyond a particular date? Why, that is to say, should he consider it uninteresting and irrelevant to imagine situations and events for any dates beyond a particular date? There seem to be two possible reasons. First, it may be that his feelings in the present will be the same no matter whether he does or does not form expectations for those dates beyond his elected horizon. Secondly, the constraints upon the play of imagination, imposed by his judgement of what is possible, may in regard to those distant dates be almost powerless, so that there is nothing which does not seem a possible consequence of no matter what action-scheme, and no choice amongst action-schemes, on the basis of expectations about those distant dates, is possible. This second reason we may express, in view of our definition of expectation as imagination constrained by bounded uncertainty, as the impossibility beyond a certain distance into the future of forming *expectations* at all, because the constraint disappears.

One of the assumptions underlying our scheme of thought is that decisions aim at experiences by anticipation for the decision-maker. If, then, distance into the future can in some way prevent expected events or situations (that is, particular events or situations which are looked on as possible consequences of an available act) from becoming the basis of experience by anticipation when the decision-maker commits himself to that act, it follows that mere remoteness of date can make some expectations irrelevant to decision. 'In some way'; in economic contexts there is a clear-cut principle which makes the present effect and relevance of supposed future states or events, even when looked on as certain, a decreasing function of their futurity; this is the principle of discounting at compound interest. Interest itself is a consequence of uncertainty; thus even this first reason for neglect of dates beyond a 'horizon' may rest ultimately, in economic contexts, upon uncertainty.

The second factor which imposes a horizon upon the imaginative creation of the future is that uncertainty becomes more and more unbounded by considerations of what is possible, the more remote the date considered. Our scheme of thought enables us to quantify this relaxation, so that we can speak of uncertainty as an increasing function of futurity. Two authors in particular, Mr J. Mars of Manchester University and Dr Joseph Haring of Columbia University, New York, have developed explicit theories in this respect and we shall consider their work below. Meanwhile let us point out that, to which ever of our two reasons we refer the existence of a horizon in any particular case, the ultimate foundation upon which such reason lies is uncertainty itself. The concept of horizon is inextricably bound up with that of uncertainty. It may be asked whether there is not something of paradox in the statement that creation of the future fails as imagination becomes less constrained. But in this statement we mean, of course, creation of a future *relevant to decision*. When the decision-maker is free to suppose that any act can have any consequence without restriction, there is no basis of choice of act. The boundedness of uncertainty is essential to the possibility of decision.

Our two reasons are linked together in another way, besides their common dependence on uncertainty. Under the economic aspect of affairs, the characteristics of a thing are often reflected in its market value. If expected outcomes which would otherwise have a value in the present are cut off by a horizon from being taken into account, the action-scheme to which they belong will be correspondingly less valued. This lower value can be looked on as due either to the non-existence, in the decision-maker's thoughts, of these outcomes or to the reduction of their present value to something negligible by discounting at a very high interest rate. This linkage of the two reasons has its own aspects of theoretical interest which we shall consider below.

In what follows we shall examine the concept of *expectation horizon* in a particular economic context, that of the business-man's task of deciding which of a number of available uses for his 'fortune', or money capital at command, he shall adopt. The set of available uses may include a number of specifications, widely diverse in technical purpose and design, of pieces of industrial equipment which the fortune might be used to buy. We have shown in chapter XVII the framework of calculation for setting up a hypothesis of the demand price, or investor's valuation, of a proposed piece of equipment. A set of such hypotheses, perhaps spread over a wide range, is a typical face-value variable to which our focus values construction may apply. For the purpose of this chapter we shall recapitulate the scheme of capitalization of expected earnings which must underly the valuation.

Let c_i be a hypothesis entertained by a businessman about the number of money units that some specified piece of industrial equipment will earn, net of all expenses of operating the equip-ment, in the ith future unit time interval from the viewpoint. Let r per time unit be the rate of interest which he would have to pay to an ultimate lender of the money needed to buy this piece of equipment. Then the contribution of the ith time unit to his valuation of the piece is

$$k = c_i \frac{1}{(1+r)^i}$$

and his total valuation, or demand price which, with a given set of hypotheses c_i, he would regard it as just worth while to pay for this piece, is

$$v = \sum_{i=1}^{\infty} c_i \frac{1}{(1+r)^i}.$$

If there is a market supply price s at which the equipment could in fact be bought, the investment-gain from buying this equip-ment, according to the set of hypotheses c_i, is $G = v - s$. The investment-gain thus defined is a typical face-value variable, from the economic field, to which the notions of potential surprise and focus values might be applied.

There is no reason in the abstract why the focus values construction should not be applied to the decision-maker's set of hypotheses concerning the equipment's net earnings of some one interval i, instead of to his hypotheses concerning the sum of the discounted equivalents of its earnings in all intervals. Thus if, for example, the interval in question is the fifth, c_5 can be looked on as a set of hypotheses forming a continuum, and the potential surprise associated with each hypothesis as a function $y = y(c_5)$ of the face values c_5. Since in general c_5 can be a hypothesis of negative or positive net earnings, a focus gain $c_{5,g}$ and a focus loss $c_{5,h}$ can be determined by the decision-maker in the sense of the most interesting hypothesis of positive earnings and the most interesting hypothesis of negative earnings. If we now regard i as a variable instead of a unique specified date, the focus gains $c_{i,g}$ can be treated as a function of i, and likewise the focus losses $c_{i,h}$ as another function of i. Finally by abandoning the notion of discrete instalments of earnings belonging to numbered intervals of finite length, in favour of that of a continuous variable t measuring futurity from the viewpoint, and an instantaneous rate of earnings $c = c(t)$, we can draw the functions $c_g = c_g(t)$ and $c_h = c_h(t)$ as continuous curves.

Dr Joseph E. Haring has most ingeniously suggested how the investor's horizon can be interpreted by means of a construction using curves essentially similar in meaning to those we have called $c_g = c_g(t)$ and $c_h = c_h(t)$, which we will refer to as the focus gain earnings curve and the focus loss earnings curve. He begins with the widely accepted idea that what we can reasonably assume about the situation or events of any future date becomes vaguer and more precarious as we shift our thoughts to more and more remote dates. To this idea he gives precise expression in terms of the focus value earnings curves. For any date t there will, he says in effect, be some numerical level of the focus loss earnings which is the greatest that the investor would tolerate. If the actual focus loss earnings for that date, which he ascribes to a specified piece of equipment, are numerically greater than that level, he will reject the proposal to buy that piece of equipment. Moreover, while the curve expressing for each futurity the maximum tolerable loss may show this boundary as a function increasing numerically with increase of futurity, and may even show it as increasing at an increasing rate, yet the focus loss earnings curve itself, of any project, will beyond some particular futurity begin to increase numerically faster than the boundary and therefore, if for near future dates the focus loss earnings are tolerable, they will beyond some futurity cease to be so. The futurity at which they do so is, in Dr Haring's construction, the investor's *horizon* for the particular project.

Dr Haring's suggestion seems to us eminently reasonable. The investor is not prepared, Dr Haring says in effect, to give any weight to the claims of an investment project in so far as those claims involve the acceptance of the possibility of a negative rate of earnings of more than a certain level. The degree of possibility in question is that of the focus value of the negative earnings hypotheses. The maximum tolerable loss in this sense might be a constant, but greater generality is achieved, in Dr Haring's theory, by assuming it to be a function (plausibly, an increasing function) of futurity. So far as it is possible to ignore the possibility of negative earnings of more than the tolerable amount, the rest of the project's career may be attractive. With a piece of industrial equipment, however, it will in fact be possible to avoid excessive negative earnings, provided these only occur beyond a certain futurity. For the investor can plan (thus we feel justified in elaborating some-what Dr Haring's construction) to stop the operation of the equipment in good time, avoiding both the prime and overhead running expenses beyond the appropriate date. The question whether to buy the equipment or not then turns upon whether its expected early career, within the horizon, is sufficiently attractive in comparison with other available uses of capital.

Dr Haring suggests alternatively that the horizon might be defined by reference to a curve of minimum tolerable focus gains, if the focus gain earnings curve of a proposed investment, lying above the minimum tolerable level for early dates, crossed the curve of minimum tolerable focus gains from above at a nearer date than that at which the two loss curves intersected. It is not quite so easy to rely upon this part of Dr Haring's construction, because if uncertainty tends to become unbounded as we look at remote future dates, it seems to follow that the focus gain earnings curve of a project, just as much as its focus loss earnings curve, will beyond a particular date bend upward and rise more and more steeply so as to be very unlikely to cross from above the curve of minimum tolerable focus gains.

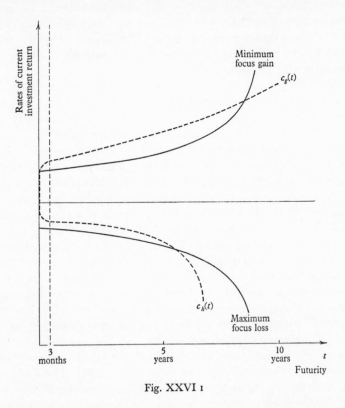

Fig. XXVI 1

Fig. XXVI 1 reproduces the relevant parts of Dr Haring's diagram. His vertical axis is labelled '*Rate* of current invest-ment returns' [our italics]. Plainly, when the proposal to invest a given sum in a fully specified piece of equipment is being considered, it is immaterial whether the net supposed, or required, earnings of any date are looked on as a rate per unit of investible capital or as the absolute earnings of the quantity of investible capital required to buy the piece of equipment.

Indeed, if the investible sum is taken as the unit, the two figures for net earnings are one and the same.

In his extremely interesting review article 'A Study in Expectations'* published in 1950, Mr J. Mars has diagrams where, for each year in the stretch of future time represented by the abscissae, the ordinate shows four hypotheses concerning the gross profit to be earned by a piece of equipment in that year. For the purpose of these diagrams Mr Mars has eschewed our term focus value and refers to the uppermost of the four curves as 'the most favourable expectation', that is, 'the

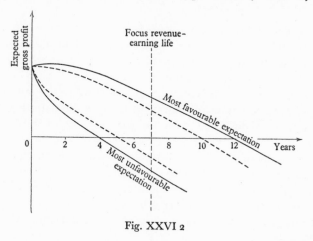

Fig. XXVI 2

expectation of a gross profit under the most prosperous conditions possible in that year', and to the lowest curve as 'the expectation of a gross profit under the most depressed conditions possible in that year'. These two curves spring from a common point representing the known conditions at the viewpoint, and thence diverge, quickly at first and then more slowly, but both of them, beyond a certain date, sloping downwards and eventually becoming negative. Springing from the same point and lying within the former curves, but also diverging from each other and from the former curves, are two curves representing the extremes of the *inner range* on our own definition. Fig. XXVI 2 reproduces Mr Mars's diagram VI.

* *Yorkshire Bulletin of Economic and Social Research*, vol. II, no. 2 (July 1950), pp. 63 to 98 and vol. III, no. 1 (February 1951), pp. 1–35.

Mr Mars now discusses the relation between the gross profit hypotheses for individual years, on the one hand, and on the other the focus-outcomes of the investment as a whole:

A problem at once arises, as Diagram VI shows. There are some years in which there are no negative values [of gross profits] and others in which there are no positive values. The focussing process in those years cannot be a polarisation process, yielding a focus gain and a focus loss. The only possible polarisation consists in selecting the extremes of the inner range as quasi focus values. Thus in Diagram VI there would be only a major and a minor quasi focus gain in the first four years.

We think that Mr Mars's argument interprets quite differently from ourselves the notion of focus value. If no hypotheses of loss are accorded even the smallest degree of possibility, then there is only one focus value, that of gain. There is nothing, however, to prevent this focus gain, referring to the outcome of prospective operations in a single year, from contributing to the calculation of the focus gain for the investment as a whole. Similarly in those years where only losses are looked on as possible, a focus loss on supposed operation of the equipment could contribute to the focus loss on the project of buying the equipment, *provided* there was an intention to continue operating the plant in those years where only a loss was thought possible. This brings us to Mr Mars's concept of the horizon. Mr Mars says:

It is immediately evident from Diagram VI...that it is not only necessary to study the focus gains and losses of each year, but also the focus period of the revenue-earning life which is that [one] among the many expectations of the revenue-earning life of the durable good, which possesses the highest discounted desirableness.

It is evident from Mr Mars's diagrams that his decision-maker looks to a stretch of time when the most favourable expectation of gross profits is still positive, though destined later to become finally negative, while the most unfavourable expectation of gross profits is already negative. Somewhere within that stretch he counts, in his thoughts at the viewpoint, on having to abandon the operation of his equipment.

This notion is not so essentially different from Dr Haring's as might at first appear. Both Mr Mars and Dr Haring regard the decision-maker as setting a 'floor' below which annual earnings, according to the 'most favourable' or 'focus gain' expectation, must not sink. In Mars's view this floor is zero, in Dr Haring's view it is above zero.

The theories of Mr Mars and of Dr Haring which we have discussed seem to us to explain why a decision-maker feels the need to cut off his expectational vista by a horizon, and to explain also how he comes to locate that horizon at a particular futurity in each particular instance of decision. We turn now to use the notion of horizon, thus explained, to explain a further phenomenon, that of the so-called interest-inelasticity of investment.

Given, for each ith future unit interval, a unique hypothesis c_i of the earnings, net of running costs, of a specified piece of equipment, the demand price or greatest worthwhile offer for this piece of equipment is as we saw

$$v = \sum_{i=1}^{\infty} c_i \frac{1}{(1+r)^i},$$

where r is the market interest rate applicable, at the viewpoint, to loans of term i unit intervals. Without much sacrifice of generality we can take r to be uniform for all terms. Then it is plain that v will be a decreasing function of r. The inducement to buy the piece of equipment at any given supply price is thus strengthened by a fall in r; and even if we regard the supply price as an increasing function of the number of such pieces of equipment ordered per unit of time, still there will not on this account be any increase in the supply price unless such an increase in orders has in fact occurred. Thus we may say that the inducement to order pieces of equipment of the specified type will be strengthened by a fall of r. But 'the specified type' can be any type, and our principle, if it applies to any type, applies to all types.

One caution we must here observe. Productive resources required for the production of one type of equipment will very often be of the same kind as those required for another type. A rise of prices of such resources, brought about by an increase in the production of one type of equipment, may well tend to discourage the production of other types of equipment. But such instances can only occur incidentally to an increase in the pace of investment as a whole, in equipment of no matter what sorts.

In face of this result, how are we to explain the statements of some businessmen themselves, implying that their decisions to invest in particular pieces of equipment would still have been taken even if the interest rate had been somewhat higher, and that in cases where they had rejected a proposed investment, a lower interest rate would not have induced them to accept it? We shall propose two entirely distinct lines of thought on which these two aspects can be reconciled. The first line applies the idea of horizon, and only relies on the notions of focus gain and focus loss in so far as they clarify that idea. The second depends directly and essentially upon those notions.

Let us suppose, then, that a businessman has in mind for each ith future unit interval a single hypothesis c_i of the net earnings in that interval of a proposed piece of equipment, the c_i for different intervals differing in general from each other. Now if his valuation v exceeds by a large gap the supply price s that he would have to pay for the equipment, any increase of the interest rate r which lowers v by less than that initial gap may still be followed by a decision to invest in the equipment. If such a gap exists, how is it that it has not long since led to a decision to buy this piece of equipment? Plainly the gap itself may have come abruptly and recently into existence. Its birth would be part of a change of expectations due, perhaps, to sudden understanding of the commercial possibilities of a new invention, or to the assuagement of fears by a conference or an election, or to great changes in a tariff or a tax, or to some other such news, acting on expectations like a twist of the hand upon a kaleidoscope. Thus that *some* decisions to invest are held to have been insensitive to interest rate increases which did, or might have, occurred just before they were taken, need not surprise us. In a corresponding way, some decisions against investing, which were taken or would have been taken despite reductions of the interest rate, can also be understood But at all times, and whether or not businessmen's expectations have just been transformed, there will be in the mind of many a businessman an investment proposal which seems to him barely more or barely less attractive than keeping the necessary funds in his bank or lending them at agreed interest to others. How is it that a number of such 'marginal' proposals are not rendered attractive and embarked on whenever the interest rate falls?

Taken together, our valuation formula and the assumption we made, in embarking on the first line of reconciliation, that the businessman fills each empty box of the formula, each c_i, with one and only one numerical value, leave us no escape from the conclusion that he will be compelled to alter his valuation whenever the rate of interest alters. In short, there can be on these assumptions no *qualitative* reconciliation of fact and formula. The only possibility is a quantitative reconciliation: is the change in v induced by any feasible change in r so small as to be 'imperceptible', or to seem negligible, to the businessman? To study this we must find out what is the order of magnitude of changes in v which correspond to changes in r of a kind which occur in practice.

The variety of patterns in which the series of c_i could be filled in is evidently limitless. We could have larger numbers in the early intervals and smaller ones in the later, or vice versa; or a humped distribution with the larger numbers in the 'middle distance' under some interpretation of the latter; and so on and so on *ad infinitum*. But all the simpler patterns can be represented in an extreme form by merely supposing that c_i is zero for all except one single interval, so that the entire supposed net earnings c of the equipment are concentrated at a single instant, at a futurity of x time units from the viewpoint. By taking c as our unit and writing u for its viewpoint equivalent value when discounted at an interest rate r we have $u = (1+r)^{-x}$. It is easily verified that at levels of r within a range of, say, 2–10%, the natural logarithm $\rho = \log_e (1+r)$ differs numerically so little from r itself that in theoretical argument we may treat ρ as the interest rate. Then $u = e^{-\rho x}$. By allowing x to vary we can see how changes in the futurity of the earnings affect the responsiveness of u, the discounted value of the earnings, to changes in the interest rate. This responsiveness will be measured by the elasticity

$$\frac{\partial u}{\partial \rho} \frac{\rho}{u} = -\rho x$$

which is proportional to the futurity x. We can conclude that of several proposed investments conforming to the foregoing assumptions, all having equal discounted values, that is, demand prices for the equipment, that particular one whose assumed returns are most distant will undergo the greatest change in its viewpoint value as a consequence of a shift of the interest rate between any two stated levels.

A more natural assumption about the net earnings of a piece of equipment is that they will be one and the same amount c in every unit interval up to some futurity T and zero in every interval beyond that date. The earnings can then be thought of as a flow continuing at all instants of futurity x at an instantaneous speed c, and for the viewpoint value of this flow when every element of it is discounted at an interest rate r per time unit we have

$$v = c \int_0^T e^{-\rho x} dx$$

$$= \frac{c}{\rho} \left(1 - e^{-\rho T} \right).$$

The connection between the supposed economic life T of the equipment, on the one hand, and the responsiveness of v to change of r, on the other, can be illuminated as follows.

When r shifts from one particular level to another, the resulting change in v can be thought of as composed of the changes in the discounted values u of those variously dated individual elements, $c(x)\,dx$, which together compose the whole life earnings of the equipment. Which of these elements, by the change of its own discounted value u, will contribute most to the change in v? More comprehensively, what will be the shape-type of the function connecting the futurity x of an element of assumed earnings with the size of the change, brought about by a change of r, in its discounted (viewpoint) value? We have

$$u = u(\rho, x) = c e^{-\rho x},$$

$$\frac{\partial u}{\partial \rho} = -x c e^{-\rho x}; \tag{1}$$

$$\frac{\partial \left(\frac{\partial u}{\partial \rho} \right)}{\partial x} = (\rho x - 1) c e^{-\rho x}; \tag{2}$$

$$\frac{\partial^2 \left(\frac{\partial u}{\partial \rho} \right)}{\partial x^2} = \rho c e^{-\rho x}(2 - \rho x); \tag{3}$$

and from $(\rho x - 1) \, ce^{-\rho x} = 0$ we have

$$x = \frac{1}{\rho} \qquad (4)$$

at which value expression (3) is positive. Since also expressions (1) and (2) both tend to zero as x tends to infinity, it follows that as x increases from zero through all positive values, $\partial u / \partial \rho$ first sags to a minimum at $x = 1/\rho$ and then rises, at first with increasing and later with decreasing steepness to approach zero

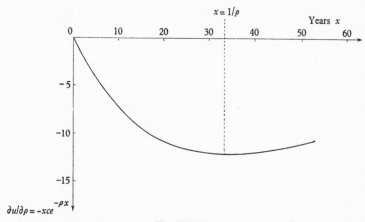

Fig. XXVI 3

asymptotically. This shape-type of $\partial u / \partial \rho$ is illustrated in Fig. XXVI 3 for values

$$c = 1, \quad \rho = 0 \cdot 03.$$

Consider, now, some pieces of equipment each assumed by the decision-maker to have net earnings at a uniform rate of c per time unit at all instants up to a futurity of $x = T$ and at a zero rate beyond T, and suppose that for the first of these pieces $T = 1/2\rho$ while for the second it is $T = 1/\rho$. The addition of the extra segment of economic life from $T = 1/2\rho$ to $T = 1/\rho$ will less than double the value of the net earnings discounted to the viewpoint, but will more than double the total absolute amount of the increase of discounted value which would be brought about by a given reduction of the interest rate. It follows that the second piece of equipment, for which

$T = 1/\rho$, will have its discounted value or demand price increased in a larger proportion by a given reduction of the interest rate, than will the first piece, for which $T = 1/2\rho$. When we reflect that in practice ρ is within the range of, say, 2–10 % per annum, and that even the latter gives $1/2\rho$ a value of five years and $1/\rho$ a value of ten years, it is apparent that those calendar segments which lie near enough to the viewpoint, to be much illuminated by knowledge of the viewpoint situation, are not the same as those where interest rate changes have powerful leverage on discounted values.

Fact and logic are reconciled, save for one step. We have shown that the assumed earning life of a piece of equipment can be too short for the value of the equipment to be powerfully affected by interest rate changes. How many unit intervals forward from the viewpoint, then, can the earning life extend and still be 'too short'? We have shown that this depends on the interest rate itself, and that if this rate is expressed as r per time unit, 'too short' may be interpreted as, say, less than $1/3\rho$ time units, so that if the time unit is a year and $r = \frac{1}{20}$, 'too short' means less than seven years. One question remains: Why should the assumed earning life be set at something less than seven years?

We are evidently asking why the decision-maker's *horizon*, when he is choosing amongst available uses for funds he has at command, and contemplating an investment in equipment, should be set at only a handful of years ahead. The reasons are those we have discussed at the beginning of this chapter, they reside in the fact that beyond a vista of at most a few years his uncertainty becomes unbounded.

It is, then, uncertainty which accounts for the interest-inelasticity of investment, according to this our first line of explanation. Beyond a year or two the fog thickens and, increasingly, things unthought of can happen. But with interest at 5 or 10 % per annum, a year or two, or even four or five years, is not enough to give any leverage.

It would be different if interest were at 30 or 35 % per annum. For then the peak of its influence, on the present value of equal instalments of net earnings, would come upon those instalments at a futurity of about three years. And although the *market* rate of interest on well-secured loans in a wealthy country never approaches 30 % per annum, it is a quite natural thing for the investor to express to himself the dangers inherent in relying on remote supposed earning power, by privately discounting all earnings at a rate which comprises not only the market rate of pure interest but also a risk premium or risk allowance having the same formal character of a percentage per annum. The adoption of this form for a risk allowance is peculiarly apt; for its proportionate effect increases with the remoteness of the earnings being discounted, and if set high enough it can virtually abolish the relevance of all earnings of a futurity of more than a few years.

It appears, then, that several superficially diverse ideas are essentially one and the same. To reject any investment, as some businessmen say they do, unless it holds out to them some hope of 'paying for itself in three years' (or even in two years), that is, of yielding in the first two or three years of its life net earnings equal in total to the purchase price of the investment, is in effect to ignore all possibilities of positive net earnings beyond those early years; to ignore those remoter earnings is in effect to impose a horizon cutting off the vista of expectation at a certain distance from the viewpoint; the reason for such cutting off is that given time enough, anything can happen; that 'time enough' is, at most, only these first few years ahead of the viewpoint; and that when anything can happen as a sequel to each and every available present action, there is no basis of choice between them; finally, to allow for the rapidly increasing uncertainty and unreality of suppositions about remoter dates by applying a high percentage per annum as a 'risk discount' is again, in effect, to ignore all but the nearest years' possibilities of earning: the wheel has come full circle, the whole argument in all its forms is simply that uncertainty cuts off from relevance all those years whose discounted earnings would be noticeably altered by a shift, such as could occur within a space of a few months, between two ordinary levels of the interest rate.

Testimony and theory about the influence of changes of the interest rate on the inducement to invest can be reconciled along a quite different route from the foregoing. Instead of supposing the businessman to assign to each future interval a unique hypothesis about the net earnings in that interval of his proposed piece of equipment, let us revert to our own scheme of thought, and suppose that for each interval he has a pair of standardized focus levels of earnings. Let us also suppose that one of these is positive and the other negative; that is to say, one of them is a hypothesis that gross receipts will exceed running costs, the other that running costs will exceed gross receipts. Let us further suppose that the standardized focus gain of the action scheme (that is, the proposal to buy this piece of equipment) is equal to the result of discounting the positive focus earnings of each interval to the viewpoint and adding the discounted equivalents; and similarly that the standardized focus loss is equal to the corresponding calculation with the negative focus earnings. Now, if two distinct rates of interest are used for discounting the positive focus earnings of each interval, the lower of these two rates will give a higher discounted value to the earnings than the higher rate does. But not only so. The lower rate will also give a greater importance to the focus *loss* earnings of each interval, when these are discounted to the viewpoint, than the higher rate does.

For if I am to be fined £1000 in a year's time, how much would I pay now to be excused that fine? If money can now be lent at 20 % it would not be worth my while to pay more than £835, but at 10 % it would be worth while to pay £909.

The outcome of the entire action-scheme which consists in buying a piece of equipment can be a loss if, merely, the total discounted net earnings are insufficient to cover the purchase price of the equipment. Thus the focus loss of the action-scheme can correspond to net earnings which are non-negative in every interval. If in every interval the hypothesis of net earnings on which the focus loss is based is non-negative and in some of them positive, the discounted total of net earnings will of course be *increased* (numerically and algebraically) by a fall in the interest rate used for discounting, and thus the deficit of total discounted net earnings, compared with the purchase price, will be reduced. That is to say, the use of a lower interest rate for discounting the hypothetical net earnings will have made the focus loss numerically smaller. But if each hypothetical instalment of net earnings, on which the focus loss is based, is itself a *loss*, a fall in the interest rate will numerically increase the discounted equivalent of that loss, and so will numerically *increase* the focus loss of the action-scheme. Now when, at a given relatively high interest rate, the focus gain and loss of such an action-scheme are plotted as a point on the gambler indifference map, and the focus gain and loss at a lower interest rate are plotted as another point, the latter will stand above *and to the right* of the former. It may thus well stand on a *lower* indifference curve instead of a higher (see Fig. XXVI 4).

It will be the more likely to stand on a lower rather than a

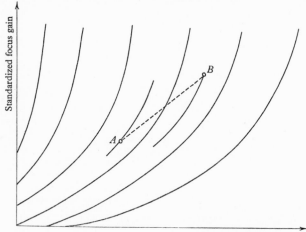

When the focus loss of an investment scheme corresponds, not merely to an excess of plant construction cost over total discounted expected earnings net of running costs, but actually to a negative total of expected earnings net of running costs, a *lowering* of interest rates will numerically *increase* both the focus gain and the focus loss, so that the representative point of the investment scheme will move to the right as well as upward, e.g. from *A* to *B*, thus possibly moving the scheme to a lower gambler indifference curve.

Fig. XXVI 4

higher indifference curve if either or both of two conditions are satisfied. The more distant from the viewpoint is the main weight of the negative focus earnings of the individual intervals (the more distant are those intervals which have the numerically highest level of negative net earnings) the greater will be the leverage of any given reduction of the interest rate in increasing numerically the (standardized) focus loss of the action-scheme. Thus if those intervals with specially large positive focus earnings are near to the viewpoint, while those with specially large negative focus earnings are remote from it, an interest rate reduction will affect the gambler indifference map position of this action-scheme more adversely (pushing it farther to the right for a given distance upward) than if specially large numerical focus operating profits and losses had been found in one and the same group of intervals. Secondly, the more convex to the loss axis are the gambler indifference curves, the more distinctly will any given upward and rightward movement appear adverse.

XXVII

A THEORY OF THE INTEREST RATE

By a *bond* we mean here the promise made by a borrower, in return for a loan of money, to pay stated sums of money at stated calendar dates to the lender. The lender, when he makes the loan, cannot know at what dates he will wish to have cash instead of the bond. If there is an organized bond market, however, he can look forward to being able in case of such need to sell his bond. But he cannot, when making the loan, tell at what price such a sale, at a date now unknown to him, will be possible. Such a sale may have to be at a price less than the sum he now lends, or less than the debt which will still at that time be outstanding. To give him a presumption that this will not be so, and also to compensate him for the irksome uncertainty in which the making of the loan will therefore place him, the 'representative lender' requires that the total of the promised payments shall exceed the 'principal sum' which he lends. If i time-units is the deferment of any promised payment A_i from the date when the principal P is lent, then we can find some proper fraction r such that

$$P = \Sigma \frac{A_i}{(1+r)^i}$$

and we define r as the interest rate per unit of time on this particular loan. The market mechanism ensures that all borrowers of the same standing can on any one date obtain the same principal sum for the same schedule of promised payments. That is to say, interest rates will be uniform throughout the market on loans of similar term, and regarding such loans we can speak of 'the' interest rate. To sell a bond, no matter whether newly created or old, is the same thing as to borrow, to buy an old or new bond is the same thing as to lend, and P of the foregoing formula is therefore the price of bonds.

We now state a theory of the determination of the interest rate as follows: The interest rate will change unless for every existing bond there is a willing holder at the prevailing interest rate. To give content to this formal statement we have to show on what the willingness of any wealth-owner to hold bonds depends; to establish the circumstances in which there will be a function connecting the number of bonds which can find a willing holder, with the prevailing interest rate, and to see broadly what is the character of this function, and whether it can allow of any range of indeterminacy such that, when by the bodily shift and alteration of shape of this function, the rate

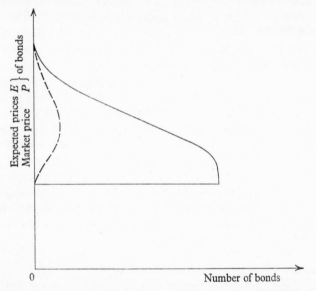

The continuous curved line represents the number of bonds finding willing holders at each market bond-price P, these being holders who entertain expected bond-prices above P. The intermittent line represents the number of bonds finding willing holders amongst wealth-owners entertaining each expected bond-price (E).

Fig. XXVII 1

has been left stranded at some particular level, it may remain there in spite of some appreciable reverse shift of the function.

Let us at first suppose that each wealth-owner, looking forward to the nearest date which he deems it worth while to consider for speculative purposes, has in mind a level which he feels certain that the price of bonds will stand at on that date. So long as we exclude the possibility of holding wealth in any form except bonds or money, we need not suppose this image-date to which the expected price refers is the same for all wealth-owners; for it is only if there is some third rival use for wealth, that the proportionate speed of capital gain, reckoned as a daily, annual, etc. percentage on the price paid for a bond, will vitally affect our argument. We shall refer to each wealth-owner's *expected price* of bonds. Let us further at first suppose that the interest yielded by each bond during the short expectation-interval is so small as to be neglected. On these assumptions a wealth-owner whose expected bond-price is above the prevailing market bond-price will wish to hold bonds, and one whose expected price is below the prevailing price will wish to hold money. With a *given* set of expected bond-prices, one for each wealth-owner, it will thus be possible to draw a curve $N = N(P)$ connecting, as in Fig. XXVII 1, each hypothetical price P of bonds (with which, of course, the corresponding hypothetical interest rate varies inversely) with the number N of bonds which, at that rate or price, will find willing holders. Since the lower the market-price the larger, in general, will be the number of wealth-owners whose expected prices exceed that market-price, the curve will slope down from left to right. If all expected bond-prices remain unchanged, a net addition to the number of bonds outstanding will require a lowering of the market-price: in other words, a raising of the interest rate. A change of the expected bond-prices of some or all wealth-owners will call for the drawing of a fresh curve. Any such curve as we have defined will be the result of cumulating a distribution-curve n (E) showing, for *each* expected bond-price E, the number n of bonds which will be willingly held by the wealth-owners entertaining that particular expectation. If the relevant distribution clusters about a central value the cumulated curve will evidently have an S-shape as illustrated in Fig. XXVII 1. The intersection of the curve $N(P)$ with a perpendicular erected on the horizontal axis at a distance from the origin representing the number of bonds in existence will give the equilibrium price of bonds as in Fig. XXVII 2, and, on a suitable scale, the equilibrium interest rate. The scale for the latter will be obtained, if the bonds are perpetuities, by dividing the absolute or coupon interest payment per bond per unit of time by each price of a bond. Since the interest rate will tend to infinity as the bond-price tends to zero, any finite interval extending

16-2

upwards from the zero of the bond-price scale will contain infinitely many graduations of the interest-rate scale, no matter what the interval of this scale in terms of percentage points. No zero of the interest rate can be shown since a zero interest rate corresponds to an infinite bond-price. Nonetheless to each bond-price, in all cases and not only with perpetuities, there will correspond one and only one interest rate.

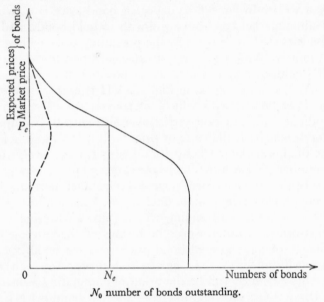

Fig. XXVII 2

Even in the *ceteris paribus* sense, the dynamics of such a system as we have described are exceedingly difficult to guess at. Unless the curve has some horizontal segments, any change in the number of bonds outstanding will, unless it changes expectations in an exactly appropriate manner, entail a change in the interest rate. An 'appropriate' type of change of expectations to preserve the interest rate unchanged in the face of, for example, a net increase in the quantity of bonds outstanding, would be a raising of expected bond-prices on the part of a number of wealth-owners whose former expected prices were in the neighbourhood of the former market-price. This is, however, the opposite of what we should regard as the natural result of an increase in the number of bonds outstanding. Most members of the market who were aware that such an increase was about to occur would say to themselves that with no change in expectations the market bond-price would fall, and so they might well lower their own expectations and precipitate a fall and magnify the fall that would otherwise have occurred.

All this is merely part of the quite general assertion that we cannot tell how a change in some public aspect of the market, such as a change in the number of bonds existing, will change expectations, that is, the 'shape and position' of the cumulated curve $N(P)$. The character of the effect on expectations may depend, not only on a vast number of variables other than the number of bonds existing itself, including the history of this number, the history of other aspects of the market, and the personal history of each marketer, but also on what we have called in Part (I) of this book inspiration, thoughts untraceable to the past. Thus a *ceteris paribus* dynamics would be purely arbitrary. A *non-ceteris paribus* dynamics, except a very rough and very short-term one, is, in our view, impossible. Is it, then, any use measuring or discussing elasticities on a curve $N(P)$? This is possible on the one assumption, concerning the effects of a change of N on the shape of the curve, which though arbitrary is arbitrary in a very simple and obvious way, namely, that the effect is *nil*.

It is plain that the more nearly horizontal is the shape of the curve $N(P)$ in the neighbourhood of the prevailing market interest rate, the less will this rate be affected by an increase or decrease of N which leaves expectations, and so the form of the curve, unchanged. But it is interesting to consider that since this horizontality is the reflection of a local concentration of expected prices, one price for each of a *limited* total number of marketers, i.e. wealth-owners, it implies that in other parts of the range of interest rates or bond-prices there must be some corresponding thinning-out of expected prices and a correspondingly greater sensitiveness of the interest rate to changes in N. There is indeed something that we might very roughly call a 'law of constant total sensitivity' without, however, seeking to give sensitivity and constancy an exact arithmetical interpretation (see Fig. XXVII 3).

We must now recognize that there is a very serious objection to the foregoing scheme as it stands. There is, indeed, a contradiction in some degree between our explanation of the fundamental necessity of interest as a safeguard and compensation in face of uncertainty, and our supposition that each wealth-owner has in mind a unique price which he expects bonds to stand at on some specified future date. The contradiction is perhaps not as serious as it appears thus baldly expressed, since

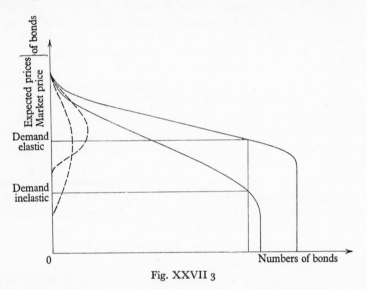

Fig. XXVII 3

the bond-holder's expectation date can be very near to his present, while his uncertainty concerns the whole prospect of the bond's life to maturity. Still, it would improve our analytical scheme if we could at the same time abolish the contradiction and dispense with the unrealism of supposing that wealth-owners feel certain what the price of bonds will be even at a near future date.

Let us, therefore, next suppose that each wealth-owner, again looking to his nearest speculation date, forms a potential surprise curve $y(P)$ concerning the price P which bonds will stand at on that date. The extremes of the inner range of this curve are the highest and the lowest price which he deems perfectly possible for that date. As a first approximation it may be reasonable to assume that if the market-price lies above the upper extreme he will be a Bear and an unwilling holder of bonds, while if the market-price lies below the lower extreme, so that he will be surprised if, over his speculation interval, the price of bonds does not rise, he will be a Bull and a willing holder. If the market-price lies anywhere in his inner range, he may well feel no incentive either to buy extra bonds or to sell those he has; he will be in a neutral or passive equilibrium.

Such a modification of our scheme has a number of great advantages. It abolishes the contradiction between our fundamental explanation of the nature of interest and the assumption that some bond-price expectations are treated as single-valued and certain. It allows for some insensitiveness in the response of the interest rate to new issues of bonds or redemptions of existing bonds. Above all, however, it enables us to account for the simultaneous holding of money and bonds by the same individual, which in case of uniquely certain expectations, would be unaccountable save for the money held from the transactions motive.

It will simplify our statements about these new assumptions if we agree to mean by 'an individual' a person who will hold either one bond or no bonds. In this way the number of bonds finding willing holders is made equal to the number of persons who entertain the appropriate forms of y-curve or, more precisely, y-curves with suitable inner ranges and therefore suitable extremes of those ranges. No generality is lost, for it matters nothing for our analytical purpose whether n bonds are held by one person having given expectations or by n persons all having relevantly identical expectations.

To illustrate diagrammatically the distribution of holders of different expectations of this new type, each consisting of an upper and a lower extreme of the inner range of a bond-price y-curve, we evidently need three dimensions, one for each of the two extremes and a third to show the number of individuals who entertain each such pair of extremes (see Fig. XXVII 4). On axes u and v lying at right angles to each other in a base-plane we mark respectively the lower extremes (algebraically increasing towards the right) and the upper extremes (increasing from the origin towards the distant edge of the paper) of the inner ranges of price y-curves, and on a third axis z

perpendicular to the base-plane we mark the numbers of individuals entertaining the pair of price extremes represented by each point in the base-plane. When thus plotted, these numbers may reasonably for the purpose of analysis be taken to form a surface $z(u, v)$. The profile formed by the meeting of this surface with a vertical wall erected along a 45° line in the base-plane will be simply a distribution-curve of holders of single-valued expectations, that is, of individuals for each of

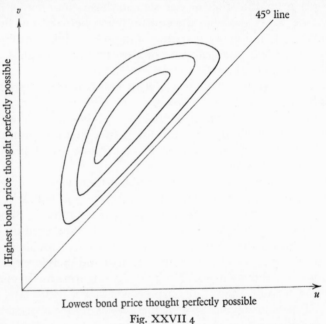

Fig. XXVII 4

whom some single price is both the highest and the lowest which they regard as perfectly possible. Since each person's highest possible price cannot be lower than his lowest possible price, the meaningful part of the surface $z(u, v)$ will lie wholly on or to the left of the 45° line. If there are no individuals who entertain single-valued expectations the surface will fall to zero along that line. There will surely be some price too high for anyone to regard it (in the situation as he knows it at some particular historical instant) as a possible one to prevail at his near-future image-date (speculation date); again, a zero price is lower than any price which can then prevail. Thus we may suppose the

surface to rise to a summit or a cental plateau in the way indicated by the contour-lines or equal z-lines of Fig. XXVII 4.

Any vertical section through the hill, parallel to but distanced
from the 45° line, will give us the distribution curve, over a
range of highest or a range of lowest prices, of individuals whose
highest and lowest prices are separated by a constant absolute
difference common to all of them. A more interesting vertical

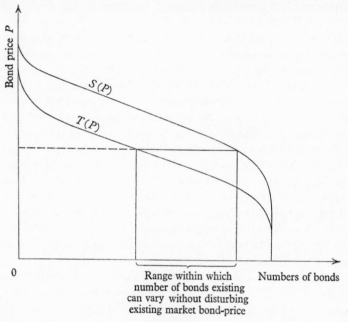

Fig. XXVII 5

section for us, however, is one made parallel to first one, then
the other, of the base-plane axes. A vertical section made parallel
to the axis of upper extremes of the price y-curve will give us the
distribution of individuals entertaining various highest possible
prices for some one lowest possible price P_{L_1}. Taking the total
of all these individuals (each counting, according to the convention we have adopted, as a holder or potential holder of one
bond) we have the number of extra bonds which would be
bought if the market-price fell from just above to just below
the level P_{L_1}. Thus we can plot on a diagram like that of
Fig. XXVII 5 a point on a curve showing the levels to which

the market-price would have successively to fall in order to gather in enough willing holders for successively larger total numbers $T(P)$ of bonds outstanding. By taking sections through the hill, parallel to the axis of highest prices, at some other point on the axis of lowest prices, and taking the total number of individuals in this section, we can plot another point on the curve; and so on. In the end we shall obtain a curve of similar shape-type but somewhat different meaning to the single curve of Fig. XXVII 1.

If we now proceed to take sections parallel to the axis of lowest prices we shall obtain, in the same manner as above, a curve showing to what successive levels the market-price must rise in order to turn 'neutral' holders into Bears and cause the number $S(P)$ of bonds finding willing holders to shrink to successively smaller amounts. Again we shall have a curve of shape-type broadly similar to the one generated by sections parallel to the axis of highest prices, but lying everywhere above it.

In Fig. XXVII 5 we can see the effect of our assumptions in creating, for any quantity of existing (i.e. outstanding) bonds, a range of bond-prices at all of which there may be sufficient willing holders. Alternatively we can say (as shown explicitly in Fig. XXVII 5) that at any given market-price of bonds the number of bonds which can find willing holders can be anything within some determinate range.

A question which will be immediately asked, concerning a theory of interest on the lines we have suggested, is how changes in the size of the economy's money stock affect the interest rate. The answer is that they affect it, if at all, either (1) by inducing the retirement of some existing bonds (this might, of course, be the actual means or mechanism of an increase in the stock of money) or the issuance of new bonds in order to replenish the balances which some individuals or firms hold in the production-consumption circuit or for other transactions purposes; or else (2) by changing the 'shape and position' of the expected price curves. An increase (for example) in the stock of money which changes neither the quantity of bonds nor the state of expectation cannot, under our scheme, affect the interest rate. Have we any historical evidence of the reality of such an indifference, or perverse reaction, of the bond-market to changes in the quantity of money? The Dalton incident provides it in abundance. Between September 1945 and November 1946 the quantity of money in Britain, reckoned as the aggregate of cash outside the banking system and money owed by the commercial banks to their customers, increased extra-seasonally by some £650 million. The yield of long-term bonds fell from about 3 % per annum to about 2½ %. In February 1947 the fuel crisis so destroyed any possibility of belief that the Government had its affairs under control, that the belief in a continuing fall in the interest rate, which the Chancellor of the Exchequer had so vigorously fostered as a means to achieve the fall itself, recoiled upon him in its collapse and started a movement to get rid of the over-priced bonds. This carried the interest rate back by August 1957, in spite of a gentle *continuing* increase in the quantity of money, to a higher level than it had stood at before the 'cheap money drive'.

Our scheme is presented, of course, as an indication of how the problem of interest rates may be attacked and not as a theory complete in all details.

XXVIII

PROFIT AND THE RANGE
OF NON-REVISION

Is *profit* something expected or something actually received? If both, do these two things influence or determine one another? What is the consequence of inequality between them? Is profit a distributive share of income? If so, to what factor of production does it go? Is it the consequence of luck or of skill? These questions and a great many that may be added to them show that no unique idea can fill all the roles which economic theory finds reason to gather under the name of profit. Can we, nevertheless, find some unified conception or scheme of thought in which all necessary meanings and aspects of 'profit' can find a place? We believe that such a scheme can be built upon a foundation which has existed for many years, if we can adapt that foundation, as so much of economic theory needs to be adapted, to assume uncertainty instead of undoubtedly correct foresight. This foundation is the 'Concept of Income' explained by Professor Erik Lindahl in his contribution to the *Economic Essays in Honour of Gustav Cassel*.* In what follows we shall try, first, to review the entire clan of ideas which have gathered themselves under the name *profit* and arrange in an orderly scheme those which seem to belong rightfully there; secondly, to explain concisely Professor Lindahl's concept of income; then to see what this concept becomes when we substitute *uncertain and diverse* for *certain and unique* expectations; and lastly to show how all the essential meanings of profit find their natural and necessary place in the scheme thus evolved.

Let us try to separate the meanings of *profit* by setting down a list of questions:

1. Does profit belong to a future or a past time interval?

2. Is profit something of specified amount looked forward to with a feeling of certainty?

3. Or is it a set of hypotheses to which are assigned various degrees of plausibility?

* London, 1933.

4. Is profit measurable absolutely or does it arise only from the comparison of two courses of action or two situations?

5. Can profit be imputed to a factor of production through the marginal productivity of that factor, or is it a residual?

6. Is profit something which is sought to be maximized, and does it thus play a part in allocating resources?

7. Or is it something ascribed to pure luck and uncontrollable circumstance?

8. Is profit something that has arisen, in an interval already past, in a manner and degree which were expected, or is it on the contrary something that has arisen and was not expected? Is it the difference between something that was expected and the corresponding thing that has been realized?

9. Is profit a prize, something hoped for by many though only able to go to a few?

10. Or are we to think of it as a reward already in the hands of those who have in some way deserved it?

11. Is profit the prize, or the reward, of uncertainty-bearing?

12. Or of decision-making?

13. Or of exceptional knowledge or of skill in forecasting?

14. Or is profit the spoils of monopoly power or of special bargaining power?

15. Is profit something implicit in the nature of a person's 'structure of expectations' or 'expectational vista', so that profit necessarily exists for any person who entertains plural hypotheses about the future course of events or about the consequence of each of several rival courses of action which are open to him, or is profit something which only arises as a consequence of the failure of experienced actuality to conform to what had been expected?

Plainly almost all of the concepts which these questions distinguish must find a place in any adequate scheme of thought about profit, and we shall try to devise a scheme of cross-classification and labelling which will include them all, so that later we can pigeon-hole each notion of profit that arises from our attempt to elaborate Professor Lindahl's concept of income. We could proceed by making a straightforward list of definitions, many of which would have features in common with several others in a complex pattern. We could then simply number the items in the list and pigeon-hole any notion of

TABLE I

Ex Ante A

Unique hypothesis alone carrying potential surprise less than the absolute maximum, $y < \bar{y}$	κ
Many hypotheses carrying $y < \bar{y}$, from which focus values are selected	λ
Excess over an absolute zero gain	I
Excess over the gain ascribed to a rival policy	II
Imputed to a factor of production through marginal productivity	(i)
Residual expected to remain after imputed income shares have been allowed for	(ii)
A simple maximand	1
The aim of a maximax strategy	2
The aim of a minimax strategy	3
The aim of a strategy seeking the highest attainable gambler indifference curve	4
Something about whose size no definite hypotheses are examined, the source of it being thought of as pure luck and uncontrollable circumstance	5
The prize of uncertainty-bearing	a
The prize of decision-making	b
The prize of exceptional knowledge or of skill in forecasting	c
The spoils of monopoly	d
Something implicit in the person's expectations existing at a single location of his viewpoint	E
Something arising from a comparison of his expectational vista existing at one viewpoint with that existing at another	G

profit by citing the appropriate number. However, our distinctions fall into groups and it will be useful to indicate this structure. Moreover, the first distinction, between the forward-looking and backward-looking concepts, is of such overwhelming importance that it ought to be specially marked. Thus it seems better to set out the whole list of definitions in the form of two columns, one headed *ex ante* and the other *ex post*, and within each of these columns to indicate the grouping of definitions which form alternative answers to some one question, or which are the two sides of a dichotomy, by using several sets of labels such as Greek letters, large and small Roman numerals and so on. The result is the scheme shown in Table 1.

A person who, having adopted a sufficiently explicit policy for his own economic conduct (and being willing to make an assumption about the policies to be followed by his heirs), more especially in the matter of saving and dissaving, feels able to name uniquely and for certain, for each identified calendar interval (such as the year 1970) lying still in the future, the value

TABLE I

Ex Post	*B*
Unique, actual and recorded result	μ
Many hypotheses carrying $y < \bar{y}$	λ
Excess over absolute zero gain	*I*
Excess of an actual outcome over what might have been achieved by a different policy	*II*
Imputed to a factor of production through marginal productivity	(i)
Residual actually remaining after payment of income shares imputed through marginal productivity	(ii)
Something which has emerged and is ascribed to pure luck	5
The reward of having borne uncertainty	*a*
The reward of having made decisions	*b*
The reward of having applied exceptional knowledge or skill in forecasting	*c*
The spoils of monopoly	*d*
Something arising from the passage of the viewpoint through some time interval	*G*

in 'today's' money units of the services he or his heirs will obtain in that interval, net of expenses incurred in obtaining them, from his own exertions and the use of the property he now possesses, can compute the *present value* of this series of expected services. This will be done by discounting each element of services at that rate of interest at which a loan could today be made for a term equal to the futurity of that element. Now let us for simplicity of illustration suppose that the expected services, instead of forming a flow continuous in time, are concentrated in instalments at the end of calendar intervals. Then if the person assumes that the mutual relations* of the

---

* If at date o a loan for a term of M time units, say years, can be made at an interest rate of $R_{0.M}$ per year, and at that same date o a loan for a term of N years can be made at an interest rate of $R_{0.N}$ per year, these two rates, $R_{0.M}$ and $R_{0.N}$, together imply that when the viewpoint shall have reached date M, a loan for a term of $(N-M)$ years will be able to be made at an interest rate of $R_{M.N}$ such that a given money sum, discounted from N to M at rate $R_{M.N}$ and from M to o at rate $R_{0.M}$, will have the same 'present' value (that is, value discounted to date o) as if it were discounted from N to o at rate $R_{0.N}$.

interest rates prevailing at his viewpoint for loans of various terms accurately reflect the rates which will prevail at future dates, he can compute the capital value which his series of expected services will have when discounted to any date not later than the earliest of the instalments. Thus if we suppose his viewpoint to be at 31 December 1962 and the earliest instalment to be at 31 December 1963, and if he feels sure that the interest rates which will prevail on that future date will be consistent with those ruling at his viewpoint, he can compute the capital value which the series of instalments has at his viewpoint and also that which it will have when his viewpoint shall have reached the end of 1963. That second computation will give a larger figure than the first, because each instalment is nearer in time to the end than to the beginning of 1963. The difference between these two capital values would, according to Professor Lindahl's concept, provided the person is not a creditor to whom interest-yielding money debts are owed, be the income of this person for the year 1963.

It is easily seen that if the rate of interest is one and the same for loans of all terms, the income defined as above is quantitatively identical with annual interest at this rate on the capital value which the series of expected services has at the viewpoint. A numerical example will illustrate this and we can afterwards prove it analytically. Thus suppose that, when the viewpoint is at 31 December 1962, 100 money-units' worth of services are expected at the end of each of the years 1963, 1964 and 1965, and that the rate of interest is 10 % per annum. Then the capital value at the viewpoint will be

$$V_0 = \frac{100}{1 + \frac{1}{10}} + \frac{100}{(1 + \frac{1}{10})^2} + \frac{100}{(1 + \frac{1}{10})^3} \simeq 248 \cdot 7$$

and at 31 December 1963 it will be

$$V_1 = 100 + \frac{100}{1 + \frac{1}{10}} + \frac{100}{(1 + \frac{1}{10})^2} \simeq 273 \cdot 6.$$

The difference between V_1 and V_0 is 24·9 and this is approximately equal to 10 % of 248·7.

Suppose now that with the viewpoint at 31 December 1962 the three instalments of service, each worth 100 money units, had been dated respectively 1 January 1963, 1 January 1964 and 1 January 1965. This situation appears strikingly different from the former one, for now the earliest instalment, instead of making a contribution to income by appreciating in present value as the viewpoint advances towards it, is about to be swept into the past and deleted altogether from the total capital value of the expected services. The sharp contrast of the two situations is due merely, however, to our having assumed that the services become available in discrete packets or instalments rather than in a continuous stream. When we turn to the continuous case it is plain that all the time some of the services are ceasing to be a prospect and are realizing themselves at the viewpoint, each element or infinitesimal packet of them being as it were actual for a fleeting moment and then disappearing into the past. The services which are thus born and extinguished in a moment cannot themselves be stored up, but they can be re-embodied, by an act which will have the character both of saving and of investment, in new capital goods representing a new additional stream of expected services. The idea, that the value of the services located in some very short identified calendar interval is deleted from the capital value of the stream of expected services by the passage of the viewpoint through that interval, must be represented in any formula intended to show this capital value as a function of the distance of the viewpoint from some fixed past date, or as we can say loosely, 'as a function of the passage of time'. To obtain such a formula, let us use the following symbols:

s the distance of a variable point of time from some fixed earlier point.

t the distance of the person's viewpoint from the fixed date $s = 0$.

$f(s)$ the value in money units of stable purchasing power of the services expected by the person to be yielded per unit of time at date s by all the concrete property he owns at the viewpoint and by his own powers.

r rate of interest ruling at the viewpoint on loans of all terms.

ρ $\log_e (1 + r)$.

v capital value, at the viewpoint, of the expected services.

Then we have

$$v = \int_t^\infty f(s) \, e^{-\rho(s-t)} \, ds$$

and

$$\frac{dv}{dt} = \rho \int_t^\infty f(s) \, e^{-\rho(s-t)} \, ds - f(t).$$

The interpretation of this result is plain. As the viewpoint advances through time, the capital value of the series of future services, each element of which is valued with certainty and its value discounted at given interest rates, undergoes two sorts of change: each element of services except that element which the viewpoint is about, as it were, to swallow, appreciates by reason of the lessening distance separating it from the viewpoint; and the element which the viewpoint overruns is deleted and the capital value diminished by the value of that element. The first of these changes is represented by the term ρv and the second by the term $-f(t)$.

The term ρv, then, is what Professor Lindahl means by income. The term $-f(t)$ is something entirely different and distinct from income, and while ρv represents an *inflow* or accretion of wealth to the capitalized total, $-f(t)$ in contrast represents an *outflow* or depletion of the total capitalized value of those services which are still in the future. We need a name for the term $-f(t)$, and I propose we should call it 'realized receipts'.

I come now to the third part of my task, namely, to explore the consequences of substituting, in Professor Lindahl's concept, *uncertain and plural* for *certain and unique* expectations.

A person who at some particular viewpoint is seeking to reckon his income in Professor Lindahl's sense is in much the same position as the possessor of a sum of money who is considering how to use it. The income-reckoner will have in mind many different *policies* each laying down the essential character of an economic career and prescribing the type of uses to be made in the future of his presently-owned property and of his personal capacities. His income will plainly be different, in general, if he chooses this policy rather than that. One policy will consist, for example, in consistently audacious responses to every situation as it arises, another in consistently cautious responses, and so on. One policy may offer an easy and another require a strenuous life. In deciding upon one policy rather than another he is indeed 'investing' the resources he now possesses, he is committing them to a course of action. It is evidently neither useful nor psychologically possible for a man to commit himself irrevocably to a detailed plan of action covering any long stretch of the future. But in order to take rationally the decision (which must of logical necessity be in fact taken, consciously or by default) upon his immediate next step, what to do now, he needs to have in mind a policy in the sense we have indicated, for not all of the possible immediate steps are equally well suited to open out effectively the types of opportunity a given policy calls for. What can effectively be decided upon is an immediate step or act; what gives meaning to this step is the further situations and possibilities for action to which this step is thought capable of leading.

For any one policy the income-reckoner will have in mind a variety of courses of events to which this policy seems to him capable of leading, and to each course of events there will correspond a particular capital value of the services, valued in viewpoint money units and discounted at viewpoint interest rates, which the person will obtain from the use of his property and his own powers if that course of events is realized. Thus we can say that each policy will have in the person's mind a range of imaginable capital values, and to each of these we can think of him as attaching its own degree of potential surprise. It is surely plausible to think that the resulting potential-surprise curves will have the same sort of basin shape as those of the investor. For the income-reckoner the independent variable will be capital value, and for each policy there will surely be a range of such values, by no means negligible as a proportion of the capital values representing its extremes, over which potential surprise will be zero. Further it seems to me reasonable to assume that there will be another range of capital values representing 'neutral' outcomes of the policy in question, outcomes any one of which constitutes in his view neither success nor failure and gives, in the imagining of it, neither pleasure nor pain. This 'neutral' range will generally, I think, be much narrower than the inner range and lie within it, and perhaps we can even assume without loss of anything important in generality that the neutral range will be a single capital value, lying somewhere inside the inner range. If these suggestions are accepted, we can apply to the income-reckoner's mental process the same concepts of the ϕ-surface and focus values as I have used in Part III to analyse that of the investor.

Let us then suppose that for every *policy*, in the sense I am giving to this word, a primary focus gain and a primary focus loss can be determined, and can be standardized, by the income-reckoner, and let us suppose the resulting points to be plotted by him on a gambler-indifference map where, however, we use the 'south-east' as well as the 'north-east' quadrant, in order to make all gambler indifference curves intersect the vertical (gain) axis as in Fig. XXVIII 1. Since 'negative focus gain' must be regarded as another name for focus loss, that segment of any gambler indifference curve which lies between the positive ray of the (horizontal) focus-loss axis and the negative ray of the (vertical) focus-gain axis must be simply a straight line joining points on these two rays equidistant from the origin. Every point on this segment is required to represent a focus loss equal to that represented by the intercept of the gambler indifference curve on the positive ray of the focus-loss axis. We can see at once two possible notions of what a policy promises in comparison with the neutral outcome, and these are two concepts of the 'absolute' profit of any policy when that policy is considered by itself. Since each of these is a possible means of comparing the profitability of different policies, we have also two concepts of profit as a differential advantage of one policy compared with another. One concept of the 'absolute' profit of any policy is simply its standardized focus gain, but this interpretation of 'profit' is open to an obvious objection. The comparison of policies by means of their respective standardized focus gains would lead to a simple 'maximax' strategy where danger in a positive sense was neglected. Our other concept of the absolute profit of a policy is the intercept on the gain axis of the indifference curve containing the point belonging to that policy. This intercept we may call the 'gain-equivalent' of the policy. The corresponding differential profit is of course the difference between gain-equivalents when one policy is compared with, for example, the 'next-best'.

The construction which gives us these four concepts of profit is open to a criticism which, however, is perhaps no more serious than that which we can direct against the assumption, in value analysis, of the mutual independence of supply and

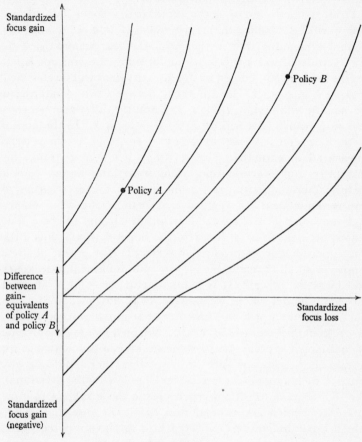

Fig. XXVIII 1

demand. The gambler indifference curves themselves, in their shape and position, are not strictly independent of the set of y-curves (potential surprise curves), considered as a whole, of the policies the person has in mind. Some policy, or at least the initial step of some policy, he is in the nature of things bound to adopt, whether by deliberate choice or only by default, and so the particular capital value that he considers as 'neutral' will be selected with a view to what seems possible: it will not make good sense for him to treat as 'neutral', in the meaning we are giving to this word, an outcome to which every available policy assigns very high potential surprise.

Profit defined merely as the standardized focus gain of any policy will be classified in our scheme as A, λ, I, $*$, 1, $*$, E, the symbol $*$ meaning that in the particular respect indicated by the location of this symbol in our formula, the concept is left unclassified. Profit defined as a gain-equivalent will be classified as A, λ, I, $*$, 4, $*$, E. The difference between two standardized focus gains will be A, λ, II, $*$, 1, $*$, E and the difference between two gain-equivalents will be A, λ, II, $*$, 4, $* E$. In the first of these four concepts we may say that profit is the extent (measured in capitalized value) to which a man thinks his enterprise and exertion may yield something better than a merely tolerable existence, in the second the possibilities of positive enjoyment are weighed against those of positive misery and the balance is 'profit'. Can profit, in any of these four senses, be looked on as the prize the hope of which calls forth some special type of productive service? Will profit, in these senses, be small or negligible for some kinds of income-reckoner and large for others? It is plain that in the kind of abstract economic model where we assume away any meaningful distinction between past and future so that uncertainty is absent, no profit in these senses could exist. Not only would the outcome of each possible policy be presumably known precisely and for certain, but it is even difficult to see how there could be any place in such a model for free choice of policy by the individual. We should have to suppose each person to be subject to some influences which constrained him to choose just that policy which other individuals expected him to choose in reckoning the outcomes of their own policies.* But even in non-static models where we admit an uncertain future, and largely even in the real world, it is possible for some suppliers of productive services to contract out of uncertainty, regarding the payments they will receive for the services they undertake to furnish, for

---

* The question of the nature and conditions of equilibrium has been examined in a classic article by F. A. Hayek on 'Economics and Knowledge', *Economica*, new series, vol. IV, no. 13 (February 1937).

some time ahead. Thus even in such models, uncertainty, though it cannot be eliminated, can be shifted. For contractual income-receivers, that is in especial, wage and salary earners and those who habitually hold fixed interest securities, profit in these four senses will be relatively small. It will surely be large for 'enterprisers', those who command large funds which they commit to the construction of particular kinds of factories and plants and concrete production systems, who both make the decisions about the specific form that these investments shall take, and who stake their reputations and even their personal capital, or as we can say in a broad sense their 'fortunes', on the success of the productive units which they create. Thus it seems that we might select decision-making and uncertainty-bearing as the economic roles which men come forward to perform because of the prize of profit in the sense we have been discussing. Is the formal distinction we have made between these two roles a meaningful one? The form in which we specially want to put this question is: Can there be any decision-making of a valuable kind, where the decision-maker stakes *nothing* on the success of his selection of one course of action out of many which are open to him? Surely a decision made by a person who in all strictness stood neither to gain nor to lose anything whatever, either material or moral, whether in wealth, reputation or self-esteem, would be no better than one arrived at by some random, inanimate procedure. The knowledge, skill, imagination and nerve which must be brought to bear upon the selection of one course of action out of many possible ones, if there is to be any 'tension' and coherence in the making of this choice, will not be summoned unless there is something important at stake for the decision-maker. Thus I doubt whether the functions of decision-making and of uncertainty-bearing can be even conceptually separated in any way which is useful for our purpose. The remaining blank space in our classifications of these four concepts of profit is the one which would name them imputed or residual constituents of income. It could be held, I think, that the idea of imputation, of *zurechnung*, belongs properly only to static models where we abstract from uncertainty and from the possibility of differences between past and future. But if we ask whether the existence of a large number of able and daring enterprisers in command of large funds would, if all of these enterprisers had rough knowledge of the numerical and financial strength of their own body, tend to make each of them set his standardized focus gain for each policy lower than he would if no such large supply of 'enterprise' existed, many economists, I think, would answer Yes. For my own part I should rather be inclined to answer No. For full employment and prosperity still depend largely on the pace of innovation and the readiness and power of the private enterpriser to promote it, and without full employment the profits, expected as well as realized, in most senses would surely decline. This space in our classification asks, then, a question which in the context of these first four concepts of profit I think is meaningless.

So far we have considered only the thoughts of a single person at a single momentary viewpoint without saying anything explicit about the past events and the chain of situations which have led up to the situation existing at his viewpoint, and which must surely have been largely responsible for forming the expectations he now entertains. In the role of detached observer we turn now to consider two locations at once of the person's viewpoint and the differences, in various respects, in the arithmetical sense, between the situations existing at them and between the person's *ex ante* and *ex post* views of the short time interval separating the two locations of the viewpoint.

During the interval information will have reached him of a great variety of events which will have occurred in the interval and of new aspects of events which were already past at the earlier location of his viewpoint. In the light of this extra knowledge he will, in general, alter the shapes and locations of the potential surprise curves of the policies he has in mind, and if we regard him as still in process of deciding amongst these policies, or if we regard him as only provisionally committing himself at any one time to any one policy, there will be differences between the earlier and later gain-equivalents of different policies amongst which he still feels himself free to choose. If at the earlier viewpoint the preferred policy was policy P_1, with a gain-equivalent g_1, and at the later viewpoint the preferred policy is P_2 with a gain-equivalent g_2 (no matter, for the purpose of definition, whether P_1 and P_2 are or are not one and the same policy) we have a difference $g_2 - g_1$ which seems to me to be a concept worthy of attention, coming under the heading of profit.

If $g_2 - g_1$ is positive this will mean that the events of the just-elapsed interval have made the person feel richer; for his preferred policy now stands on a higher gambler indifference curve than did the policy which at the earlier viewpoint he had deemed to be the best, and so his prospect in some sense promises better than it did before. We can infer that he will tend, as a consequence, to increase the amount of his intended spending on consumption. Thus if many individuals simultaneously experience a positive difference $g_2 - g_1$ we can infer that there will be an appreciable extra stream of consumption spending over the near future which may not be offset by decreased spending on the part of others. Thus it follows that the occurrence of profit of this type can tend to increase employment and prosperity. This concept of profit, which we might call 'dynamic increment of gain-equivalent' will be classified as A, λ, I, $*$, 4, a and b, G. A negative increment, a decrement, would presumably tend to reduce consumption spending and depress employment and output in a symmetrical way.

What sort of events would bring about a dynamic increment of gain-equivalent? It is plainly impossible to make a comprehensive list even of the broad headings under which the 'public' events with this effect might be classified, while the 'private' events might be largely beyond the power of any person, except the individual concerned, to imagine with any particularity and precision. By 'public' events we mean those known to everyone, by private events those known to, or those closely affecting, only the individual himself. Modern dynamic economic theory, more particularly of the kind which we have called elsewhere 'calculable dynamics', speaks as though the only kind of event which would affect the views of enterprisers about the future behaviour of any variable were the past behaviour of a few broad, public aggregates. In the extreme case we have future revenue, in some sense, from a given type of business regarded simply as a function of recent past revenue from that type of business. Are not the expectations of business men moulded by hundreds of elements of news of every kind, of comment, personal well-being or unhappiness and all the varied stages of interpretation and assimilation through which these elements pass in their minds? The retort may be that without such simplifications there is no possibility of constructing a 'calculable dynamics' by which, from data consisting of two or three past values of a mere handful of variables, we can prognosticate the future course of the main economic aggregates through several years ahead. But if so, is not a calculable dynamics of this kind a mistaken ambition?

Let us, nevertheless, make some concession. It is, after all, a universal habit of economists, not merely in their attempts at an economic dynamics, to wring every drop of understanding of the economic process, that they can possibly get, out of functions involving only one independent variable. Let us, then, consider whether there is some other concept of profit, upon which we could, without doing too much violence to our sense of realism, suppose the dynamic increment of gain-equivalent mainly to depend.

The passage of the viewpoint through the interval will have substituted a unique and recorded quantum of services, accruing to the person from the use of his equipment and of his own powers during the interval, for the set of diverse hypotheses about this quantum which he entertained while the interval still belonged to the future. If we suppose him to have assigned degrees of potential surprise to these hypotheses, and if indeed we suppose the hypotheses to have formed a range of a continuous variable so that we can speak of a y-curve, then if the actually realized quantum of services turns out to be equal to one of the hypotheses which carried zero potential surprise, that is, one which belonged to the 'inner range' of the y-curve, there is nothing on the face of this situation which would entitle us to say that the realized result had diverged from what the individual had expected. On the other hand, we do not know whether the individual may not have said to himself 'Within the inner range of hypotheses, the realization of any one of which would not surprise me, I can specify a narrower range of possible quanta of services, such that if the actual quantum fell outside this range, this would not itself surprise me, but it *would* cause me to revise my expectations about the further future beyond this immediately future interval'. What does seem to us to follow of logical necessity is that this second range, within which the actual quantum of services has to fall if it is not to cause a revision of expectations, must lie wholly within the inner range (where $y = 0$) of the y-curve. For it seems evident that if the actually realized quantum of services is such as to cause the individual surprise, it must be inconsistent with essential elements of that whole structure of thought and assumption upon which his vista of expectations has hitherto been based. Let us, as in chapter xxv, call this second range the range of non-revision. Then what I am asserting is that no actually realized quantum of services can fall within the range of non-revision, and yet fall outside the range of hypothetical quanta, for each of which potential surprise was zero.

Now if we are determined to select a single variable as the one upon which the individual's expectations of the further future, and in particular the shape and location of the curve assigning degrees of potential surprise to hypotheses concerning the capital value of his preferred policy, depend, we might choose the excess of the actually realized quantum of services over the largest quantum in the range of non-revision or (according to circumstances) the excess of the smallest quantum in the range of non-revision over the actually realized quantum. The variable thus constructed will be zero as long as the actual quantum falls inside the range of non-revision. However, it seems to me doubtful whether we could usefully call this variable a concept of profit. On the other hand, if the actually realized quantum falls outside the inner range ($y = 0$) of hypotheses concerning it, then the difference between this actual quantum and the upper (or, according to circumstances, lower) extreme of the inner range does seem to deserve a place in our classificatory scheme, for this is, I think, the analogue, in our construction, of Keynes's 'windfall profit' which, in the *Treatise on Money* of 1930, was the chief influence determining the volume of output as a whole. Let us then call this concept 'windfall realized receipts'. Its classification in our scheme can at first be written B, μ, I, (ii), *, *, G. The first of the two questions we have here left for discussion is whether windfall realized receipts can be ascribed to 'pure luck'. The concept of focus-outcomes, as far as the reader may feel able to accept it, implies that outcomes to which some appreciable degree of potential surprise is attached may yet be the ones upon which a decision-maker's attention is most intensely concentrated. Thus I incline to say that any windfall realized receipts to which any degree of potential surprise less than the absolute maximum, $y = \bar{y}$, was attached, ought not to be classified as due to pure luck; but any part of the windfall realized receipts which had carried the absolute maximum of potential surprise ought to be so classified.

In trying to answer the question whether windfall realized receipts are to be looked on as a reward for some particular type of performance or service, we have to remember that realized receipts themselves, in so far as they are of an amount which carried zero potential surprise, are not a part of *income*, according to Professor Lindahl's concept as I have extended it, but are merely that part of the person's capitalized wealth that becomes available for him to consume or invest. They are his off-take from his capitalized wealth, whereas his income is the natural growth of that capitalized wealth through the drawing nearer to the present of the elements of service on which it is founded. Thus the proper classification of *windfall* realized receipts is a little doubtful. I think, however, that in so far as they carried less than the absolute maximum of potential surprise, they can be legitimately regarded as a reward, *ex post facto*, for the combined achievement of skill, decision-making and the bearing of its attendant uncertainty.

This point of our argument is the natural place to turn aside for a moment to emphasize again the profound, fundamental importance of distinguishing absolutely between *ex ante* and *ex post* magnitudes. There is a total difference of character and meaning between the forward-looking and the backward-looking types of concept. There are passages to be found in the literature, where writers speak as though the profit in hope of which a person allocates resources to a certain type of production, and the profit which he actually receives as a consequence of having engaged in that production, were necessarily equal and could be treated as one and the same. The orthodox theory of income shares belongs in origin and in its essential nature to a static, timeless economics where the distinction between past and future has no place or meaning. To say, even by implication, that the profit which a man has actually received from having produced a certain object, was, itself and without any even conceptual distinction, the very thing which induced him to undertake that production, is manifestly nonsensical.

Let us now return to the question whether any variable, that can properly be included as a concept of profit, can be treated in a highly abstract and simplified model as the sole, or at least the predominant, 'independent' variable governing the dynamic increment of gain equivalent. We have seen that, on the one hand, the excess (respectively, shortfall) of the quantum of actually realized receipts compared with the largest (respectively, smallest) hypothetical quantum in the range of non-revision can scarcely be looked on as a concept of profit; yet it is this variable, rather than windfall realized receipts, which can reasonably be treated as the variable on which the dynamic increment of gain-equivalent depends. On the other hand, windfall realized receipts *can*, I think, properly be included as one of the essential meanings of 'profit'. Only one solution suggests itself: it is to ask whether any reasonable assumption or definition will enable us to argue that the two things will approximate to each other so that they can be treated as one and the same. What is there that we can adjust, by definition, for this purpose? We have so far not discussed at all the *length* of the interval between the earlier and later locations of the viewpoint. But our natural temptation will be to treat this interval as vanishingly short. Now the more distant the future date we look at, the greater, in general, will be the divergence between the extremes of the range of possibilities, in this matter and that, to which we now assign zero potential surprise. But we certainly also expect that as that date is approached, and the nearer part of what is now still the unknown future becomes the known past, we shall be able to *narrow* those ranges of hypothetical events carrying zero potential surprise, we shall be able to exclude, or disregard as potentially highly surprising, some still future events because of the answering of certain questions by the events which will have happened in the meantime and the new knowledge which these answers will constitute. Thus regarding *distant* future dates the 'inner range' of hypotheses concerning any type of outcome will usually, I think, spread widely, on either side, beyond the extremes of that range within which actual events would afford no ground for revising expectations concerning the further future, no ground for increasing the potential surprise attached to some hypotheses about events of the time beyond the date in question. Indeed, if we look at a short interval which is sufficiently remote in the future, it seems likely that, while the *inner range*, $y = 0$, concerning any outcome will be extremely wide, the *range of non-revision* of expectations concerning the further future will have vanished altogether and will be of zero width. If so, can we not argue that as we shift our attention from a short interval remote in the future to ones which are successively nearer the viewpoint, the two ranges will tend more and more closely to coincide? Now the short interval which concerns us in the present context is the one lying immediately ahead of the viewpoint, the one with the least possible remoteness. Thus it may be that we can treat the range of non-revision as roughly co-terminous with the 'inner range' of hypotheses concerning the size of realized receipts. If so, we are enabled to treat the amount of 'windfall realized receipts' as the independent variable on which the dynamic increment of gain-equivalent depends; and we can then define the 'elasticity of gain-equivalent' in the obvious way as the proportionate change in gain-equivalent associated with a given proportionate difference in windfall realized receipts.

XXIX

ORDER AND DECISION
IN ECONOMICS

The paradox and dilemma of a philosophy of history is this: that a knowledge of 'laws of history', of historical cause and effect, of some inescapable principles which govern the course of events, is useful only if *decision* is real, that is, non-illusory, non-empty, non-impotent. But if decision is real there can be no basis of a predictive theory of history, there can be no reliable laws of historical cause and effect, nothing to tell the decision-maker that if he presses this or that political or economic button the consequences will certainly be just such and such. Laws of history, it seems, are either otiose or non-existent. The resolution of this paradox, which we have offered in this book, seems on reflection perhaps obvious: there are no laws of certainty about what *will* happen when a human individual does this or that, but there are constraints as to what range of diverse things *can* happen. There is not certainty, therefore there can be decision; but there is *bounded* uncertainty, therefore there can be meaningful choice even in face of the absence of certainty. This is our whole thesis, it is this case which we have in the preceding chapters sought to establish, to elaborate in its detailed meaning and consequences, and to apply in some measure to the situations, viewed in an essential rather than a conventional light, in which men find themselves, especially under the economic aspect of things.

As part of this scheme of thought, and in order to establish its logical possibility and coherence, we proposed to assume that decision is in a special sense 'uncaused', that the range of thoughts amongst which choice is made is in part 'inspired' from a source not susceptible of investigation. We elected to suppose that the range or set of diverse imagined sequences of situations (or, indifferently, of events) of which the decision-maker could say to himself 'this, or this, or this,...any one of them could be the sequel of this specific act which I am contemplating', is not deducible by a detached observer from a knowledge of the past no matter how complete. We supposed that decision is creative in that the past does not determine the list of rival imagined outcomes which may arise in the decision-maker's mind concerning any act open to him; and that decision is rational in that he will necessarily choose that act whose imagined possibilities (visible after a drastic simplification whose nature and justification we indicated) afford him the most desired total experience by anticipation. Thus we said that uncertainty on one hand and creative imagination on the other are inseparable; that decision is choice amongst mental constructs each of which is a set of imagined, not actual nor 'objective', outcomes, and that for inclusion in such sets the necessary condition is a degree of possibility; and finally that degrees of possibility are to be identified by location on the scale of a non-distributional uncertainty variable.

The difference between this view, on the one hand, and on the other such views as can be inferred from the theories of human action or of the nature of history which are to be found in social sciences such as economics, is essential and radical. In economics of the accepted, Western, maximizing kind we are confronted with a basic contradiction: men are choosers; they choose the best, each for himself; what is the best can always be known to each person, either by merely consulting his own tastes or by applying the techniques of engineering or, where knowledge lacks a *simple* precision, by applying statistical techniques which turn ignorance of the particular into knowledge of the aggregate. Thus that action which will attain 'the best' can always be discovered, its prior discovery is part of that policy of rational action which is attributed by economics to the Economic Man in his modern sophisticated form; and all men in some degree approximate to this, or would wish to. And so we have man in this situation: what is 'the best' for him is known to him uniquely and for certain; how to attain it is dictated by circumstances, and can be inferred from them. What, then, is left for him to do in the way of *choosing*? Where is there room for his judgement, for the artist's discernment of beauty, for the inspired creation of what is essentially new?

Conventional economics is not about choice, but about acting according to necessity. Economic man obeys the *dictates* of reason, follows the *logic of choice*. To call his conduct choice is surely a misuse of words, when we suppose that to him the ends amongst which he can select, and the criteria of selection, are given, and the means to each end are known. The theory which describes conduct under these assumptions is a theory of structure, not of creation of history. Choice in such a theory is empty, and conventional economics should abandon the word. Is the only alternative to a theory of necessary action a theory of non-rational, of arbitrary action? The escape we have suggested consists not in abandonment of rationality, not in abandonment of the adoption of the means which will lead to the selected end, but in abandonment of the postulate that the available ends are given. The escape from necessity, we suppose, lies in the *creation of ends*, and this is possible because ends, so long as they remain available and liable to rejection or adoption, must inevitably be experiences by imagination or anticipation and not by external occurrence. Choice, inescapably, is choice amongst thoughts, and thoughts, we suppose, are not *given*.

What is the place of conventional economic theory in such a *theory of action* as this book seeks to supply? It is part of that natural law upon which our theory of action relies to provide *order*, to make decision non-powerless. In that theory, the decision-maker looks upon each act available to him as having a range of diverse possible outcomes, but their diversity is in every direction bounded by the inability of things to move, physically, politically, psychically, institutionally, at more than some speed which we can seek to name. In the non-human world we suppose that there is structure, so that physical, chemical and electrical occurrences have classifiably stable patterns of earlier and later sets of circumstances or phases; so that they have regularity. In the biological world we suppose that such stability is true of some aspects, though we believe also in genetic mutations and the occurrence of unaccountable 'sports'. In the conscious world our theory of action supposes that there can be 'inspiration', that is, unaccountable thoughts. But even in the human world thoughts and decisions can be *partly* explained. The individual is pressed upon by circumstances visible to others as well as himself. In so far as these circumstances are economic, what economic theory seeks to explain is the character and direction of such pressures.

Anticipation we have defined as that imaginative experience which takes it for granted that the action scheme to which the decision-maker has committed himself *can* have as desirable an outcome as one which he specifies to himself, and *cannot* have a more undesirable outcome than another which he specifies. The act to be discovered is the one, out of all those available, which will give him the preferred such dual experience by anticipation. In order that he may thus choose amongst available acts, he needs to be able to find for each act a barrier in both directions, towards both poles of the axis of desirability-undesirability. The 'existence', in the logical sense, of these barriers, the semantic basis of such an uncertainty-bound, lies in the decision-maker's taking for granted an orderliness in his environment, which he expresses to himself as the prevalence of natural law. Within the meaning of natural law he needs evidently to include law about the propensities of human nature. Just, for example, as massive objects have physical inertia, so human beings find their desires for a given extra supply diminishing in strength as the supply already at command increases. Physical law and psychological law can both be looked on as parts of natural law. Economic theory is an endeavour to systematize part of psychological law. Its purpose and proper duty is descriptive, to define the kind of things that can happen, not to try to say what particular thing will, on a particular historical occasion, be the fact.

A theory is an account of orderliness, and a detailing of a ground for belief in this order. Economic theory is an account of the orderliness of society in its business. In this book we have sought to supply a *general* theory of decision, but this we have illustrated from economic examples. This has for us a special value, for economic theory shows better, as yet, than any other of the sciences of man's nature how the self-interested exertion and enterprise of individuals, in natural interaction, can yield a cosmos in which uncertainty is present but bounded and in which non-illusory, non-empty, non-powerless decision can therefore be conceived to exist.

BIBLIOGRAPHY

The theory presented in this book has been discussed, in some one or more aspects, in the following books and articles.

I. BOOKS

Carter, C. F., in *Uncertainty and Business Decisions*, ed. C. F. Carter, G. P. Meredith and G. L. S. Shackle (Liverpool University Press, 1954), 1st ed. pp. 48–57; 2nd ed. (1957), pp. 48–57, 142–52.

Cohen, John. *Chance, Skill and Luck* (London: Penguin Books, 1960), pp. 26–7.

Coward, Dag, *Økonomisk risiko og usikkerhet* (Oslo: I kommisjon hos bedriftsøkonomens forlag, 1953), pp. 89–97.

Eastham, J. K., in *Dundee Economic Essays* (Dundee, 1955), pp. 49, 50.

Edwards, Ward, in *Expectations, Uncertainty and Business Behaviour* (New York: Social Science Research Council, 1958), pp. 45–7.

Egerton, R. A. D. *Investment Decisions under Uncertainty* (Liverpool University Press, 1960), pp. 6–12.

Gallie, W. B., in *Uncertainty and Business Decisions*, ed. C. F. Carter, G. P. Meredith and G. L. S. Shackle (Liverpool University Press, 1954), pp. 1–10.

Georgescu-Roegen, Nicholas, in *Expectations, Uncertainty and Business Behaviour* (New York: Social Science Research Council, 1958), pp. 21, 22.

Jöhr, Walter Adolf, *Die Konjunkturschwankungen* (J. C. B. Mohr, 1952), pp. 372, 396, 399–402, 406, 408, 410, 412.

Keirstead, B. S., *An Essay in the Theory of Profits and Income Distribution* (Oxford: Basil Blackwell, 1953), pp. 17, 19, 20, 25, 29–34.

—— *Capital, Interest and Profits* (Oxford: Basil Blackwell, 1959), pp. 29, 30.

Lachmann, L. M. *Capital and Its Structure* (London School of Economics, 1956), pp. 26–9.

Maggi, Raffaello. *Momenti dinamici dell' economia* (Rome, 1958), pp. 46, 47, 285–93.

Meredith, G. P., in *Uncertainty and Business Decisions* (Liverpool University Press, 1954), 1st ed. pp. 35–47; 2nd ed. (1957), pp. 35–47, 85–9.

O'Connor, D. J., in *Uncertainty and Business Decisions* (Liverpool University Press, 1954), pp. 11–18.

Papandreou, Andreas, G., *A Survey of Contemporary Economics*, vol. II (New York: Richard D. Irwin, 1952), pp. 209, 210.

Pen, J., *The Wage Rate under Collective Bargaining* (Cambridge, Mass.: Harvard University Press, 1959), pp. 189–94.

Seidenfus, H. St, *John Maynard Keynes als 'Psychologue'* (Berlin: Duncker and Humblot, 1956), pp. 111, 113, 115, 116, 125, 126.

Watkins, J. W. N., in *Uncertainty and Business Decisions* (2nd ed. Liverpool University Press, 1957), pp. 107–21.

Williams, B. R., in *Uncertainty and Business Decisions* (Liverpool University Press, 1954), 1st ed. pp. 63–5, 70, 71; 2nd ed. (1957), pp. 122–33.

Wray, Margaret J. *The Women's Outerwear Industry* (London: Gerald Duckworth and Co., 1957), pp. 300–2.

2. ARTICLES

Åkerman, Johan. 'De ekonomiska beslutens katalysatorer', *Ekonomisk Tidskrift*, vol. LVIII (December 1956), pp. 203, 214–18.

—— 'Professor Shackle on Economic Methodology', *Kyklos*, vol. XI (1958).

—— 'Shackle's System and Theories of Business Cycles', *Metroeconomica*, vol. XI, fasc. I–II (Aprile-Agosto 1959), pp. 3–11.

Angell, James W. 'Uncertainty, Likelihoods and Investment Decisions', *Quarterly Journal of Economics*, vol. LXXIV (February 1960), pp. 3–7, 14.

Arrow, K. J. 'Alternative Approaches to the Theory of Choice in Risk-taking Situations', *Econometrica*, vol. XIX (October 1951), pp. 405, 415, 419, 420, 432–4.

Brockie, M. D. 'Expectations and Economic Stability', *Weltwirtschaftliches Archiv*, vol. LXX (1953).

Carr, J. L. 'Uncertainty and Monetary Theory', *Economics*, vol. II (Spring 1956), pp. 82–9.

Carter, C. F. 'Expectation in Economics', *Economic Journal*, vol. LX, no. 237 (March 1950), pp. 92–105.

—— 'A Revised Theory of Expectations', *Economic Journal*, vol. LXIII, no. 252 (December 1953), pp. 811–20.

Dickson, H. 'Ovisshetens roll i ekonomisk planering', *Ekonomisk Tidskrift*, vol. LII (June 1950), pp. 69–83.

Duncan, David C. 'Shackle's Theory of Expectations and the Definition of Rationality', *Occupational Psychology*, vol. XXXI (July 1957), pp. 177–84.

—— 'The Concept of Potential Surprise: can it Serve Better than Probability as a Means of Analysing Uncertainty?', *Metroeconomica*, vol. XI, fasc. I–II (Aprile-Agosto 1959), pp. 21–36.

Egerton, R. A. D. 'Investment, Uncertainty and Expectations', *Review of Economic Studies*, vol. XXII, no. 58 (February 1955), pp. 143-50.

—— 'The Holding of Assets: "Gambler-preference" or "Safety first"?', *Oxford Economic Papers*, new series vol. VIII (February 1956), pp. 51-9.

Foldes, Lucien. 'Uncertainty, Probability and Potential Surprise', *Economica*, vol. XXV, no. 99 (August 1958), pp. 246-54.

Fossati, Eraldo. 'Note sur un essai d'approche probabiliste à la théorie économique', *Economie Appliquée*, vol. X (January-March 1957), pp. 45-7.

Gorman, W. M. 'A Note on "A Revised Theory of Expectations",' *Economic Journal*, vol. LXVII, no. 267 (September 1957), pp. 549-51.

—— 'How Surprising is a Chain of Coincidences?', *Metroeconomica*, vol. IX (August 1957), pp. 112-15.

Gould, Gerald. 'Odds, Possibility and Plausibility in Shackle's Theory of Decision', *Economic Journal*, vol. LXVII, no. 268 (December 1957), pp. 659, 660.

—— 'Odds, Possibility and Plausibility: A Further Examination', *Economic Journal*, vol. LXVII, no. 268 (December 1957) pp. 661-4.

Guitton, Henri. 'La théorie du temps et de l'incertitude de Shackle', *Revue d'Economie Politique*, vol. LXIX (Janvier-Fevrier 1959), pp. 79-81.

Hahn, F. H. 'Uncertainty and the Cobweb', *Review of Economic Studies*, vol. XXIII, no. 60 (1955-6), pp. 65, 66, 73-5.

Hamblin, C. L. 'The Modal "probably",' *Mind*, vol. LXVIII, no. 270 (April 1959), pp. 234, 238-40.

Hart, Albert Gailord. 'Shackle's System and the Theory of Liquidity Preference and of Money', *Metroeconomica*, vol. XI, fasc. I-II (Aprile-Agosto 1959), pp. 37-43.

Hillebrandt, P. M. 'The Economic Theory of the Use of Pesticides. Part II. Uncertainty', *Journal of Agricultural Economics*, vol. XIV, June 1960, pp. 52-61.

Johnson, H. G. 'A Three-dimensional Model of the Shackle ϕ-surface', *Review of Economic Studies*, vol. XVIII, no. 46 (1950-1), pp. 115-18.

Keirstead, B. S. 'Profitti, aspettative e impressa', *Economia Internazionale*, vol. IV (November 1951), pp. 868, 869, 874-7.

—— 'Professor Shackle on Time in Economics', *Metroeconomica*, vol. XI, fasc. I-II (Aprile-Agosto 1959), pp. 44-50.

Krelle, Wilhelm. 'Unsicherheit und Risiko in der Preisbildung', *Zeitschrift für die gesamte Staatswissenschaft*, vol. 113 (1957), pp. 635, 638, 640, 643, 646, 648-51.

Krelle, Wilhelm. 'A Theory on Rational Behaviour under Uncertainty', *Metroeconomica*, vol. XI, fasc. I–II (Aprile-Agosto 1959), pp. 51–63.

Krüsselberg, H. G. 'Kritische Betrachtungen zu G. Merks Aufsatz: Wahrscheinlichkeitstheorie und Investitionstheorie', *Weltwirtschaftliches Archiv*, Band 82, 1959.

Lachmann, L. M. 'Professor Shackle on the Economic Significance of Time', *Metroeconomica*, vol. XI, fasc. I–II (Aprile-Agosto 1959), pp. 64–73.

Landgren, Karl-Gustav. 'Nyare litteratur om risk problemet', *Ekonomisk Tidskrift*, vol. LVIII (December 1956), pp. 241–9.

Mars, J. 'A Study in Expectations (Part I)', *Yorkshire Bulletin of Economic and Social Research*, vol. II (July 1950), pp. 63–98.

—— 'A Study in Expectations (Part II)', *Yorkshire Bulletin of Economic and Social Research*, vol. III (February 1951), pp. 1–35.

McManus, Maurice. 'Transformations in Economic Theories', *Review of Economic Studies*, vol. XXV, no. 67 (February 1958), pp. 99–102.

Merk, Gerhard. 'Wahrscheinlichkeitstheorie und Investitionstheorie', *Weltwirtschaftliches Archiv*. vol. LXXXI (1958), pp. 69–78.

Nicholson, M. B. 'A Note on Mr Gould's Discussion of Potential Surprise', *Economic Journal*, vol. LXVIII, no. 272 (December 1958), pp. 830–3.

—— 'Probability and Economic Decision Taking', *Manchester School of Economic and Social Studies*, vol. XXVII (September 1959), pp. 221–39.

Niehans, Jürg. 'Reflections on Shackle, Probability and our Uncertainty about Uncertainty', *Metroeconomica*, vol. XI, fasc. I–II (Aprile–Agosto 1959), pp. 74–88.

Parker, H. R. 'Voluntary and Forced Decisions', *Metroeconomica*, vol. IX (August 1957), pp. 116–24.

Pen, J. 'Naschrift'. *De Economist*, vol. CIV (March 1956), p. 205.

Puthucheary, J. J. 'Investment Incentive and Income Tax', *Public Finance* (*Finances Publiques*), vol XIV, 1959, pp. 222–35.

Rijken van Olst, H. 'Onzekerheid en di beschriving daarvan door middel van het begrip "potential surprise",' *De Economist*, vol. CIV (March 1956), pp. 198–205.

Sargan, J. D. 'Subjective Probability and the Economist', *Yorkshire Bulletin of Economic and Social Research*, vol. V (February 1953), pp. 60, 61.

Shoup, Carl S. 'Some Implications for Public Finance in Shackle's Expectation Analysis', *Metroeconomica*, vol. XI, fasc. I–II (Aprile-Agosto 1959), pp. 89–103.

Watkins, J. W. N. 'Decisions and Uncertainty', *British Journal for the Philosophy of Science*, vol. VI, no. 21 (May 1955), pp. 66–78.

Weckstein, R. S. 'On the Use of the Theory of Probability in Economics', *Review of Economic Studies*, vol. XX, no. 53 (1952–3), pp. 191–8.

—— 'Probable Knowledge and Singular Acts', *Metroeconomica*, vol. XI, fasc. I–II (Aprile-Agosto 1959), pp. 104–18.

Williams, B. R. 'Shackle's ϕ-function and Gambler Indifference Map', *Metroeconomica*, vol. VI (December 1954) pp. 118–28.

Wray, Margaret J. 'Uncertainty, Prices and Entrepreneurial Expectations—An Applied Study', *Journal of Industrial Economics*, vol. IV (February 1956), pp. 107, 122–6.

—— 'Professor Shackle's Theory and Short Period Entrepreneurial Decisions in the Women's Clothing Industry', *Metroeconomica*, vol. XI, fasc. I–II (Aprile-Agosto 1959), pp. 119–36.

INDEX

outcome(s) *(cont.)*
definable by description or by utility, 63
depend on state of nature as much as on decision principle, 65
exemplified by investment gain, 137
extremely diverse, effect of, shown by gambler indifference map, 175
how potential surprise to be assigned to, 136, 137, 186
hypothesis of, defined, 4
hypothetical, expressed by potential surprise curve, are mutually contradictory, 176
imagined, cannot be called non-legitimate, 37
imagined, if comparison possible, 9
in one-one correspondence with acts, 4, 7
individual makes two orderings of, 117, 145
listable, 10
listable, if rules of game known, 6, 43
nature of, considered in detail, 136
neutral, *see* neutral outcome
not determined by previous history, 31, 272
not listable, 7, 271
of action which is still subject to choice, exists only in imagination, 143
of available actions, not to be discovered but created, 143
possibility of, judged on a basis which includes observed acts of others, 40
radically new, 10
result of luck or clever decision? 66
treated as continuously variable argument of desiredness, potential surprise and ascendancy, 145
unsurprising, need not be equally likely, 87
when judged possible, are expectations, 38

Parker, H. R., 178
past
can historian transport his 'present' into? 35
exists only in a mental act of the present, 16
'Pattern of Evidence of Rational Liklihood', 88

patterns of expected earnings, representable by supposing earnings to be zero for all but one interval, 233
Pen, J., 95, 97
Persons, W. M., 33
ϕ (phi) *(see also* ascendancy)
absolute maximum of, 150, 151
as direct pull or push on decision, 157
constrained curve of, 154, 157, 158
constrained curve of, as wire casting a shadow, 158
contour-lines of, 148, 149, 150
formal description of, 147, 148, 149
shape-types of, 147, 177
surface, conventions to be adopted for, 170
surface, evolution of, through time, 178
surface, notion of, introduced, 147
surface, profiles of, 150, 151, 152
surface, shows how ascendancy depends on face-value and potential surprise, 147
surface, stability of, depends on temperamental stability of decision-maker, 177
values of focus-elements, algebraic sum of, 156
plausibility(-ies)
and Dr Hamblin's paper, 97, 100
modal logic of, 97
rule for combination of, 98
policy(-ies) for life career
capitalization of, 259
concept of, 258
potential surprise and focus-element concepts applied to capital values of, 259
Popper, K. R., 100
portfolio, optimal number of assets in, 180, 181, 182
possibility
a more efficient and powerful uncertainty-variable than probability, 103
and ascendancy-matrix, 190
and contrasting notions, 12
and desiredness, whether to be ranked or measured, 187
and impossibility, dichotomy between suffices for basic model, 135
and long adverse odds, 84
as a cardinal variable, 135

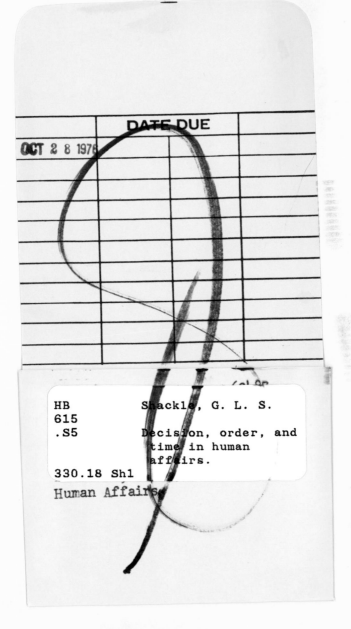